Transnational Moments
of Change

Transnational Moments of Change

Europe 1945, 1968, 1989

Edited by
Gerd-Rainer Horn
and Padraic Kenney

ROWMAN & LITTLEFIELD PUBLISHERS, INC.
Lanham • *Boulder* • *New York* • *Toronto* • *Oxford*

ROWMAN & LITTLEFIELD PUBLISHERS, INC.

Published in the United States of America
by Rowman & Littlefield Publishers, Inc.
A wholly owned subsidary of the Rowman & Littlefield Publishing Group, Inc.
4501 Forbes Boulevard, Suite 200, Lanham, Maryland 20706
www.rowmanlittlefield.com

PO Box 317
Oxford
OX2 9RU, UK

British Library Cataloguing in Publication Information Available

Library of Congress Cataloging-in-Publication Data

Transnational moments of change : Europe 1945, 1968, 1989 / edited by Gerd-
Rainer Horn and Padraic Kenney.
   p. cm.
  Includes bibliographical references and index.
  ISBN 0-7425-2322-5 (alk. paper) — ISBN 0-7425-2323-3 (pbk. : alk. paper)
  1. Reconstruction (1939–1951)—Europe, Western. 2. Europe—Politics and
government—1945– 3. Europe—Social conditions—20th century. 4. Protest
movements—Europe, Western—History—20th century. 5. Communism—Europe,
Western—History—20th century. I. Horn, Gerd-Rainer. II. Kenney, Padraic, 1963–
  D1051.T73 2003
  940.55—dc22   2003016217

Printed in the United States of America

Pictured on the cover: (standing, left to right) Piotr Niemczyk, Petr Uhl, Józef Pinior,
Adam Michnik, Jan Lityński, Mieczysław Piotrowski, Jaroslav Šabata, Ivan Lamper,
Zbigniew Bujak, Anna Šabatová, Stanislav Devátý, Václav Malý, and Ján
Čarnogurský; (kneeling, at left) Mirosław Jasiński, Zbigniew Janas, and Václav Havel;
(front, left to right) Zbigniew Romaszewski, Petr Pospíchal, Jan Urban, Ladislav Lis,
Alexandr (Saša) Vondra; (reclining, front) Danuta Winiarska, Jacek Kuroń

Contents

Acknowledgments

This book had its beginnings in a conference that we co-organized at the Rockefeller Foundation's Bellagio Center on the shores of Lake Como, Italy, in October 2000. It is quite fitting that our explorations of the theory and methodology of transnational history should have begun with the generous and efficient assistance of a foundation that has worked internationally for decades. We are grateful for its support.

Many of our contributors participated in the discussions at Bellagio. Others joined this project later. We thank them for their willingness to do so—especially as, in one case, the unexplained last-minute resignation of one author required a quick search for a replacement. We also want to acknowledge those conference participants whose contributions do not appear in this volume.

We must thank our home institutions: the University of Colorado (and in particular Patricia Murphy of the Department of History staff), the University of Huddersfield for financial assistance, and the University of Warwick for logistical support. And, last but not least, we would like to express our appreciation of the friendly and efficient support extended to us by Mary Carpenter and Laura Roberts at Rowman & Littlefield.

Introduction

Approaches to the Transnational

Padraic Kenney and Gerd-Rainer Horn

For a long time, the nation-state has shaped the contours of historical study.[1] Not least for linguistic and logistical reasons, it has made sense for historians to focus on processes occurring within one country. Moreover, the development of modern nationalism—as it has grown side by side with modern historiography—has forcefully directed attention to the organic development of states into culturally united (if not necessarily homogeneous) units and of populations into nations.

The structure of university history departments, now as before the key employers of historians, likewise actively discourages the transnational study of modern-day European phenomena. In European countries, the absolute dominance of the respective national histories in the distribution and creation of lecturer posts or professorships continues unabated. In North America, the historical interest (in both senses of this expression) in Europe continues to characterize the discipline. But, as an unintended consequence of this relative embarrassment of riches, certainly in the Western European field this has resulted in position descriptions calling for national specialisms above all else. So, in a curiously inverted logic, both European parochialisms and North American Eurocentrism forget the forest for all the trees.

Yet several phenomena urge the historian to move beyond these safer confines. First, it is hard not to notice similarities between roughly simultaneous developments in various countries. Most such similarities dwell in the footnotes of the national monograph. For some historians, however, the question of commonality becomes central, a window into processes of history. As from a room in a familiar house, the historian turns to look out this window, at the network of streets and alleys connecting many other houses. It is this perspective that we term "transnational history." Such a consistently transnational approach must also sooner or later raise the question why: Why should parties in different countries have similar programs, or social groups advance similar demands and participate in similar protests?

Transnational studies are no novelty. A number of historians have employed some version of the transnational approach, and this for some time, though most often without adopting that term. We do not enjoy neologisms more than anyone else, so what is the use of the term we employ? Perhaps the expression that first comes to mind when thinking of transnational work is *comparative history*. Why not continue to use it instead?

We are fundamentally convinced that the two concepts represent distinctly different approaches to the study of history across national frontiers. There are those authors who study two or more national cases to highlight that which is unique to each individual case. And then there are historians who study two or more national cases to highlight those elements that unite their sample, or who are interested primarily in the connective tissues themselves. In one instance, the differences tend to be at the center of attention; and in the other, the similarities. While it would be absurd to build up artificial barriers between the two approaches, it is evident that the first approach implicitly maintains barriers, while the latter moves across them. We like to refer to the former approach as comparative history and the latter as characteristic of the transnational approach, though we are acutely aware that some authors define the terms in different ways, yet others may use the terms interchangeably.

The transnational question has arisen at many times; it appears, though, with particular frequency today. For another factor bringing increased interest in transnational history is the study of great events that simply cannot be captured within the narrative of one country. Such events have occurred with increasing frequency in the modern era. One could, of course, categorize the spread of humanism, the Reformation and Counter-Reformation, and the Enlightenment (among many others) as transnational phenomena in a way. Yet, while the study of the early modern era undoubtedly shares some significant similarities with modern transnational history, the trans*national* element implies something different. At the risk of tautology, it should be clear that transnational history makes little sense when participants in a continent-wide movement are defined primarily by their common language (such as Latin) or religion, rather than by their citizenship or national identity.

It is in the modern era that one begins to observe moments in which social, political, and cultural movements, and even entire societies, even as they are bound within a narrative of the nation-state, consciously or unconsciously embrace similar experiences or express similar aspirations across distinctly national frontiers. The rise of socialist parties and trade unions in the late nineteenth century is a useful example, as is the liberal moment of 1848. In the twentieth century, such moments occurred with increasing rapidity. Contacts and cooperation among socialists were matched by similar initiatives among peasant parties, Catholic parties, and others. The often excruciatingly detailed cooperation of the European Union raises questions about the primacy of the nation-state and also of whether common identities and processes are created from above or from below.[2]

Of greatest significance to transnational history in the twentieth century were the Russian Revolution and the rise of fascism—or, more accurately, the historiography concerning those two pancontinental events. While in both cases the developments in one or two countries are central to the story and have been exhaustively researched, the fact that similar political change, or attempts at change, took place nearly simultaneously across most of Europe eventually began to turn historians' attention toward transnational processes, though most work on the spread of communism and fascism before World War II has been mononational or comparative in nature.

Looking at the topic more closely, we may speak of three broad categories of transnational history, to which we will return later in more detail. One variant of the transnational approach limits itself to the description of similarities across national frontiers. Such works may often leave unaddressed the reasons for such transnational evolutionary or, indeed, revolutionary processes, and they may directly or indirectly refer to the zeitgeist as the operative factor beyond national control. The second category embraces structural change: great economic (the Great Depression, postwar hyperinflation) or political (world wars, the European Union) events or structures that are by their very nature supranational and that may be expected to have similar effects in a number of countries. At the least, the absence of such effects (such as the relative weakness of the extreme right in interwar Britain and Czechoslovakia) requires explanation. The third category entails active efforts to spread change from country to country. The Red Army attempting to bring communism to Poland in 1918 and Nazi Germany's use of credits to exert influence on Hungarian politics are examples of this more voluntarist trend.[3]

Taking a closer look at the latter two categories of transnational work (i.e., those that endeavor to go beyond description toward the distillation of the concrete factors behind apparent transnational changes), we suggest that processes of these two types usually occur together; the postwar cases contained in this book, we believe, support this conclusion. It is unlikely that actors by themselves can bring ideas or inspirations across borders if neighboring countries are not in some way open to those gifts thanks to larger processes. On the other hand, even the most forceful transnational process cannot bring about developments in countries where people are not prepared to accept or push forward those ideas or practices.

Defining transnational history as the study of similarities, parallels, or connectors across national frontiers simultaneously begins to answer the question of the benefits and purposes of the transnational approach. What can the transnational approach do that others cannot or cannot do as well? A transnational approach may contribute to the awareness that certain phenomena thought to be peculiar to one specific national context are indeed phenomena that occur elsewhere as well. This, in and of itself, is no small matter. To take the example of the moment of liberation, the first of our three moments of change under review in this volume, it is revealing to observe that certain phenomena sometimes studied in great local, regional, or national detail are virtually unaddressed on a transnational level. Thus, the sudden emergence of institutions of local self-government (*comités de libération, comitati di liberazione nazionale, Antifa-Ausschüsse*, etc.), vaguely reminiscent of the wave of workers', soldiers', and peasants' councils in immediate post–World War I Europe, has been the subject of much local, regional, and even national research, but it remains to be adequately addressed as a transnational phenomenon. Likewise, the contemporaneous phenomenon of Left Catholicism, a Western European antecedent of subsequent Third World liberation theology, has thus far produced a fair amount of nationally specific literature, but few serious attempts to address this development on a transnational plane. So if all that a transnational approach could do is to question and dismantle national blinders, this alone would be no small matter. But there is more.

What are the objects and/or subjects of transnational studies? Here we believe that it is crucial to recognize that they may easily span the entire range of topics common to the historical discipline. To take the second of the moments of change addressed in the individual contributions here, inasmuch as some phenomena of 1968 are products of the emergence of a "consumer society," attention would be more than warranted to such "structural" transnational phenomena as demographic changes or the rise in real wages, to mention but two obvious factors. At the same time, depending on the question asked, an attempt at an analysis of some of the political manifestations of 1968 would probably necessitate a close look at the available menu of competing ideologies. This, in turn, could call for a close investigation of some prominent and many not so prominent individuals of transnational relevance—and their international contacts.

Some of the choices of the objects of study may depend on the concrete chronology and/or the actual themes chosen. Any attempt to uncover the underlying weaknesses of Stalinist regimes leading up to their near-simultaneous overthrow in 1989–1990, the third of our three moments of change, may very well focus on medium- to long-term socioeconomic or sociopolitical factors. On the other hand, a focus on the events of 1989 themselves may very well foreground individual activists and symbolic deeds. The focus on individual deeds need not forego attention to sociostructural patterns or vice versa, though the personal predilections and biases of each individual historian will undoubtedly help determine the particular pathway taken for each transnational investigation. The point is that a transnational approach is agnostic in relationship to the range of other methodologies that can be employed. Transnational history can be intellectual history or economic history, political or social history, traditional cultural history or "new" cultural history, or any combination of these and any others. Transnational history can be the domain of structuralists or voluntarists or anyone else, as long as they are researching the simultaneous emergence or the spread of phenomena across national frontiers.

A transnational approach may address the causes of and/or the reasons for the emergence of similar phenomena across national frontiers. However, few if any transnational phenomena appear simultaneously in all countries even within "just" one continent. A carefully chosen transnational approach may permit the observer to specify the range of countries affected by a given phenomenon under study and to begin the search for one or several common denominator(s). Thus, factors deemed all-important in a purely local or national study may turn out to be incidental when placed next to other similar experiences elsewhere. In many ways, this phenomenon is comparable to an Impressionist painting. Observed closely, such a painting appears to make little sense other than as a collection of color strokes in no particular order. Looked at from a distance, shapes and contours begin to emerge, while some details, striking up close, recede into the background. At the same time, of course, as any art critic knows all too well, certain individual details of Impressionist (or other) paintings may fruitfully be studied up close, as they provide important clues for the mechanics or the message of the entire work.

Transnational history is no miracle cure. History is always concrete, and for obvious reasons any satisfactory answer to virtually any significant question will need to address and untangle the web and intermixture of transnational, national, regional, and local influences. But what we are also saying is that, given a transnational historical phenomenon, it would be wholly surprising if transnational causes would be merely incidental in more than a few exceptional cases.

Our collection of essays hopes to do no more than to begin to draw the contours of what a comprehensive survey of contemporary European history may need to include. The intention of this volume was not to pretend to carry out this encyclopedic task but to give some concrete examples of the range of questions possible and the range of answers furnished by a transnational approach. As such, they may hopefully serve as inspirations for transnational works to come by future historians of contemporary Europe. For, despite some promising changes, contemporary European historical writing, in our view, as stated before, continues to suffer from a peculiar particularism.

Despite much historical knowledge on individual European countries, post-1945 transnational European history in particular has until recently remained by and large the preserve of historical sociologists and comparative political scientists. The present volume is therefore also conceived of as a contribution to the emergence of post-1944–1945 European history as a domain for research and scholarship for transnational *historians* as well.

Why should an introduction to transnational history focus on Europe? Europe, we believe, is in fact an ideal site for such study. How, after all, do processes that we call transnational, such as those mentioned earlier, spread from country to country but by modern systems of communication? We mean communication in the broadest sense: roads, rails, postal networks, telegrams and telephones, banking systems, missionaries of varying types, or armies. All of these developed rapidly in modern Europe, a continent with no major geographic obstacles to block such spread. The obstacles to the spread of ideas and practices have been immeasurably greater in Africa, Asia, South America, and Oceania. (This is not at all to suggest that such processes do not occur on those continents; postwar decolonization is excellent evidence to the contrary. But given both technological and geographic barriers, they have heretofore been generally both fewer and slower than in Europe.) North America, in turn, cannot match Europe in the sheer number of national borders (and linguistic boundaries) that must be crossed; it is therefore far less interesting as a case for transnational study. Europe is the essential laboratory, then, for transnational processes and, consequently, methodologies.

Why have we chosen to focus on the postwar era? First, the period since 1945 remains less well studied than the period 1914–1945. This is especially true of social and cultural history, but even political history is invariably less powerfully portrayed than in the cataclysmic epoch that preceded. The postwar era appears to lack a compelling grounding narrative; if there is one, it is the forward march of European prosperity and integration. This Fukuyamaesque tale neglects any sense of the European experience; at the same time, it should be obvious that, in light of integration (as well as the Cold War), nationally bounded historiography is simply inadequate to grasp the story of Europe since the fall of the Third Reich. We feel certain that transnational narratives such as those in this book offer a more dynamic view of contemporary European history: as a place and time of intense interrelation among societies, cultures, economies, and polities.

As much if not more than other historical eras, the last six decades have been marked by rapid transnational change. Thus, the second concept we engaged with in the title of the book—and in the conference call that gathered most of the contributors to this volume on the shores of Lake Como in October 2000—is the concept of moments of change or, as one of us has termed it in an earlier study, moments of opportunity and crisis. In one sense, certainly, history is always changing; but, to many observers, in some historical moments things (both structures and individuals and most certainly ideas) seem to be changing more quickly than in others.

We believe that in European history of the past half century or so, three particular historical moments of rapid and far-reaching changes can be identified: the moment of liberation, the sixties, and the fall of communism. The years most closely identified with these events and processes are 1944–1945, 1968, and 1989, though the underlying processes giving rise to the events of these fateful years began earlier and continued to influence European politics, society, and culture for quite some time after their respective high points. What guided our original conference call was not only the common adoption of a transnational approach but the focus on one of these three particular moments, however understood by each individual contributor. We believed that the combination of these two factors might provide some important keys to an understanding of the mechanisms of contemporary European history. It is for the reader to judge the results.

Before we turn to a discussion of the cases in this book, one more comment about transnational methodology and its use seems appropriate. The twelve essays included here showcase the variety of approaches possible under the transnational label, though, truth be told, some contributors would probably opt to avoid that label altogether. While we have ordered the essays in three groupings depending on the moment of change they aim to illuminate, no particular methodological inflections are associated with any one of these clusters. The precise pathway chosen to a large extent depended on the concrete problems posed and on the personal preferences of individual contributors. Yet, as is all too well-known, if methods chosen depend on the problems raised, it is no less true that certain methodologies may also preclude certain questions from ever being asked in the first place. It is precisely for this reason that we asked of all authors, regardless of their preferred historical method, be it structuralist or voluntarist or anything else, also to adopt a transnational approach. Our intention, after all, is that this book offer both a new approach to postwar Europe and a guide for those interested in transnational history anywhere, either for its own sake or in order to better understand phenomena within one national history.

This collection is intended to offer a guide to the methodological potentials, limitations, and problems of transnational history. Each of the contributors has grappled with these issues in different ways. Just as most comparative historians include (consciously or unconsciously) at least some elements of the transnational approach in their work, most (if not all) historians setting out to investigate transnational problems include elements of "simple" comparison, though the precise mix may differ widely from case to case. This kaleidoscope of possible individual approaches toward cross-national studies is reflected in the diversity of methods employed by the twelve authors included in this collection. We hope that the reader will find this useful in choosing his or her own path to transnational study or contemporary history.

We begin with two studies, the lengthiest and most geographically comprehensive in our collection, of left politics after liberation. In both cases, the authors treat topics that have traditionally been treated comparatively (if at all). As they search for common sources of similar phenomena, they both reveal the importance of underlying structures. Patrick Pasture and Aldo Agosti explore the decisions made, and the opportunities available, on the left (in Pasture's case, also on the center-right) at the close of World War II. Agosti's chapter embraces nearly the entire continent, outlining what might be termed "the communist moment" (the second such, of course, after that of 1917–1919). Except for intermittent signals from the Kremlin, interaction among parties or countries is absent in this story. Yet the continental reach invites the reader to consider common causes; these, in fact, are at the core of Agosti's concerns. The weakness of competing parties, the popular openness to parts of the communist program, and the flexibility of that program all have origins in wartime destruction, as well as in particular national circumstances.

The same holds true for Pasture's account of the quest for trade union unity. Trade unions, even more than political parties, often respond primarily to local and national socioeconomic concerns. Yet by moving beyond study of any one country to a much larger focus, Pasture demonstrates that the sources of this drive were often common and can again be traced to wartime experiences. Even where he points to differences, they are themselves frequently shared across a multicountry region. As with Agosti's work, Pasture helps us to become aware of the broad contours of a continental moment of change in Europe.

Anna Balzarro takes us more deeply into that moment, as she examines certain aspects of zones of liberation in southeast France and northwest Italy in the last year of the war. Here we are to some extent on classically comparative territory, especially if we look at certain sections of the author's treatment of memoirs. Yet the enemy is in both cases the same; the conjuncture (belief in imminent liberation) is the same; even the cast of characters has much in common, as partisans from France and Italy participate in each other's struggles. The comparative here becomes transnational, too.

Juan José Gómez Gutiérrez, in contrast, brings us a textbook example of one kind of transnational history: that of cross-national cultural influence. Here we do not encounter underlying structures but a conscious story of transnational agency. The "communist moment" was also experienced in art—or rather at the intersection of art and politics. As Gómez Gutiérrez shows, this is not simply a question of the influence on Italian artists of a style—socialist realism—originating in the USSR; rather, as artists and left politicians in Italy debated the function and aesthetics of art, they calibrated their opinions with regard to Soviet models and Soviet debates. In effect, one cannot write the early postwar history of the Italian left (and the same would be true for many other cases) without Soviet history, as Gómez Gutiérrez makes clear.

The moment of 1945 has many more dimensions than those included here. Work on the sociopolitical or economic causes and consequences of migration, for example, or on efforts at building regional alliances or networks (notably in the Balkans, but one might also include the early contacts among future members of the European Economic Community) would be equally welcome. The essays in the first section offer an introduction to the great potential for a truly transnational history of liberation.

It is more difficult to define whose year was 1968. Students, of course, or the young generation, or the left; but how to define that moment, and its desires, from a European-wide perspective? Each of our authors aims to bring greater precision to our understanding of this transnational moment.

Arthur Marwick's essay introduces us to the larger structural changes that affected all of Western Europe from the late 1950s onward. The cultural changes Marwick explores (with particular reference to France and West Germany) are more than just an expression of a zeitgeist but the expression of underlying social and economic changes since World War II. For Marwick, the remarkably similar course of the student revolt in various countries is not a coincidence but a window onto the transformation of European society.

When the subject is the aftermath of war, generational change, or an international political or cultural movement, the threads of international history may lie close to the surface. Gerd-Rainer Horn considers in his essay a case where the threads are much deeper. Worker revolt was a nearly constant presence across Europe in the 1968 era, from Spain's anti-Franco upheavals in late 1967, through the French May events and Czechoslovakia in 1968, Italy's Hot Autumn in 1969, to Portugal's revolution in 1974–1975 (and elsewhere as well). These protests often occurred in tandem with, and were supported by, student protests, but by no means always. What were the transnational links that bound or inspired worker protest? Horn finds that in this case comparative history falls short, requiring further research on the structures and agents of transnational history in 1968.

Paulina Bren brings us back to the third type of transnational study, involving conscious agents. Here we have, in fact, influences felt (and sought) across even the barrier separating the Soviet bloc and Western Europe. As Bren shows, it is one thing to list (as most studies of 1968 do) the events in Czechoslovakia's Prague Spring alongside those in Paris, Berlin, and Milan; it is another to consider precisely how echoes of events in the West were interpreted in the East and what concrete effect they might have had on Prague debates. In the encounter between "Red" Rudi Dutschke and "radical" Czech students, we can see the microprocesses of transnational history at work.

On a similar scale, Kristina Schulz maps the transnational influences of 1968 in another direction, across time. The emergence of women's movements in France and Germany in 1970–1971 Schulz traces in part to what might be termed the zeitgeist of the 1968 era, earlier themes of protest naturally spawning new ones. Yet there are other dimensions to this story, equally important. Schulz finds individual actors carrying ideas of protest across borders. Finally, by looking over a period of several years, Schulz can trace the sometimes parallel evolution of women's movements, in response to common intellectual and socioeconomic stimuli.

As several of the essays in this section point out, 1968 has remained surprisingly understudied by historians. One reason may be the lack of appropriate tools necessary to apprehend such a moment of multidirectional influences. We hope that readers will find in transnational history an opening into the moment (the long one of Marwick, the medium one explored by Schulz and Horn, and the brief moment examined by Bren) of 1968.

The moment of liberation at the end of World War II had been anticipated by resistance activists for many months. In contrast, everyone experienced 1968 as an unexpected surprise, though the peak of social movement activism occurred at widely varying times in different European states. Not only did 1989 occur like a bolt out of the blue, but it (almost) literally happened everywhere at once. What accounts for the remarkable simultaneity of the democratic revolutions across Eastern Europe?

Jarle Simensen points out that the Eastern European revolutions should actually be considered as part of an even larger wave of democratization of truly global reach. Simensen's approach to transnational studies here is actually transcontinental. Given the global dimension of his topic, he foregrounds structural conditions as responsible for democratic change, though in his concluding comments he points to the role of contingency in the historical process, and he suggests that another historical conjuncture could have produced a rather different result.

With Miroslav Vaněk, we turn to concrete historical agents in the form of Czech environmental activists. For Czech environmentalists, the German Greens performed an important role as inspiration for ecological activism. Vaněk, however, recounts the obstacles in the way of this encounter. He points out how, despite the particular severity of Czech environmental damage, ecological activism was for a very long time artificially kept at prepolitical levels by the hostile and repressive Czechoslovak state. Even as late as mid-1989, ecology protests had to, in part, rely on foreign activists to "import" the Green message.

In the transnational wave of protests against Euromissiles in the era of Ronald Reagan and Margaret Thatcher, the most serious attempts at creating a transnational network of mutual assistance and information exchange were undertaken by European Nuclear Disarmament (END) in Britain. Patrick Burke reconstructs one particular moment in this enterprise, a moment of great tensions, which at one point stretched END almost to the breaking point. Conflicting strategies over the best way to build bridges between antinuclear activists in the Eastern and the Western blocs lay at the origins of this bitter debate. Burke's detailed reconstruction of this episode may serve as a useful reminder that transnational social movement activism is not only direly needed but fraught with many pitfalls and dangers.

With Padraic Kenney's investigation of transnational opposition networks and diffusion processes, we are entering the mental and material world of underground activists. We learn about the arsenal of symbolic actions and practical solutions adopted by organizers, distributors, and couriers in the Eastern European underground. But Kenney's dynamic description and analysis also highlight another feature peculiar to the moment of 1989: the transnational radiance of Polish activism as a beacon of hope and a material mainstay of support for activists elsewhere.

Kenney's portrayal of Eastern European underground activism exemplifies the voluntarist variant of transnational history. Simensen's opening chapter in this section on 1989 approaches transnational change from the opposite angle. Vaněk points out obstacles in the path of democratic change created by Eastern governments; Burke portrays the difficulties faced by activists in the West. May this exemplary kaleidoscope of topics and methodologies serve as an inspiration for forthcoming transnational historical studies.

NOTES

1. Convention mandates that, in case of multiauthor publications, the place in the alphabetical order dictates which author gets listed first. In the case of this article, and indeed of this entire publication project, both authors are coresponsible for equal parts of the work. In the interest of "equality," we would thus like to reverse the alphabetical order here, as we prefer to give each other equal billing wherever possible.

2. Note that the European Union is not *itself* a transnational process; the study of the EU is rather an example of *inter*national history (as would be the study of the United Nations or of world trade negotiations). The EU is an underlying or supranational structure that may give rise to transnational processes that might be observed simultaneously in separate countries.

3. The contemporary processes of globalization might be considered to occupy a space between the second and third types. While globalization is on the one hand a large structure operating simultaneously on countries around the world, it is also, of course, the function of conscious actors (corporations, trade organizations, world leaders, social movements).

I

1945

1

Recasting Democracy?

Communist Parties Facing Change and Reconstruction in Postwar Europe

Aldo Agosti

THE COMMUNIST BOOM

At the end of World War II, the strength of the communist movement in Europe had enormously increased compared to the late 1930s. Both in countries liberated by the Red Army and in countries liberated by the Allied troops, the collapse of the fascist or Quisling regimes and the development, though very uneven, of the resistance movements had fostered a deep expectation of renewal in society, the economy and political institutions. In 1945–1947, Communists formed part of the government in most European countries. Apart from Yugoslavia and Albania, where they had taken power by themselves, Communists were the pivot of the "patriotic fronts" in all the countries liberated by the Red Army (Poland, Czechoslovakia, Hungary, Romania, Bulgaria) and were members of government coalitions in France, Italy, Belgium, Luxembourg, Austria, Denmark, Iceland, Norway, and Finland. The formula of antifascist unity appeared to have reasonable chances to last beyond the war and shaped in a relatively uniform way the programs of reconstruction.[1]

Of course, from various angles, Europe was already divided, though the Iron Curtain had not yet closed. The pressure of the victorious powers in their respective spheres of influence was felt well before the definitive onset of the Cold War, though it was exerted in different manners in the two halves of Europe. Nevertheless, at least for a certain time, a somewhat open conception of this influence survived among all the main partners of the Great Alliance, leaving some room for a variety of relatively flexible political and social developments.

The impressive expansion of the Communist parties has to be seen in this context, and from this point of view it obeyed the same logics both east and

3

west of the Stettin-Trieste axis, made famous by Winston Churchill in his Fulton, Missouri, speech. In general terms, this trend concerned almost all of Europe, with no distinction between winners (or allies of the winners) and defeated (or allies of the defeated), regardless of the respective countries' economic and social structures. Figures concerning individual parties will be given further on; let us simply draw an overall picture for the moment.

At the end of 1946, the membership of the Communist parties in Europe (leaving aside the USSR) amounted to between six and seven million.[2] Of course, it must be stressed that figures concerning the Communist parties of Eastern Europe could already be consciously overestimated for propagandistic reasons and must therefore be given closer scrutiny. Nevertheless, if we compare these figures both with the rough guesstimate of "one million or a little more"[3] of 1939—which refers to a context in which more than half of all European Communist parties were outlawed—and with the official data given by the Fifth Comintern Congress in 1924 (656,000 members in twenty-one countries),[4] we cannot but be impressed. Moreover, the figures on the density per one thousand inhabitants are very interesting: Between the end of 1945 and the beginning of 1946, it was less than 10:1,000 in no more than five out of twenty-three countries in which the Communists were legal and reached as high as sixty-eight in Czechoslovakia, fifty-three in Bulgaria, thirty-nine in Italy, twenty-three in Poland, and twenty in France. Already in 1924, the highest membership density rate belonged to Czechoslovakia, but even there it amounted to no more than 9:1,000, whereas it reached a mere 1.4 in France and 0.3 in Italy.

Such an organizational explosion was generally accompanied by a widening of the social base. With almost no exception, the strength of the Communist parties rested on the working class, but their social implantation was generally wider and more varied. In March 1946, the membership of the Communist Party of Czechoslovakia (KSČ) was 57.7 percent workers, 12.8 percent farmers, 9.2 percent "intellectual workers," and 4.1 percent small craftsmen and shopkeepers.[5] In many countries, and particularly in France and Italy, the Communist parties deeply penetrated the peasant world, not only the milieu of landless laborers but also the world of sharecroppers and, to some extent, even that of smallholders. France experienced what has been called a "ruralization" of the party that was linked, on the one hand, to its role in the *maquis* and, on the other, to the moderating action it tried to exert on workers' struggles. The communitarian traditions of rural areas, which had formerly been linked to other political cultures (socialist or radical), evolved to Communist predominance, while the French Communist Party (PCF) lost members in its working-class strongholds. At Renault in Boulogne-Billancourt, the ratio of members to the total number of employees fell from 23.3 percent in 1937 to 8.3 percent in 1946.[6] In Italy, the party was composed of 53.4 percent workers and 33 percent peasants, two-thirds of the latter being laborers, tenants, or sharecroppers.[7] In Poland, factory workers accounted for 62.2 percent of the Polish Workers' Party (PPR) membership and peasants only 28.2 percent; 69 percent of the latter were farmers who benefited from the agrarian reform.[8]

Generally speaking, the Communist parties exerted a great attraction over intellectuals: In France, 10 percent of *école normale* students were members of the PCF in 1946, while the party's influence in the world of arts, humanities, and, to a lesser extent, science was constantly expanding in Italy. On a smaller scale, this trend was common also in Great Britain, Belgium, and many countries of Eastern Europe.[9] In the countries occupied by the Red Army, to join the party had a clear implication of social promotion. This attracted an increasing number of clerks and public service personnel, who remained generally immune to communist propaganda in Western Europe. Those described as "clerical and administrative staff" or "employees" represented 16.8 percent of party members in Czechoslovakia in early 1947, while the percentage of workers had fallen to 45.7 percent.[10]

The electoral figures of 1945–1946 reflect the increased membership and the widening of the social base of the Communist parties. In the countries untouched by Soviet occupation, the Communists—running almost everywhere under their proper name and their own symbols, and only seldom as part of wider left coalitions—gained over 25 percent of the popular vote in France; around 20 percent in Finland and Italy; over 10 percent in Belgium, Denmark, Luxembourg, Netherlands, Norway, and Sweden; and approximately the same average level in the Berlin districts occupied by the Western Powers; only in Austria and Switzerland did they reach a poor 5 percent.[11] In the countries of Eastern Europe, the Communist vote is doubtless a less reliable indicator of their real influence, both because it is not easy to disaggregate it from the results achieved by the wider democratic or popular fronts of which they formed a part, and because already in 1945–1946, truly free elections took place only in Czechoslovakia and Hungary. At any rate, even the electoral strength of the Communist parties was remarkable, as we will see. Apart from the exceptional cases of Yugoslavia and Albania, the most impressive outcome was the result obtained by the Communist Party of Czechoslovakia, which in May 1946 won 38 percent of the vote.

The prominent role the various Communist parties had played in the resistance almost everywhere in Europe was the main reason for their general expansion.[12] In the first place, the great popularity of the USSR, which had sustained the heaviest losses in the war against Nazi Germany, projected a positive image onto the other Communist parties that were perceived as the representatives of Soviet antifascist efforts. Second, even if their language was usually moderate and the slogans of socialist revolution were not mentioned in their platforms, the radicalization of class conflict, along with the struggle for national independence, allowed the Communist parties to benefit from the great hopes for social change stirred up by victory; the Communists were indeed very skillful in cultivating these expectations. They often presented themselves to their allies as the only force able to control and channel these expectations within the framework of national liberation. They were also careful to capitalize on the radical feelings of the masses and did not disregard the possibility of appealing to them in case the struggle for power should turn out to become practicable again.

Communist party structure, which hinged on "professional revolutionaries" forged in the 1920s and shaped by the extreme situations of civil war, proved particularly suitable when facing the conjuncture of social protest, armed struggle, and repression, which marked the final stage of the war. Total devotion to the cause, courage, personal unselfishness, and the extremely high price paid in human lives (the PCF earned itself, and proudly claimed, the label of *parti des fusilés*) literally forced the Allies to take account of Communist militants and strengthened the latter's influence in a wide range of social milieus. The occupiers and the Quisling governments objectively favored this trend, because they systematically identified resisters with Communists, in order to discredit the former but thereby finally serving only to increase the prestige of the latter. Faced with all this, even the not at all unusual recourse by Communist parties to unscrupulous methods against their political adversaries (such as the brutal liquidation of Trotskyists in, e.g., the French resistance) seemed little more than a painful detail. Finally, their organizational skill had been decisive in forging structures of resistance at the local level and on the factory floor; this bestowed on them unprecedented and unexpected political weight in the immediate postwar period.

The resistance, however, was not the only factor accounting for the communist boom. The roots they had been able to grow within their respective national societies before the war counted as well. The three numerically strongest Communist parties in Europe between late 1945 and early 1946 (Italian, French, and Czechoslovak) belonged to the exclusive Gotha of the Communist parties that boasted mass support since the beginning of their history. By contrast (see, e.g., the cases of Belgium, the Netherlands, and Denmark), in countries where their development had been difficult and where their organizations remained weak, their organizational force and penetration into the tissue of unions, cooperatives, clubs, and so forth were by no means comparable to those of their social democratic rivals, even when their leading role in the resistance allowed them to narrow the gap. This distance was regularly mirrored by their electoral results. For example, in Belgium the Belgian Communist Party (PCB) grew in the first year after liberation from eleven thousand to eighty-eight thousand members, approaching the ninety-five thousand of the Belgian Socialist Party (PSB); but at the 1946 general elections, it lagged behind the PSB by twenty points (12.7 percent and 32.5 percent, respectively).[13]

Formally, this impressive communist army no longer had an international "command center"; the Comintern had been dissolved in 1943. Nevertheless, the psychological and political ties with the Communist Party of the Soviet Union had by no means loosened. The relationship of each party with Moscow remained very tight; certainly, it remained important with regard to finances, but there were also constant consultations on main political issues, both national and international. Of course, the margin of autonomous decision making of the individual parties varied according to their organizational strength, their weight in the national arena, and the role each of them had been assigned by Soviet foreign policy. Occasionally, some Communist parties could act against the Soviet party's advice. Such was probably the case of the Greek Communist Party, when it decided not to take part in the March 1946 elections. In other situations, as in France and in Italy, the ties with the USSR remained very tight, but the organizational strength and the social implantation of the Communists produced an increasing number of "endogenous" factors that played a role in party policy, a development for which the Soviet leaders themselves showed the utmost consideration.

In the countries of Eastern Europe, dependence on Soviet guidance took on a far more direct and restrictive character. Here, the growth of the Communist parties in terms of membership and votes was made easier by the close cooperation between occupiers and local Communist leaders (many of whom had been educated in Moscow). On the other hand, the collapse of the old regimes, which had generally been based on the power of landed, financial, and/or industrial elites with strong German participation, left a vacuum in which the impulse to renew institutions and to recast the political system was stronger. In these countries, the Communist parties organized rapidly and acquired key positions in the state apparatus, occupying the most important ministries (Internal Affairs, Justice, Economy). Nevertheless, their strength remained rather uneven at the beginning of the postwar period.

THE BIRTH OF PEOPLE'S DEMOCRACIES

In Yugoslavia and Albania, where the national territory had been liberated almost solely by an armed resistance that they strongly monopolized, the Communists enjoyed wide-ranging popular support and were able to take over power practically alone, notwithstanding cautionary advice coming from Moscow. As early as November 1945, the Yugoslav electors were given no choice but the list of the Communist-oriented Popular Front, which won over 90 percent of the votes; but there is little doubt that, though the traditional parties had been marginalized and prevented from exerting any effective opposition, this plebiscite expressed a deep and authentic popular consent.[14]

Bulgaria had a relatively well-rooted communist tradition, and pro-Russian feeling there can be traced back centuries. Moreover, the fact that the country would belong to the Soviet sphere of influence had never been under dispute. The Communist Party, given the support of the Soviet occupiers and the indifference of the Western Allied powers, was thus able to place under its control rather quickly all vital points of state organization.[15]

Elsewhere the situation was far less favorable to the Communist parties. Mistrust toward the occupying power was more than evident in Poland, Hungary, and Romania, where the Red Army often had recourse to pillage and violence. In each of these countries, the Communists, though rapidly growing, represented but a minority component of the "national fronts" that had led the resistance. In Poland in particular, the Communist identification with Soviet interests was a serious handicap after the wounds left by the Molotov-Ribbentrop Pact; the Polish Communist Party thus chose to enter the political arena under the new label of Polish Workers' Party (PPR). Though it extended its support among the working class and the poor peasantry (membership went up from about 20,000 in early 1944 to 235,000 in late 1945 and 556,000 one year later),[16] it had to compete with the still-vital Polish Socialist Party, which was split but deeply attached to its independence, and with the strong Polish Peasant Party. The compromise reached in June 1945 with regard to the enlargement of the Communist-controlled Lublin government (later moved to Warsaw), as well as its acknowledgment by the Western Allies, strengthened the PPR's influence, but it could not prevent an unsettled and tense situation, which lasted for a relatively long period. From 1945 to 1947, the government even had to confront an underground resistance movement, organized by moderate or right-wing survivors of the antifascist resistance. Ultimately, the Communists were able to turn to their advantage the need for order and normalcy, and with consummate tactical skill they induced the country to express its will via a referendum on a series of issues (including agrarian reform, the Oder–Neisse border, and partial nationalizations), which their reluctant allies could not reject. When the first general elections took place in January 1947, the climate was already conditioned by the pressure the PPR was able to exercise through control of key ministries, the army, and the police.[17]

In Romania, the Soviet occupation and the influence exerted by the Soviet representative in the Inter-Allied Control Committee increased the weight of the Communists, of whom there existed only a few thousand at the end of the war. General elections took place in November 1946; the result was largely favorable to the Democratic Front (of its 347 seats, 272 went to the Communists; only 96 to the opposition parties). This outcome cannot be explained only by intimidations and vote riggings, though there was no lack of both. As in Bulgaria and Yugoslavia, already before the end of the war, the unscrupulous control and use of the fundamental mechanisms of power had been employed against political adversaries much more frequently than the ballot box.[18]

In Hungary, too, the Communist Party, which had been persecuted by the Horthy regime and decimated by the purges in the USSR during the 1930s, was in 1944 a rather meager and relatively isolated force; nor was it helped by the strong anti-Russian prejudices nourished by the population and fostered by the territorial losses suffered in favor of Romania, for which the Soviets were blamed. In the November 1945 elections, the Hungarian Communist Party (MKP) won only 17 percent of the votes, against 57 percent for the Smallholder Party. The latter, however, was an accumulation of heterogeneous currents; it was not solely because of Communist skill in maneuvering that it began to disintegrate. At the same time, a strong current within social democracy favored an alliance with the MKP. The great progress in recruitment accomplished by the Communists (30,000 members in February 1945, 225,000 in July, 608,000 by January 1946), however, was difficult to translate into electoral consent. In August 1946, the bloc including the two left parties won 60 percent of the votes, but the MKP achieved only a disappointing 22 percent.[19]

The case of Czechoslovakia looked quite different. The exile government and later the provisional government of the newly liberated territory based themselves from the very beginning on a wide and relatively united alliance, headed by President Edvard Beneš, who strongly supported a foreign policy oriented toward friendship with the Soviet Union. The Communists were part of both these governments. Together with the socialists and the Populist Party, they formed a National Front, which worked out a rather advanced program of reforms. The Communist Party had emerged from the resistance as the most organized and prestigious force. Its members had increased from 40,000 in late 1944 to 475,000 in June 1945 and to 826,000 at the end of the year, which meant that one out of every nine inhabitants in the Czech lands, and one out of twenty-five in Slovakia, was a Communist Party member.[20] Its influence branched out in the network of unions, shop committees, women's and youth organizations, sports associations, and the important league of war veterans. The 1946 elections were genuinely free, at least in the sense that the four government parties were free to compete under equal conditions, even if the parties accused of having contributed to the dismemberment of the country in 1938–1939 were not allowed to participate. The KSČ won 38 percent of the vote and emerged as the most popular party in the country, although it was much stronger in Bohemia and Moravia than in Slovakia. Together with the Socialist Party, it held an absolute majority of seats in parliament.[21]

The case of the Soviet Occupied Zone in Germany (SBZ) is, of course, *sui generis*. Besides the eastern half of Berlin, it included a highly industrialized area, Saxony, and three mainly rural *Länder*. The occupying power authorrized almost immediately the rebirth of four antifascist political parties, which in July 1945 united in a Democratic Front, in whose executive organs they were represented on an equal basis and where they were bound to uphold unanimity. The German Communist Party (KPD), having reached half a million members in early 1946 (about twice the membership it had attained at the zenith of its development in the Weimar Republic), followed at first a line that has been labeled a course of "immoderate moderation," assuming a goal of consolidating a new parliamentary "antifascist" republic and relegating the socialist stage to an indefinite future.[22]

A turn that would prove fateful in the escalation toward the division of Germany occurred with the merging of the KPD and the German Social Democratic Party into the Socialist Unity Party of Germany (SED) in April 1946. This was partly the result of genuine rank-and-file pressure for unity, but the timing and modes of the merger were in fact imposed by the Soviet authorities. Though the liberty of action of the "bourgeois parties" had already been considerably limited, the local elections that took place in September–October 1946 were but a hard-earned success of the new party. Nevertheless, they were the starting point for the SED to spread its control over the entirety of political life in the SBZ. With six hundred thousand trained and disciplined members (the factory cell once again became the nucleus of its structure), the party undertook a strong campaign of "denazification"; at the same time, the room for the other political organizations was restricted, and their independence became merely formal.[23]

Many different factors played a role in the relatively steady march of the Eastern European Communist parties toward the monopoly of power: tactical skill, extent of infiltration of noncommunist organizations, recourse to intimidation facilitated by the Soviet occupier and the Communists' control over the police, as well as their genuine capacity for building mobilization and consent. It is not at all easy to assess what weight may be attributed to each individual factor. In each of the cases mentioned earlier, the programs of the Communist parties called for political, social, and economic reforms that appeared necessary in order to reconstruct disrupted economies and to overcome their historic backwardness or, as in Czechoslovakia, to quickly recover the levels of prewar development. The Communist challenge to the democratic and even to the socialist parties, which, often weak and split, were usually not very consistent in their appeals for radical innovations, resulted in a noteworthy following among the most important social groups. Intellectuals, deceived by prewar governments and often fascinated by Marxism and its promise of equality and social redemption, were rather prone to the Communist message. In any case, many of them considered that, in the geopolitical situation that the outcome of the war had reserved for their countries, the future belonged to the Communists; thus, the most reasonable thing to do was to join them, if only in order to mitigate their excesses and encourage democratization. Elements among the intelligentsia hitherto firmly belonging to the socialist and peasant parties were pushed in that direction.

For the peasants, the prospects of an agrarian reform based on the distribution of land meant the fulfillment of a centuries-old aspiration. The initially rather moderate plans worked out by the Communists in this domain induced peasants to embrace the Communists' economic programs. The fear of an eventual collectivization of the land persisted, but this did not prevent the peasants from welcoming the liquidation of the large landowners, who had oppressed them for centuries, and to praise above all the Communists for such a favorable turn of events.

More than anyone else, workers and technicians, as the classes most interested in reactivating industrial production, saw Communists as the leading force of social and civic progress. Thus, the Communists, though often a minority, could exploit a situation in which any opposition to their reconstruction programs was tantamount to the sabotage of the national interest.[24]

Another factor the Communist parties of Eastern Europe were able to turn to their advantage was the strong presence of nationalist feelings. In 1945–1946, Communists were the most active promoters of the expulsion of the German populations not only from the Slavic countries but also from Hungary and Romania. In Slovakia, the Communist leaders Vladimír Clementis and Gustáv Husák were as much if not more intransigent than their nationalist allies in urging the expulsion of the Hungarian minority. The Romanian Communist Lucretiu Patrascanu was criticized even by the Soviets for the discriminatory measures he adopted against the Hungarians in Transylvania. All this created a serious potential for conflicts among a variety of countries; such problems would have certainly emerged sooner or later had Soviet control not been imposed onto that part of Europe. For the moment, however, with the exceptions of Hungary and partly of Poland, the Communists succeeded in presenting themselves as the guarantors of the "sacred egoism" of their respective countries.

Last but not least, the Eastern European Communists were favored by their outward appearance of ruthless determination and inner resolve in pursuing their aims. In fact, significant differentiations existed already in their ranks, which could be explained by generational conflicts and different political sensibilities. One such factor undercutting party unity was the experience of the "muscovites"—those cadres trained in the USSR at the Comintern school in the tragic atmosphere of repression during the 1930s. Another was the experience of those party members who had fought in the Spanish Civil War; another one yet that of the exiles in the democratic countries; not to speak of the survivors of the Nazi concentration camps (the so-called *kazetniki*) or of those who had come to the fore in the resistance. All these differences would weigh heavily in the future, but for the moment they seemed canceled out by an apparently complete unity of goals.

The overall picture offered by the Eastern European countries in the two years following the end of World War II was thus marked by notable similarities but also by deep differences. In any case, at least until the end of

1946, it was not an experience of "sovietized" countries. It is still an open question whether Stalin from the beginning planned to shape these countries into economic and political satellites of the USSR and to impose on them a uniform social and institutional model, imitating the Soviet one; or whether, in an international situation less tense than the one that eventually became reality, he would have been satisfied with a "finlandization" of this part of the continent, a status favoring peaceful coexistence guaranteed by nonhostile governments, conditioned but not necessarily controlled by the Communist parties.[25] Whatever the case may be, as late as autumn 1946 the model of "popular democracies" in Eastern Europe remained compatible with forms of pluralism totally unknown in the history of the Soviet Union. Apart from Yugoslavia and Albania, the nationalization of the main economic sectors proceeded gradually (as late as the end of 1947, the private sector supplied about two-thirds of production in Poland and Hungary), and the agrarian reform was based on the principle of parceling out and redistributing the big landed estates, whereas planning responded most of all to the need to reconstruct a seriously damaged productive apparatus.[26]

Some attempts were made to frame this evolution in a theoretical model. All the Communist leaders—and not only in Eastern Europe, as we will see—in 1944–1946 extolled the virtues of "national," "specific" roads to socialism, clearly distinct from the Soviet experience of "proletarian dictatorship." Although Joseph Stalin never stated publicly his opinion about the social nature of the regimes developing to the west of the USSR's borders (he simply declared that the advent of socialism by parliamentary means was not impossible), a spokesman as authoritative as the Soviet-Hungarian economist Evgeni Varga talked about "democracies of a new type," where the old state apparatus was to be deeply transformed, while at the same time keeping "the outward forms of parliamentary democracy" and a mixed economic structure. In such a state, political power could be exerted by national coalitions of different political parties, expressing an alliance based on the predominance of the working class in conjunction with the peasantry, but open to the urban middle classes, intellectuals, and a part of the bourgeoisie itself, aiming to block the road toward the return of fascism by means of far-reaching social reforms. There was a clear connection to the earlier evocation of the desirability of a "democracy of a new type" at the time of the Spanish Civil War, although the historical precedent was not explicitly recalled. It is hard to say to what extent these sorts of theories (which were particularly favored by the Polish secretary-general, Władysław Gomułka)[27] reflected a true aspiration to build socialism in a way clearly distinct from the Soviet model, thus bypassing the stage of proletarian dictatorship, and how much they represented merely tactical acrobatics, concealing the purposeful pursuit of power by the Communist parties. To be sure, these new theoretical departures met with some "leftist" resistance—in the Polish party, for instance—and they were only halfheartedly welcomed by the Yugoslavs, who thought that the national peculiarity of their experience should by no means dilute their revolutionary and communist identity. It was the Yugoslav Communists who first described their own new state as a "people's democracy," though they regarded this formula as a simple variation of "proletarian dictatorship" or "Soviet democracy."[28]

TO THE WEST OF THE IRON CURTAIN

At the end of the war, two countries found themselves in conditions roughly similar to those of the future "people's democracies"; their destiny, and the destiny of their Communist parties, were, however, notably different. In Austria, a portion of which was occupied by Soviet troops, a provisional coalition government was formed in April 1945, with the participation of the Socialists, the People's Party (Catholics) and the Communists, the latter controlling no less than nine ministries. The November elections, however, saw a clear success of the first two parties and a stinging defeat for the Communist Party, which barely obtained four seats with 5 percent of the votes. This result was far from a reflection of the central role the Communists had played in the underground resistance to Nazism. On the other hand, social democracy, as the heir of a massive organized force, had also never compromised itself either with the clericofascist Dollfuß regime or with the post-Anschluss governments; its prestige among the working class was essentially untouched. The second postwar government saw the presence of only one Communist minister. In 1946 and 1947, an important part of the economy was nationalized (as much as 70 percent of industrial production was now state controlled), but the political system rapidly consolidated itself in the form of a parliamentary democracy, strongly characterized by the features of a consociational agreement between the two major parties.[29]

Finland, having withdrawn from the alliance with Nazi Germany and sided with the Allies in September 1944, was able, once the war was over, to avoid Soviet occupation. In addition, from the very beginning the USSR appeared reluctant to assert the overwhelming weight it could have exerted on its neighboring country, and the Soviet leadership adopted a line that has been called a course of "confident moderation."[30] In the process, it probably overrated the strength of the Communist Party (which had 150,000 members and notable influence in the trade unions) and underestimated the inner unity of social democracy. Elections took place already in March 1945, at a time when cooperation between Moscow and the Allies was still in full force, and they did not give rise to recriminations or reciprocal accusations of interference. The moderate and center parties garnered 101 seats, with the left obtaining ninety-nine seats. Forty-nine out of these ninety-nine seats were held by an alliance of the Communist Party with various left socialist organizations. A coalition government was formed by the Agrarian Party, the Social

Democrats, and the Communists. Since the latter controlled the Ministry of the Interior and the police, and as the government began significant economic reforms and purged the state apparatus, the situation was not dissimilar to the state of affairs within the Central European countries. Nevertheless, in 1945 and for part of 1946, the Soviet leadership, having in Andrei Zhdanov an influential spokesperson, tended to put the brakes on that part of the local Communist leadership aiming to embark on a more radical course. Despite occasional tactical turns, for the Soviets it was enough to have a friendly government in Finland, not interfering with Soviet foreign policy and unwilling to put in question the boundary changes achieved during the Winter War of 1940.[31]

As mentioned earlier, the progress of the Communist parties was not less impressive in the countries that had not been affected by Soviet occupation. Even in Sweden, which had stayed out of the war, the Communists were able to exploit the popularity of the USSR and the admiration for the first-rate role their brother parties had played in the other Scandinavian countries. They won a significant 10.3 percent of votes and fifteen seats in the 1944 election, repeating this performance in 1946. Their progress was remarkable in terms of membership, too. In 1946, they counted forty-four thousand members, four times more than before the war.[32] In Denmark, too, the active role played in the resistance considerably strengthened a party that, before the war, had barely been more than a small sect. The Danish Communist Party had two ministers in the government formed immediately after liberation, and in the 1945 elections it jumped from forty-one thousand votes and three seats obtained in 1939 to a quarter million votes (12.5 percent) and eighteen seats.[33]

The case of Norway is more interesting yet. The workers' movement in this country had nourished a radical, pugnacious tradition, as a result never quite feeling satisfactorily represented by social democracy, and it was further reinvigorated by the resistance experience. Communist Party membership multiplied by five, and its influence considerably increased within the trade unions, in which it was able to hold sway over roughly 30 percent of the rank and file immediately after the war. The daily newspaper *Friheten* was for a certain period the second largest daily in the country. In the 1945 elections, the Norwegian Communist Party (KPN) polled 11.9 percent of votes and gained 11 seats, exceeding 20 percent of the vote in the major cities. The KPN was represented in the government by two ministers and, though paying lip service to the unification with social democracy, did little to obtain it, jealous as it was of its own radical traditions and culture. But the most remarkable peculiarity of the KPN was the real presence of a lively inner-party debate, taking on aspects of open and public struggles between various tendencies.[34]

The de facto division of the Netherlands into two parts, the south liberated by the Allies as early as autumn 1944 and the north occupied by the Germans until May 1945, caused divergent political orientations within the Dutch Communist Party (CPN). Under the influence of its "historical" leader, Paul De Groot, the idea of "dissolving" the party into a wider progressivist grouping prevailed. The nucleus of this organization was to be the network of small groups that had crystallized around the journal *De Waarheid*, which had acquired an extensive readership during the resistance. Only later on, under the pressure of the Belgian and French brother parties (who certainly also gave voice to Soviet "advice"), was the Communist Party rebuilt in its original independent structure. Despite fair success in the 1945 elections, where the CPN garnered 10.3 percent of votes, and despite the remarkable influence of their independent trade union federation, which at the height of its influence came close to obtaining half of the membership of the social democratic union federation, as early as late 1945 the Communists found themselves as isolated as they had been in the prewar period.[35]

In Belgium, the PCB entered the government of national unity in September 1944, immediately after liberation, but displayed a rather conflictual attitude toward it and finally left the government two months later. The PCB claimed one hundred thousand members, ten times more than before the war; it also created a trade union of its own, the *Comité de lutte syndicale*, which was influential in some industrial areas and proved able to conquer positions among the middle classes as well, particularly among teachers and clerks. In the elections of February 1946, the PCB got over 12 percent of the vote within Belgium as a whole, reaching up to 30 percent in parts of Wallonia (21.6 percent in Wallonia as a whole) and 17.4 percent in Brussels, but only 5.5 percent in Flanders. A government of left-wing parties, without the participation of the Catholics, was then formed in a context polarized by the confessional divide and exasperated by the controversy over the "royal question," due to the Belgian king's attitude toward the Nazi occupier during the war. This government lasted only a year. In March 1947, the relationship between the uneasy allies had become very tense, with the four Communist ministers opposing the rise in the price of coal demanded by the business community. In the process, the PCB left the government.[36]

In Great Britain, the Communist Party (CPGB) had reached the zenith of its organizational strength in 1943 with sixty thousand members. After the opening of the second front, recruitment slowed down; in 1946, its membership had plummeted to little more than forty thousand. The British electoral system allowed few successes for Communist candidates who were not supported by Labour, but the results of July 1945 were worse than expected, with only two members of Parliament elected. However, the unforeseen Labour victory was at the same time the result of a social and political atmosphere to which CPGB activism had contributed in a major way. Communist strength in the unions had increased impressively. The party daily, *The Daily Worker*, had a print run of over one hundred thousand copies for some years. Among cultural and academic circles, CPGB influence was quite extensive as well (the "historians' group" alone, which included people such as E. P. Thompson, Christopher Hill, and Eric J. Hobsbawm, numbered more than one hundred members).[37]

As we have seen, the most brilliant exploits in terms of both electoral growth and organizational expansion were accomplished by the Communist parties of France and Italy, where it was clear that conquering power through revolution was totally unrealistic. In each country, the respective Communist party formed a constituent part of coalition governments, in which they gave proof of remarkable moderation to the point that, at least at first, their contribution was seen even by the political and economic elites as a guarantee against uncontrolled social upheavals. Their commitment to stimulating production and reining in strikes was strong and clear in France as well as in Italy.[38]

Of course, such a "constructive" attitude can be explained also by the fact that, outside the areas that the Yalta agreement had acknowledged as its sphere of influence, the USSR wished no revolutionary upheavals; on the contrary, it feared them above all else. In this respect, the political situation in the immediate post–World War II era had deeply changed compared to the "red years" after World War I. The complaints about the "missed revolutionary opportunity," echoed in late 1960s historiography,[39] have simply ignored this irrefutable fact. There is no doubt that the leaders of the two major Communist parties in Western Europe were fully aware that they were acting in a context of international relations in which the classic revolutionary perspective was blocked a priori, as the fatal Greek experience had proven from the end of 1944 onward. The Communists' expressly declared goal was to recast the democratic republic on the basis of a wide-ranging social consensus, aiming to establish antifascism as the key concept in the distinction between the politically legitimate and the politically unacceptable. The features of this project remained rather vague, even though they echoed the definitions of "progressive democracy" that were, as we have seen, also current in the countries liberated by the Red Army. It is hard to say whether Palmiro Togliatti and Maurice Thorez, when speaking of this issue, were thinking of a transitional stage to socialism or simply giving a theoretical justification to a tactic aimed at maximizing the influence of the Communist Party and legitimating it within the existing system of representative democracy. In any case, the political lines of the PCF and the Italian Communist Party (PCI) developed in a notably different way.

The strength of the French Communist Party (eight hundred thousand members at the end of 1946) was essentially similar to that in the era of the popular fronts in the 1930s. But the party now gained mass support in the rural areas, among the middle classes, and, most of all, among intellectuals. The General Trade Union Federation (CGT), numbering four million members, was now firmly controlled by the Communists, who represented about 80 percent of the delegates at the April 1946 CGT congress. The PCF emerged from the first elections in October 1945 as the strongest party in France, scoring 26.2 percent of votes. Together with the Socialists, it held the absolute majority of seats in the Constituent Assembly elected on that occasion. After one year of precarious stability and a long debate on the new forms of the state, the elections of October 1946, held to designate the first parliament of the Fourth Republic, gave the Communists 28.3 percent of votes. These results convinced them that the time had come to launch the candidacy of their leader, Maurice Thorez, for the post of prime minister. The breach of party discipline by about twenty Socialist deputies did not allow Thorez to win the parliamentary vote. It was an alarming but underestimated signal. The alliance with the Socialists, the keystone of PCF tactics in this conjuncture, showed thinly veiled flaws, and the isolation of the PCF in the national political arena clearly began to emerge.[40]

Only eight months after the liberation of Italy, the force of the Communist Party in Italy was even more impressive than that of its brother party beyond the Alps. The Fifth Party Congress at the end of 1945 claimed just under 1,800,000 members. The Communist position in Italian society was the direct result of a long phase of expansion. Never before in Italy had a mass party reached a comparable size. In late 1946, its membership for the first time exceeded the two million mark. This impressive organizational force was reinforced and supported by a wide network of mass organizations spread all over the country and combined with the decisive influence the Communists held in the united trade union federation. Nevertheless, the elections to the Constituent Assembly (2 June 1946), which took place together with the referendum on the republican form of government, gave the PCI only 18.9 percent of the popular vote, a result significantly below its expectations, leaving it to trail far behind Christian Democracy and even (though barely) the Socialist Party. Actually, the party had not been able to find its way into the middle-class electorate. Its impressive organizational structure was not matched by comparable political influence.[41]

There is no doubt that the widespread and sociologically diverse influence of the party, which was a reality despite the disappointing electoral returns, was also the result of the political strategy it had worked out during the resistance. The participation of the PCI in the governments of antifascist unity, which followed in quick succession from 1945 to 1947, and the choice to privilege the alliance of the three mass parties were the coherent expression of an orientation toward "progressive democracy." This, in and of itself, did not represent an exception to the general trend within the Communist movement in those years. The most original contribution of the Italian Communists, and of Togliatti himself, was in rethinking the kind of party that should be constructed to conform to and benefit from this strategy. The PCI was the only Communist party that, without openly questioning the concept, dropped the Leninist model of party building. Both the strategy of "progressive democracy" and the conception of the "new party," however, met with significant, though seldom explicit, opposition in the rank and file and even within the middle cadres of the party, among whom a rebellious and "class-against-class" consciousness had not completely disappeared. The new line of the PCI and the organizational changes that accompanied this turn constituted a profound change, which was not accepted without mental reservations by all members. Some sectors of the party complied with the official party line only, or mostly, because they thought its stated moderation was a tactical trick aimed at cheating the adversary or a provisional device imposed by an unfavorable situation, which the party would get rid of as soon as possible, in order then to apply its allegedly "true" policy—namely, the Communist seizure of power.[42]

The tolerance of such views was implicitly and sometimes explicitly supported by statements made by Togliatti and other prominent party leaders. This policy of *doppiezza* (duplicity), however, ultimately evolved toward the absolute predominance of the moderate view, both because of Togliatti's political initiative and because of the conditions under which political and social conflicts occurred in Italy at that time. The moderate line it adopted in 1944, followed by its stubborn effort to work out a blueprint for a democratic state together with the parties who had been part of the antifascist resistance front, allowed the PCI to establish itself permanently as one of the major political forces in the country. The total commitment of the party to constructive collaboration within the Constituent Assembly survived even the ousting of the left parties, most notably the PCI, from the coalition government in May 1947.[43]

SIGNALS OF GLACIATION

All things considered, for at least eighteen months after the end of the war, the communist movement in Western and Southern Europe seemed to enjoy excellent health, and its perspectives looked, if not equally promising everywhere, at least open to positive developments. There were at least three exceptions.

In Spain, even after the defeat suffered in 1944, the Spanish Communist Party (PCE) continued to concentrate its efforts on building an effective guerilla movement. But the groups it succeeded in organizing were never able to stir up a general insurrection. Still, from 1945 to early 1947, they caused considerable troubles to Franco's regime, particularly through sabotage actions. Repression, however, was merciless and effective. The *guerilla* was able to survive precariously for some years, but this was due more to the geography of the country than to tangible support of the rural population.

The PCE soon realized that the method of armed struggle was not suitable, and it attempted to overcome its isolation, supporting the exiled Republican governments and even joining them with its own ministers. Nevertheless, mutual suspicion dominated its relations with other antifascist forces.[44]

In Portugal, Antonio Salazar had shown, in the summer of 1945, some intentions of holding democratic elections, and he had promulgated a relatively wide-ranging amnesty. Yet the illusions of democratization soon vanished and repression intensified anew. In spite of all difficulties, the Portuguese Communist Party had about seven thousand members and remained by far the strongest and best-organized force within the broad opposition to Salazar.[45]

In Greece, harsh repression targeted the Communist Party (KKE) after the defeat of the uprising of December 1944. In the following year, almost twenty thousand militants were arrested, while another eighty thousand were sought by the police. Even before the elections of March 1946 sanctioned the victory of the monarchist right over the liberals (an outcome favored also by the boycott of the KKE), civil war broke out in the country. The reestablishment of the monarchy after the September 1946 referendum convinced the KKE that there were no chances of reentering the scene as a legal force; moreover, the increasingly generous aid the guerillas received from the Yugoslav government, cautiously supported by the USSR, beguiled the Communists with the short-lived hope of a military victory.[46]

The developments of the situation in Greece and the concern for the future of Turkey gave U.S. president Harry Truman the occasion to proclaim his doctrine: The United States was now engaged to "support free people who are resisting attempted subjugation by armed minorities or by outside pressures" in whatever country the "free institutions" (i.e., the regime of "free enterprise") were endangered. Actually, the American move was but the last stage of the increasing deterioration in the relationships between the former allies. As early as late 1946, signals of a change in the international situation and the progressive carving out of the spheres of influence by the two opposing blocs had become patently obvious. The room left for government coalitions based on antifascist unity, which had depended on the prospect of cooperation between the Great Powers in reorganizing Europe, was closing again. From late 1946 to early 1947, the Communist parties of Eastern Europe sped up the monopolization of political power, intensified their pressure against the "bourgeois" opposition, and in fact absorbed the socialist parties. Only in Czechoslovakia and to a certain extent in Hungary did this trend look not yet irreversible. On the other hand, the position of the Communist parties in the governments of Western Europe became day by day increasingly precarious.

In France, disagreements between the PCF and the socialists sharpened at first vis-à-vis the colonial question: The Communist deputies, with the exception of the ministers in office, voted against the government, which opposed any negotiation with the Vietnamese guerillas. But the breaking point was eventually reached in the area of wage policy. After some hesitations, the CGT supported a spontaneous strike in the Renault firm, which had been nationalized after liberation. The Ramadier government asked again for a vote of confidence on its economic policy, and all the Communist deputies voted against. Without even the formal proclamation of a government crisis, the Communist members of the cabinet were ousted.[47]

In Italy, the PCI was having a hard time on the knotty problem of Trieste, which was claimed by Yugoslavia.[48] The unity pact binding the two Italian workers' parties was questioned by an influential minority of the Socialists, who promoted a split in January 1947. De Gasperi, who was also under intense economic and political pressure by the United States, seized the opportunity to proclaim a crisis situation within the ruling coalition, and the left parties emerged out of it considerably weakened. Less than three months later, the disagreements about economic policy brought to an end the tripartite alliance. A new government was formed by Christian Democracy with the support of supposedly neutral "technical experts," while the PCI and the Socialists were excluded.[49]

In Great Britain, too, the "critical support" of the CPGB to the Labour government was gradually replaced by bitter accusations against the "reactionary trend" of government politics. As mentioned earlier, the Belgian Communists left the government in March, while the Danes, the Norwegians, and the Dutch had done the same in the course of 1946, in different circumstances and on different grounds. Only in Finland and Iceland did the "front organizations" controlled by the Communists remain in government until 1948.

The decisive turning point was the Marshall Plan, which the American secretary of state announced on 5 June 1947. After some hesitations, the USSR came to perceive the conspicuous economic aid promised to the European countries as a maneuver aimed to interfere with their reconstruction efforts and to submit Soviet economic policy to American control. Were Marshall Plan aid extended to Eastern Europe, they believed, it would seriously weaken Soviet influence and endanger the social and economic changes the governments of those countries were enacting under Communist pressure. Nevertheless, many Communist parties, in both the East and the West, were not against the American offer on principle. The PCI, for example, had considered accepting it for a while, if only "Italy's independence" was safeguarded. The Polish and the Czech parties, too, looked ready to participate in the Paris conference, which would define the terms of the European Recovery Program. Only the Soviet veto forced them to withdraw.[50]

Even before George Marshall launched his plan, Moscow had been more and more inclined to consider the national articulation of the Communist parties: the promotion of the various "national roads to socialism"—

a henceforth unacceptable undermining of Soviet leadership. The Soviets perceived the Western "bloc" in formation as a geostrategic threat to all of Europe, above all because of the attraction it could exercise on the more unstable Eastern European countries. Fearing that their alliance system would be weakened, the Soviets came to see a new phase of permanent international conflict as inevitable. In this context, the foundation of the Cominform in September 1947, though neither implying a global challenge to the West nor constituting an offensive move aiming to undermine the opposing bloc, denoted a return to the isolationist tradition of earlier stages of Soviet foreign policy, and in this way it seriously contributed to the Cold War.[51]

Generally speaking, the Communist parties of Western Europe were not helped by the creation of a new organizational bond. Though not aspiring to rebuild the Communist International, the Cominform established nonetheless an explicit connection among the USSR, the Communist parties in power in the "people's democracies," and the two main Western parties, the PCI and the PCF. At the same time, international communism now theorized the splitting of the world into two opposing "camps" as an accomplished fact that characterized the latest stage in world politics. In the view of the Cominform, a socialist, anti-imperialist camp committed to the defense of peace now faced an aggressive, warmongering, reactionary imperialist camp.[52] The characterization of the former as "democratic" betrayed the attempt to exploit the bonus points the Communists had acquired in the antifascist struggle and was designed to facilitate the creation of a new alliance against the new enemy: American imperialism. In fact, the definitive separation of the Communist parties from their former allies ensued, leading to their increasing political isolation and to a retreat into sectarianism. A particularly serious consequence was the quick deterioration—everywhere except in Italy—of the relationship with the Socialist and Social Democratic parties. This ended rather suddenly any perspective of reunification and instead entrenched the terms of a deep and permanent split. This split was nourished both by the ideological differences on a series of fundamental issues (the role of state institutions, the conception of democracy and liberty, the function of culture and the role of intellectuals) and by a set of international options, in a sense much more clear-cut than the ones of the interwar period.

The centripetal trend of the communist movement, of which the Cominform conference had been a clear signal, was to be considerably strengthened by a totally unforeseen event. The decisive break between the Soviet Union and Yugoslavia occurred in 1948, and the immediate alignment of all Communist parties to the former served as proof that no alternative existed within the communist system. There was only the choice between total submission to the leading state and party, on the one hand, and dramatic internecine conflict, on the other.

Around mid-1947, therefore, while Europe was being divided into two opposing blocs, the destinies of the Communist parties were proceeding along divergent roads. In the eastern part of the continent, not only were they consolidating their position within the respective governments, but they identified themselves increasingly with the state. This placed all opposition in an increasingly difficult situation and anticipated the opposition parties' eventual marginalization and outlaw status. Eight countries (actually seven plus the SBZ), spread over a surface of more than a million square kilometers and with a population numbering over one hundred million people, thus became Communist. The process was not identical everywhere and was characterized by different rhythms and different degrees of participation and mobilization. But the stages were more or less the same: The Communist parties swallowed the Socialist parties through more or less spontaneous mergers, got hold of the decisive levers of the state, and oversaw omnipresent mass organizations, in the process increasing their membership beyond all proportion. Their control over civil society turned inflexible. The army and police lost all remaining autonomy, the educational system was now completely reformed and "nationalized," and the privileges of the churches were abolished (and soon their rights drastically reduced), exploiting their inner divisions. In fact, the border between "people's democracy" and "proletarian dictatorship" disappeared, and the Soviet model became once again the sole example to be imitated. Behind the screen of some residual elements of pluralism, the primacy of the Communist parties became reality in the shape of an unadulterated dictatorship. The control of the secret police, often infiltrated by Soviet agents, was fundamental in the new mechanics of power. They controlled the levers of repression against any form of dissent and carefully watched over the maintenance of the existing equilibrium.[53]

In Western Europe, meanwhile, even before the Cold War had started, the communist movement was beginning to enter a phase of decline. With the important exceptions of France and Italy, this trend was mirrored in both decreasing membership and narrowing electoral influence. Only where a true refoundation of the state had occurred, and where power had been vacant for a certain time, had the Communist parties been able to benefit from the situation and create strongholds bound to withstand external pressures for decades. But in the majority of countries in the West, the state structures had resisted qualitative change, and the strength of the Social Democratic movement, with its thick network of socioeconomic parallel organizations, had been, if not untouched, at least fully reestablished. The influence the Communists had gained during the resistance experience, though initially mistaken as a sign that communism had finally obtained a permanent and central place in Western as well as Eastern European societies, was already in decline.

NOTES

1. See Eric J. Hobsbawm, *The Age of Extremes: The Short Twentieth Century 1914–1991* (London: Joseph, 1994), 166–67; Donald Sassoon, *One Hundred Years of Socialism: The West European Left in the Twentieth Century* (London: IB Tauris, 1996), 93–97; Charles S. Maier, "I fondamenti politici del dopoguerra," in *Storia d'Europa*, Vol. I: *L'Europa oggi* (Turin: Einaudi, 1993), 324–33.

2. Branko Lazitch, *Les partis communistes d'Europe 1919–1955* (Paris: Les Iles d'Or, 1956); R. Neal Tannahill, *The Communist Parties of Western Europe* (Westport, Conn.: Greenwood, 1978), 249–64.

3. Paolo Spriano, *I comunisti europei e Stalin* (Turin: Einaudi, 1983), 3–11.

4. Annie Kriegel, "La Terza Internazionale," in *Storia del socialismo*, Vol. III: *Dal 1918 al 1945*, ed. Jacques Droz (Rome: Riuniti, 1978), 123.

5. Gordon Wightman and Archie H. Brown, "Changes in the Levels of Membership and Social Composition of the Communist Party of Czechoslovakia 1945–1973," *Soviet Studies* 27, no. 3 (1975): 396–417.

6. Stéphane Courtois and Marc Lazar, *Histoire du Parti Communiste Français* (Paris: Presses Universitaires de France, 1995), 240–41.

7. Renzo Martinelli, *Storia del partito comunista italiano: Il "partito nuovo" dalla Liberazione al 18 aprile* (Turin: Einaudi, 1995), 38–40.

8. Figures reported in Zbigniew K. Brzezinski, *The Soviet Bloc: Unity and Conflict* (Cambridge, Mass.: Harvard University Press, 1967), 10–11.

9. Courtois and Lazar, *Histoire du Parti Communiste*, 243–45; Tony Judt, *Past Imperfect: French Intellectuals 1944–1956* (Berkeley: University of California Press, 1992); Nello Ajello, *Intellettuali e PCI 1944–1958* (Rome: Laterza, 1979), 3–112; Neal Wood, *Communism and British Intellectuals* (London: Gollancz, 1959); Geoff Andrews, Nina Fishman, and Kevin Morgan, eds., *Opening the Books: Essays on the Social and Cultural History of the British Communist Party* (London: Lawrence & Wishart, 1995).

10. Wightman and Brown, "Changes in the Levels of Membership," 399.

11. For an overall picture, see Geoff Eley, *Forging Democracy: The History of the Left in Europe, 1850–2000* (Oxford: Oxford University Press, 2002), 290.

12. Eley, *Forging Democracy*, 287–89.

13. José Gotovitch, "Histoire du parti communiste de Belgique," *Courier Hebdomadaire du CRISP* 1582 (1995): 30; Pascal Delwit, "Le pragmatisme du socialisme belge," in *La Gauche en Europe depuis 1945*, ed. Marc Lazar (Paris: Presses Universitaires de France, 1996), 233–34.

14. Joze Pirjevec, *Il giorno di San Vito: Jugoslavia 1918–1992: Storia di una tragedia* (Turin: Nuova ERI, 1993), 203–21; Paul Shoup, "The Yugoslav Revolution: The First of a New Type," in *The Anatomy of Communist Takeovers*, ed. Thomas T. Hammond and Robert Farrell (New Haven, Conn.: Yale University Press, 1975), 264–65. For Albania, see Stephen Peters, "Ingredients of Communist Takeover in Albania," in *The Anatomy of Communist Takeovers*, ed. Hammond and Farrell, 290–92.

15. Elene Valeva, "The CPSU, the Comintern and the Bulgarians," in *The Establishment of Communist Regimes in Eastern Europe 1944–1949*, ed. Norman Naimark and Leonid Gibianskij (Boulder, Colo.: Westview, 1997), 41–54.

16. Brzezinski, *The Soviet Bloc*, 10.

17. Krystyna Kersten, *The Establishment of Communist Rule in Poland, 1943–1947* (Berkeley: University of California Press, 1991); Norman Davies, "Poland," in *Communist Power in Europe 1944–1949*, ed. Martin McCauley (London: Macmillan, 1977), 42–48.

18. Bela Vago, "Romania," in *Communist Power in Europe 1944–1949*, ed. McCauley, 123; Richard Crampton, *The Balkans since the Second World War* (Edinburgh: Pearson, 2002), 75–83.

19. Bennett Kovrig, *Communism in Hungary: From Kun to Kádár* (Stanford, Calif.: Stanford University Press, 1979), 164–219, 448; George Schöpflin, "Hungary," in *Communist Power in Europe*, ed. McCauley, 98–100; Bela Zhelitski, "Postwar Hungary," in *The Establishment of Communist Regimes*, ed. Naimark and Gibianskij, 73–92.

20. Wightman and Brown, "Changes in the Levels of Membership," 401.

21. Jacques Rupnik, *Histoire du parti communiste tchécoslovaque: Des origines à la prise du pouvoir* (Paris: Presses de la Fondation des Sciences Politiques, 1981), 167–79; Igor Lukes, "The Czech Road to Communism," in *The Establishment of Communist Regimes*, ed. Naimark and Gibianskij, 243–65.

22. Lucio Caracciolo, *Alba di guerra fredda: All'origine delle due Germanie* (Rome: Laterza, 1986), 64; Eric Weitz, *Creating German Communism 1890–1990: From Popular Protest to Socialist State* (Princeton, N.J.: Princeton University Press, 1997), 307–10.

23. Martin McCauley, "East Germany," in *Communist Power in Europe 1944–1949*, ed. McCauley, 60–67; Hans W. Schoenberg, "The Partition of Germany and the Neutralization of Austria," in *The Anatomy of Communist Takeovers*, ed. Hammond and Farrell, 375–77; Enzo Collotti, *Storia delle due Germanie 1945–1968* (Turin: Einaudi, 1968), 426–505; Norman M. Naimark, *The Russians in Germany: A History of the Soviet Zone of Occupation 1945–1949* (Cambridge, Mass.: Harvard University Press, 1995).

24. This analysis is substantially shared by Brzezinski, *The Soviet Bloc*, and François Fejtö, *Histoire des démocraties populaires*, Vol. I: *L'Ere de staline 1945–1952* (Paris: Seuil, 1952).

25. See Mikhail Narinsky, "Sovetskaya vneshnaya politika i proiskhozhdenie kolodnoi voiny," in *Sovetskaya vneshnaya politika v retrspektive* (Moscow: n.p., 1993); Richard Raack, *Stalin's Drive to the West 1938–1945: The Origins of the Cold War* (Stanford, Calif.: Stanford University Press, 1995); Vladislav M. Zubok and Constantine Pleshakov, *Inside the Kremlin's Cold War: From Stalin to Khruschev* (Cambridge, Mass.: Harvard University Press, 1996).

26. Laszlo Nagy, *Le democrazie popolari 1945–1968* (Milan: Saggiatore, 1969), 70–96.

27. Inessa Iazhborovskaja, "The Gomulka Alternative: The Untravelled Road," in *The Establishment of Communist Regimes*, ed. Naimark and Gibianskij, 122–37.

28. Brzezinski, *The Soviet Bloc*, 25; Richard J. Crampton, *Eastern Europe in the Twentieth Century* (London: Routledge, 1994), 241–42.

29. Schoenberg, "The Partition of Germany," 378–81; Kurt R. Luther and Peter Pulzer, *Austria 1945–1995: Fifty Years of the Second Republic* (Oxford: Ashgate, 1998), 15–18.

30. Kimmo Rentola, "The Soviet Leadership and Finnish Communism 1944–1948," in *Finnish Soviet Relations 1944–1948*, ed. Jukka Nevakivi (Helsinki: Department of Political History, 1994), 217.

31. Anthony F. Upton, "The Communist Party of Finland," in *The Communist Parties of Scandinavia and Finland*, ed. Anthony F. Upton (London: Weidenfeld & Nicholson, 1973), 237–39; Rentola, "The Soviet Leadership," 220–34; Jukka Nevakivi, "The Soviet Union and Finland after the War," in *The Soviet Union and Europe in the Cold War 1943–1953*, ed. Francesca Gori and Silvio Pons (Basingstoke, U.K.: Macmillan, 1996), 89–105.

32. Ake Sparring, "The Communist Party of Sweden," in *The Communist Parties of Scandinavia and Finland*, ed. Upton, 78–80.

33. Peter P. Rhode, "The Communist Party of Denmark," in *The Communist Parties of Scandinavia and Finland*, ed. Upton, 16–21.

34. Per Selle, "The Norwegian Communist Party in the Immediate Postwar Period," *Scandinavian Political Studies* 3 (1982); Terje Halvorstadt, "Peder Furobotn, the Norwegian Communists and the Comintern 1939–1950," in *Communism: National and International*, ed. Tauno Saarela and Kimmo Rentola (Helsinki: Studia Historica, 1998).

35. Gerrit Voerman, "La crise du Parti communiste néerlandais," in *Communisme* 29–31 (1992): 62–67.

36. Gotovitch, "Histoire du Parti communiste de Belgique," 30–31.

37. Henry Pelling, *The British Communist Party: A Historical Profile* (London: Black, 1975), 127–43; Noreen Branson, *History of the Communist Party of Great Britain 1941–1951* (London: Lawrence & Wishart, 1997).

38. Marc Lazar, *Maisons Touges: Les partis communistes français et italien de la Libération à nos jours* (Paris: Aubier, 1992), 27–57; *L'Altra faccia della luna: I rapporti tra PCI, PCF e Unione Sovietica*, ed. Elena Aga-Rossi and Gaetano Quagliariello (Bologna: Mulino, 1997).

39. See, above all, Fernando Claudin, *The Communist Movement: From Comintern to Cominform* (Harmondsworth, U.K.: Penguin, 1975).

40. Courtois and Lazar, *Histoire du Parti communiste français*, 238–47; Maxwell Adereth, *The French Communist Party: A Critical History 1920–1984: From Comintern to "the Colours of France"* (Manchester: Manchester University Press, 1984), 130–45; Philippe Buton, *Les lendemains qui déchantent: Le Parti communiste français à la Libération* (Paris: Presses de la Fondation Nationale des Sciences Politiques, 1993), 195–296.

41. Renzo Martinelli, *Storia del Partito comunista italiano*, 92–111.

42. Aldo Agosti, *Palmiro Togliatti* (Turin: UTET, 1995), 312–14; Bruno Groppo, "Il 1956 nella cultura politica del PCI," in *La sinistra e il '56 in Italia e in Francia*, ed. Bruno Groppo and Gianni Riccamboni (Padova: Liviana, 1987), 192–97; Martinelli, *Storia del Partito comunista italiano*, 110–11.

43. Angelo Ventrone, *La cittadinanza repubblicana: Forma-partito e identità nazionale alle origini della democrazia italiana (1943–1948)* (Bologna: Mulino, 1996), 31–36.

44. Antonio Elorza, "Dalla guerra antifascista al mito della Resistenza in Spagna 1936–1949," in *Antifascismi e resistenze*, ed. Franco De Felice (Rome: NIS, 1997), 238–46; Guy Hermet, *Los comunistas en España: Estudio de un movimiento político clandestino* (Paris: Ruedo Ibérico, 1972), 49.

45. Dawn L. Raby, *Resistencia antifascista em Portugal* (Lisbon: Salamandra, 1988), 104–14; José Pacheco Pereira, *Álvaro Cunhal: Uma biografia política: "Duarte," o dirigente clandestino* (Lisbon: Temas & Debates, 2001), 491–658.

46. Richard Clogg, "Greece," in *Communist Power in Europe*, ed. McCauley, 193–97; Artem A. Ulunian, "The Soviet Union and the 'Greek Question': Problems and Appraisals," in *The Soviet Union and Europe in the Cold War*, ed. Gori and Pons, 144–60.

47. Roger Martelli, *Communisme français: Histoire sincère du PCF 1920–1984* (Paris: Éditions Sociales, 1984), 105–19; Grégoire Madjarian, *Conflits, pouvoirs et société à la Libération* (Paris: Union Générale d'Éditions, 1978), 359–74; Buton, *Les lendemains*, 297–312.

48. Roberto Gualtieri, *Togliatti e la politica estera italiana: Dalla Resistenza al trattato di pace 1943–1947* (Rome: Riuniti, 1995), 120–23; Elena Aga Rossi and Victor Zaslavsky, *Togliatti e Stalin: Il PCI e la politica estera staliniana negli archivi di Mosca* (Bologna: Mulino, 1997), 131–56.

49. Severino Galante, *La fine di un compromesso storico: PCI e DC nella crisi del 1947* (Milan: Angeli, 1980), 29–183.

50. Scott Parish, "The Marshall Plan, Soviet American Relations and the Division of Europe," in *The Establishment of Communist Regimes*, ed. Naimark and Gibianskij, 267–90.

51. Silvio Pons, *L'impossibile egemonia: L'URSS, il PCI e le origini della guerra fredda (1943–1948)* (Rome: Carocci, 1999), 32–36.

52. Anna di Biagio, "The Establishment of the Cominform," in *The Cominform. Minutes of the Three Conferences 1947/1948/1949*, ed. Giuliano Procacci (Milan: Fondazione Giangiacomo Feltrinelli, 1994), 11–34.

53. Crampton, *Eastern Europe*, 240–55.

2

Window of Opportunities or Trompe l'Oeil?

The Myth of Labor Unity in Western Europe after 1945

Patrick Pasture

Labor unity is one of the great myths of modern times. It was a major concern of organized labor in Western Europe during the whole twentieth century; however, it was never achieved. On the contrary, anyone studying the organization of the European working class is rather struck by its fragmentation and, even more so, by the amount of competition and political struggle among the different factions. This is particularly true for the trade union movements, on which this chapter concentrates. At times, however, labor unity, here understood as political unity among Communists, Socialists, and Christians,[1] seemed to be imminent. One of those "moments of opportunity" was the liberation and the first years or months after World War II. Apparently, war had produced the circumstances that made labor unity possible.

UNITY AT LAST? A REAL HURRICANE—THE LOCAL FACTOR

No doubt many countries experienced intense mobilizations in favor of labor unity, "a real hurricane," as one Belgian Christian trade unionist in 1944 put it.[2] Unified trade union movements, designed to overcome the former pluralism of political trade unions or *Richtungsgewerkschaften*, were created all over Europe, although in some countries "unified" trade unions simply added to the existing diversity.

Often unitary initiatives indeed arose from the grassroots level, in particular from local movements within firms, thus introducing a new dynamic into the trade union movements of Europe. This was, for example, the case in northern Italy and among the miners of Dutch Limburg and the Belgian metalworkers' communities of Liège and the Borinage. In Germany, too, the unified trade union movement had a strong basis on the factory floor.

The local unitary unions or labor councils, often animated by Communists, also created tensions within the leadership of the preexisting trade union federations. These differences are usually interpreted in terms of an opposition between old and bureaucratic leaders and the newly emerging, radical rank and file. However, in reality this phenomenon was largely confined to certain regions or industries.[3] This suggests that the common interpretation of an opposition between leadership and rank and file may be too simplistic. In Belgium, for example, the call for unity was hardly heard outside the metalworkers' and mining communities of Liège and the Borinage, and such calls were noticeably absent in the highly unionized Flemish towns. As I will emphasize later, a closer look at the formation of the major unified trade union movements nuances the importance of the local dimension, and it reveals that unification was often the result of a political decision made at the highest levels.

War and Resistance

Unified unions were often rooted in common experiences during the war. In general, the war led to a radicalization of the imagination, in the sense that radical change was felt possible and imminent; the destruction offered opportunities to make a fresh start. In these circumstances Marxist analyses, and thus also the idea of class unity, almost by definition were more likely to be welcomed than in times of prosperity. Certainly in France and Italy, Socialists were strongly influenced by the notion and the ideology of the desirability to unify the working class. French and Italian Socialists also underwent a common process of radicalization. Most definitely, they were staunchly opposed in principle to the idea of working-class division. Moreover, the war strengthened the idea of unity through mutual collaboration, particularly in the resistance, in exile, and in the shared experiences of imprisonment and persecution, which in itself was enough to enhance solidarity and the sense of unity.

In France, contacts between the General Confederation of Labor (CGT)—from which Communists had been excluded after the signing of the 1939 Nazi-Soviet Pact—and the French Confederation of Christian Workers (CFTC) go back to February 1940, when activists of both unions published a *Bulletin d'Information Ouvrière*. On 15 October 1940, both unions signed a manifesto listing twelve principles on which unanimity was reached. Further contacts in the resistance led to a common plan for postwar reconstruction and even an appeal for a political strike in the summer of 1944.[4] A few weeks earlier, in June 1944, representatives of the major political currents active in the Italian resistance since 1943, in which Communists were the main organizational force, signed a "pact of trade union unity," the Patto di Roma, which served as the basis for the creation of the unitary Italian General Confederation of Labor (CGIL).[5] Especially in the north (Turin, Milan, etc.), unified trade unions firmly rooted in the resistance mushroomed literally everywhere.

The case of Austria and Germany is more ambivalent, although Communist as well as Socialist and Christian trade unionists after the war considered themselves to stand on the side of "sacrifice and resistance," the Christians easily ignoring the ambivalence they had exhibited in this regard in 1933.[6] Nevertheless, in Austria, too, the foundation of an all-inclusive confederation in April 1945 resulted from illegal contacts between former trade unionists and the (more overtly political) conversations and shared experiences in the concentration camp of Dachau.[7]

At the international level, Communist and non-Communist trade union federations, led by the British Trades Union Congress (TUC), the Soviet trade union confederation, and the American Congress of Industrial Organizations (CIO)—the rival center of the larger American Federation of Labor (AFL)—in October 1945 joined forces to create the World Federation of Trade Unions (WFTU). The WFTU also had its roots in wartime antifascist initiatives and must be regarded as an expression of the prevailing spirit of labor unity and solidarity with the Soviet Union, at the same time undoubtedly promoting the idea of unity as well.[8] The intense acquaintance with the example of the ideologically undivided trade unionism in Britain and the United States, without the virulent hostility toward Christianity that still largely prevailed in the continental Western European secular labor movements, exerted considerable attraction over both Socialist and Christian labor leaders in exile, thus contributing to the popularization of the idea of labor unity. The concrete impact of exile activists on postwar trade union reconstruction, however, was rather limited.

The unions of all three (former) Axis countries held in common a strong motivation to overcome prewar trade union divisions. Austrian unionists in particular were convinced that the internal conflicts between the unions had contributed to the inability of labor to respond effectively to the world economic crisis of the 1930s and to prevent the rise of fascism and its seizure of power.[9] In Italy, the personal experiences of the historical leaders Achille Grandi among Catholics and Pietro Nenni among Socialists convinced them strongly to favor labor unity, with both men frequently referring to the "pernicious effects of the divisions of the working class" in 1920–1922.[10]

After the war, the Allied occupation authorities in the Axis countries undoubtedly tried to shape the renascent trade union structures in the image of the trade unions in their own countries that, apart from France, boasted unified organizations. They all agreed in preventing the former Richtungsgewerkschaften to reestablish themselves. They were especially concerned that a divided trade union movement could become an element of instability.

The impact of Allied policies on the new trade union structures was nevertheless limited, even in the British and American zones of Germany where labor relations were controlled by the respective occupation authorities for much longer than in Austria and Italy.[11] In the latter countries, the Allied impact on events (at least in regard to trade union organization) in 1945 was negligible.

AMBIVALENT LEGACIES:
FASCIST AND CORPORATIST EXPERIENCES

Paradoxically perhaps, some experiences of fascism also contributed to the formation of unified trade unions. At the very least, and in different ways, they had their part in the depoliticization of the working class. The antipolitical and antidemocratic fascist discourse had alienated workers from the political parties already in the 1930s. Furthermore, with the disappearance of many prewar trade union leaders, prewar oppositions may have vanished as well.[12] Moreover, fascists had installed corporatist labor structures, proving that it was in principle not impossible to streamline some prewar factional divisions. In Austria, in the context of the Catholic-corporatist regime, contacts between Christian and free trade union leaders from 1935 onward led to a certain rapprochement.[13] In Germany, recurrent proposals to transform the German Labor Front after the war into a broad centralized trade union with compulsory membership likewise point to the importance of this factor.[14]

In the occupied countries, fascists had also tried to install corporatist and fascist unitary structures. In the Netherlands and in Belgium, fascists in 1940 exerted pressure to constitute "united" trade unions as a first step toward the creation of a National Socialist Labor Front. After some earlier initiatives in Belgium had failed, a unified trade union federation, the Union of Manual and Intellectual Workers (UTMI), was established in November 1940. Most Flemish Christian and a handful of Socialist trade unionists agreed to join the UTMI, hoping thereby to maintain their autonomy and influence in the new structure; but when, in August 1941, it became all too apparent that this would not be the case, the vast majority of these activists withdrew from this venture and went underground.[15]

It is most doubtful, however, that in the end such experiences with fascist "unified" labor organizations had any positive effect on discussions about trade union unity after the war. On the contrary, such forced "unification" often increased tensions between the unions. In the early days of the occupation in the Netherlands, the Socialist and the Catholic trade unions took some initiatives to unite the three main confederations into one single structure. Such a unitary federation, however, did not materialize; already on 16 July 1940, the Socialist unions were put under fascist restraint (but continued to function), while the confessional unions were left in peace for the time being. In the summer of 1941, the Germans imposed *Gleichschaltung* on all unions, but the confessional trade unions refused to comply and were liquidated. By contrast, many Socialist union officials participated in this operation, which shocked the confessional unions and destroyed mutual trust.[16] In Belgium, apart from the tensions resulting from the experience with the UTMI, the well-known postwar conflicts surrounding the repression of the collaborators and the return of King Leopold III (issues whose origins could be traced back to the occupation period) deeply divided not only the country but the unions as well.[17]

These experiences undoubtedly contributed to the weakening of the labor movement after the war, and in particular of the moderate Socialist union leaders most directly involved in collaborationist ventures. The highly controversial attitude of the Dutch Socialist union leaders, even if some had used their position to resist Nazification, not only blurred the relations with the Catholic and Protestant unions but also caused a deep rift within their own rank and file and ultimately gave way to more radical left-wing actions on a local level.[18] In France, some CGT and CFTC unions collaborated with the Vichy regime, undermining in particular the right-wing faction in the CGT.[19] The collaboration of the prewar Socialist Party leader, Hendrik De Man, contributed to the weakness of the Belgian Socialist trade union movement after the war as well, particularly in Wallonia.

On the other hand, contacts were established during the war between labor leaders and representatives of the bourgeoisie, employers and bankers, finding common ground on some basic economic and political issues. These contacts expressed the corporatist mood of the times but also reflected the prevailing mood of secrecy. They did create a sense of "unity," in particular within the respective headquarters of the trade unions involved. In this context, we may refer to the negotiations that led to the so-called Social Pact in Belgium and the Stichting van de Arbeid in the Netherlands.[20] But this particular dimension of cooperation is not the sense in which labor unity is understood in this chapter.

If we look at the geography of trade union unity after the war, we cannot fail to notice—although it is rarely done in practice—that unified trade unions were established above all in the (former) Axis countries. The longevity and intensity of fascist rule had destroyed the prewar political networks and trade union organizations. This made it more difficult to restore old pluralist traditions and easier to start from scratch with unitary federations. But even in Italy, particularly in the south, in 1945 traditional divisions between "white" and "red" unions reappeared within those trade unions that were reestablished by well-known local party leaders. At the same time, new divisions were created, for instance, at the instigation of Action Party followers and supporters of Dino Gentile in Naples. After the unified trade union committees of northern Italy merged within the CGIL, a clear division between north and south remained on many issues.[21] Elsewhere, one could suppose that the old structures simply had survived and that institutional inertia was too ever-present to permit unification. But there were additional reasons why trade union activists preferred not to go along with unitary unions.

UNITY IN DIVERSITY: THE POLITICAL PARTY DIMENSION

When speaking about trade union unity, one should not ignore that, where it became reality, it came about against the background of the restoration of political diversity. Admittedly, there were some plans for labor unity made during the war that foresaw the creation of large popular parties encompassing the entire working class. Some of those plans, as in the case of the German Goerdeler Kreis, predicted a retreat of the role of political parties.[22] However, most prewar political parties, be it in a renewed shape, returned as main protagonists in the revitalized European postwar democracies.

The political landscape as such, however, underwent a thorough renewal. Fascist parties were not restored, and new parties saw the light of day, incarnating the spirit of unity and resistance, particularly among Catholics, such as the Popular Republican Movement (MRP) in France, the Belgian Democratic Union (UDB) in Belgium, and the Nederlandse Volksbeweging in the Netherlands. Moreover, new Christian Democratic parties emerged. These Christian Democratic parties constituted a remarkable mix of renewal and continuity. At least in theory, they stood in a direct line of continuity with prewar confessional party politics; they adopted relatively open, nonconfessional policies; and they addressed themselves explicitly to working people. Each of them included both conservative and more progressive factions, among whom were partisans of a totally deconfessionalized party.[23] The success of Christian Democracy after 1945 may well have been the main postwar political development in continental Western Europe,[24] even if contemporaries and generations of historians and political scientists have mainly stressed the breakthrough of communism as the most significant new departure.

Undoubtedly, the Communists incarnated more than any other political tendency the spirit of the resistance and renewal that reigned after the war. Since 1941, they had put all their energies into combating fascism, favoring broad popular fronts and alliances that stood in a line of continuity with their initial opening toward broader political forces in the mid-1930s.[25] Communists in the 1940s aimed at rallying as much labor support as possible behind their organizations and political objectives, and the latter included the Communists' entrance into postwar governments in order to weaken American influence in Europe and to strengthen those governments observing, at the very least, neutrality vis-à-vis the USSR. Simultaneously, they implemented a policy of moderation in the social and economic fields, postponing any revolutionary ambition to a later stage. The idea that production had to be resumed first, above any other perspective of social and political reform, let alone revolution, was shared by all major Communist trade union movements.[26]

Also, Socialist parties modified their political stance and tried to open their ranks further. The experiences of the politicians and intellectuals imprisoned in the Sint-Michielsgestel, resulting in the Nederlandse Volksbeweging (Dutch Popular Movement), deeply influenced the new Dutch Labor Party, established in February 1946 from a merger of different political groupings. This new party aimed at putting an end to Dutch pillarization. It adopted a very broad reformist concept of social class and appealed to large segments of the population, although it did not succeed in convincing Catholics or Protestants. As a result, it failed in its ambition of depillarization, and the pillars, with their respective trade unions, reappeared.[27]

In Germany, on the contrary, the intense network around the Social Democratic Party (SPD), resting on the cooperatives and cultural, educational, and social ancillary organizations, was not restored. Still, for the party as such, continuity was ensured.[28] In Belgium, the Socialist Party was even less inclined to realize a fundamental renewal. The postwar political tensions soon weighed heavily on the ideological divide between Catholics and those hostile to Catholic influence in society. Belgian Socialists rejected both Communist appeals and the openings that were created in some progressive Catholic circles.[29] Moreover, Socialist parties in Belgium, the Netherlands, and Germany remained fiercely anticommunist. The position of the French and Italian Socialists toward communism, however, was different. Both parties were divided on the subject, but the majority favored a popular front. In France, however, Léon Blum effectively opposed any attempt at a merger.[30]

The importance of these political changes for the postwar trajectory of trade unions needs special consideration, for there was a tendency toward cutting the close ties that had united trade unions and political parties before the war. In this way trade unions were "emancipated" from political tutelage. It would be a mistake, however, to believe that unions developed in a vacuum independent from politics. In fact, quite the opposite was true, since political parties played a determining role in the restoration of the postwar social and political order. Austria and Italy, where representatives of the openly political caucuses or the political parties representing Christian Democrats, Socialists, and Communists (which, incidentally, in Italy signified the failure of Allied policies striving to enhance apolitical *tradeunionismo*) made the key decisions leading toward the creation of politically all-encompassing trade union structures, are examples of the influence of political strategy in the process of establishing trade union unity.[31] Even the Free German Trade Union Confederation (FDGB), established by the Soviet military occupation authorities in the Russian zone of Germany, was conceived initially as a unitary trade union with the participation of Socialist and Christian factions alongside the Communists.[32]

Particularly in West Germany, politicians (including many former trade union officials) supported trade union unity as a factor of social and political stability in the period of reconstruction and as a buffer against the raising of demands by competing unions, above all if the latter would include separate Communist unions. Unlike Austria and Italy, though, the German political parties were not directly involved in the reconstruction of unions in the Western occupied zones and in the slow development of the unitary German Confederation of Labor (DGB).[33] On the contrary, it was precisely the desire for independence from any political party that motivated the West German *Einheitsgewerkschaft* (unified trade union).[34]

THE COMMUNIST DRIVE TOWARD TRADE UNION UNITY

As already mentioned, the Communists in particular actively promoted trade union unity after the war. Since 1942, they had striven for unified trade unions and focused on the formation of factory committees. They made significant progress in the working class and especially among groups that had been out of the reach of organized labor before the war.

In Belgium and the Netherlands, the Communists tried to fill in the gap left by the traditional Socialist and Christian unions, whose organizations had been dismantled. The Communists built up or took control over militant trade union movements, the *Eenheidsvakbeweging* in the Netherlands and the *Comité de lutte syndicale* in Belgium. These unions managed to attract new, unorganized workers in some areas and industries, including Socialist and even Catholic workers. After the war, these Communist-influenced militant organizations became the main advocates of trade union unity in both countries.[35] There were also some leftist non-Communist groups who favored and encouraged the idea of trade union unity, such as the quasi-anarchosyndicalist Mouvement Syndical Unifié (MSU) of André Renard. The MSU was particularly active among Liège metalworkers and was mainly composed of workers without strong prewar trade union traditions. (The fact that in the interwar period trade unionism had been better organized in Flanders offers a major explanation of why, in Flanders, the call for unitary trade unionism remained much weaker.)[36]

In the Netherlands, a mostly Communist new trade union federation arose from the war and became the Eenheidsvakcentrale (Unified Trade Union Federation, EVC), which originally tried to unite workers along industrial lines, irrespective of denomination or political orientation. The EVC initially appeared considerably more militant than the three competing prewar confederations, at least until the Netherlands Communist Party (KPN) eventually managed to obtain control over it. The KPN then used its leverage to impose restraint and moderation on EVC operations, in accordance with overall Communist postwar political designs. The new movement was quite successful during the first months after liberation, especially in the southern provinces and the capital city of Amsterdam; its membership equaled that of the Socialist Dutch Federation of Trade Unions (Nederlands Verbond van Vakverenigingen [NVV]) and exceeded that of the two confessional trade union confederations. It attracted formerly unorganized workers but also Socialist union activists who were disappointed by the behavior of their leaders during the war, in addition to a considerable number of Catholic workers, especially from the Limburg coal mines.

In all those cases, the Communists were quite ready to compromise in order to achieve their goals. In the Netherlands, the Communist Party strove for a merger of the EVC and the NVV. It therefore urged the EVC to restrain its radicalism (in order to facilitate its cooperation with the Dutch Labor Party and its ongoing participation within the government) and to be compliant in its negotiations with the NVV, which EVC historians have described as a "complete capitulation."[37] In Belgium, too, where the Communist position was much stronger compared to that of the Netherlands, the comités de lutte syndicale demonstrated a sometimes astounding readiness to compromise.[38] In Italy and France, the Communist-dominated unitary federations (CGT and CGIL) also followed a very moderate course.

Of course, such a nonconfrontational strategy made the Communists vulnerable to tactical maneuvers from their adversaries, in particular from the Socialists. This was certainly the case in Belgium, where the Communists had recruited considerable support and power in certain industries and regions but risked being surpassed and isolated by the reformists in a larger federation—which is precisely what eventually happened. In the Netherlands, the compliant Communist strategy also operated to reduce Communist influence, undermining the revolutionary image of the Communists and ultimately discrediting the EVC.[39]

In the Soviet zone of Germany, this moderate strategy was implemented to the maximum degree. The Soviets actively promoted the organization of a single, centralized trade union, which was to incorporate all political factions. Initially it was supported by Socialist as well as by former Christian trade unionists. This could have worked as a powerful example and attraction to the workers elsewhere in Germany (and Europe), especially in the context of Western Allied occupation authorities being very reluctant to oppose initiatives toward the building of strong unified trade unions, as desired by German trade union activists. However, in the end the example worked the other way around. According to Denis MacShane in his authoritative study, *International Labor and the Origins of the Cold War*, the Soviets first tried "to stamp out any spontaneous grass-roots working-class organization; second, to ensure that amongst the Communists it was those who had been in Moscow during the Nazi era who were in overall control; third, to find German Communists to run the unions whose acceptance of democratic centralist party discipline can be relied upon." By the time of its first Congress in February 1946, Communists occupied all important leadership posts of the FDGB.[40] Obviously, this example did not appeal to trade unionists in the Western zones, nor were the Western occupation authorities likely to allow a similar evolution in the areas they controlled.

In France, the Communists succeeded in resuming the tradition of the prewar unitary CGT after the conclusion of a pact with the Socialists under the leadership of Léon Jouhaux in 1943; for different reasons (in particular their organizational strength and the prestige they gained from their own and the USSR's resistance during the war), the Communists profited more than anyone else from the influx of new members and soon largely outnumbered the prewar reformist majority. As was the case in Italy, the Communists strove toward a "bourgeois-proletarian pact among the three mass political parties" and a return to normality.[41] However, another aim, the prevention of "the re-emergence of social democracy as a major political force," ultimately eluded them.[42]

THE ISSUE OF NEUTRALITY

The capital role of political strategies behind trade union unification raises the question of the political orientation of the unitary trade union federations. All unified trade unions classified themselves as neutral or above party divisions. However, they never espoused genuine neutrality; as important social forces, unions rely far too much on lawmaking and the political order to leave politics entirely to professional politicians. Likewise, for the political parties, unions are far too important to ignore. However, a certain level of political neutrality for the unions was an important issue in 1945, and the close formal or organizational ties that existed in many European countries before the war were not restored.

Again, the plea for political neutrality was supported above all by Communists, as it was the obvious condition for the achievement of trade union unity. In Italy, Austria, and to a certain extent also Germany, political neutrality was guaranteed by an equal or balanced representation of the different political currents within the executive bodies of the unions.[43] Fractionalization was from the very beginning much stronger in the Austrian Trade Union Federation (ÖGB), officially created in Vienna as early as 13 April 1945, than in the CGIL or the (West and East) German federations. The DGB in particular maintained more of a distance from political parties (including the SPD) and the political party system.[44] It may have contributed to the strength of the DGB. Nevertheless, "the insistence after 1945 that unions should be free of formal party links did not diminish the loyalty that [Socialist] trade-unionists felt towards their party, nor alter the overall acceptance of the party leadership as the political representative of the wider interests of the German working class and the German people," Denis MacShane concludes.[45] This applies to the Communists and Christians (to whom we will return soon) as well. Of course, the case of the FDGB is an extreme example of party-political dominance of a so-called neutral unified movement and of the application of the "transmission belt theory," by which neutrality is a first step leading to control and dominance.

In Italy, the three factions, though unequal in membership share, were granted equal representation in the executive organs of the CGIL; in reality, the Communists came to dominate. However, according to Paul Ginsborg, since decisions were made by mutual consent, paradoxically such decisions merely reflected the lowest common denominator, which was usually close to the Christian Democrat position; as Ginsborg observes, this was the logical consequence of Togliatti's alliance policy.[46]

In France and Belgium, the unified trade unions also claimed political neutrality, but they belied this claim in practice. In the French CGT, the Communists quickly occupied the key posts; they could do so because they benefited from their prestige and attraction among the population as well as from their excellent organization. The Communist tendency was much better equipped to cope with the mass influx of new members than the Socialist faction, and they benefited from the weakness of their adversaries. As stated before, the wartime record of the Socialists appeared bleak in comparison, and the prewar right wing of the CGT was compromised by the collaboration of its main leaders with the Vichy regime. Moreover, the main reformist trade union leader, Léon Jouhaux, had been deported, and he only returned to France in May 1945. Above all, however, non-Communists in the French *syndicaliste* tradition emphasized their independence from political parties and other external groups.[47] The main Communist union activists, on the contrary, occupied high positions in the French Communist Party; CGT general secretary Benoît Frachon was a member of the party's central committee since 1926. The Communists considered the CGT as both a basis for the creation of a popular front and an extraparliamentary pressure force.[48]

In Belgium, the Comité de lutte syndicale strongly advocated neutrality for the new, united trade union federation. In contrast to their counterparts in France, the Belgian Socialist union leaders were reluctant to accept such neutrality—the prewar Commission Syndicale had originally been set up as a trade union secretariat within the Belgian Workers' Party—but they were in no position to oppose it effectively; in practice, however, they maintained their connections with the renewed Belgian Socialist Party, just as had happened in the Netherlands and Germany. Most leaders of the Comité de lutte syndicale held important positions in the Belgian Communist Party and followed its directives closely—not the least its far-reaching readiness to compromise in the merger discussions.[49]

In the Netherlands, already during the war the NVV and the Social Democratic Workers' Party had agreed to end the formal organizational links between the two organizations. After the war, partly because of what had happened in the first years of the occupation, the understanding between party and union could no longer be enforced, but informal contacts were maintained. The NVV did not develop a proper political action program. Since prewar political and trade union divisions remained, de facto the NVV relied on the Labor Party for the defense of its interests; in return, the NVV received political and economic recognition and backing in its fight against the EVC. Nevertheless, both the NVV and the party had their own priorities and autonomy.[50]

ANTICOMMUNIST STRATEGIES AND SOCIALIST AMBIVALENCE

Notwithstanding the hesitations recalled earlier, European Socialists in the liberation period seemed to be overtaken by the unitary mood. Their enthusiasm for labor unity depended not only on ideology and principles but to an equal extent on strategic considerations. By no means had their prewar anticommunism vanished. But, compared to Communists, they had not performed so well during the war. Occasionally (France, Denmark, Belgium), Socialists had collaborated with the Nazis, and rare had been the cases where Socialists had played a notable role in the resistance. Especially in those countries where resistance had been strong—as in Italy (after 1943) and France—the Communists managed to outflank the Socialists.[51]

Paradoxically, though, anticommunism could be a motive to support unified trade unions. In fact, in their anticommunism the European Socialists fully supported Allied policies in trade union matters. Anticommunism certainly was a motive for the Allied authorities, backed up by the AFL, to support the formation of unified trade union federations in the western zones of Germany, as well as in Italy and Austria (although in these two countries, the Allies had no real impact on the initial organization of the trade unions).[52] Especially with regard to the Christian trade union activists operating in unified trade unions, one could count on anticommunism as an argument ensuring that moderate forces would be gaining the upper hand. In Austria, for example, the Christian Democrats would often refer to this argument within the unitary federation, although—Communists not having played a role in the establishment of the ÖGB—here the Communists remained a small minority.[53]

In Italy, such considerations turned out to be a serious miscalculation. Many Italian Socialists, and in particular the party's undisputed leader, Pietro Nenni, were in favor of close collaboration with the Communists. In general, the Italian Socialist Party, even if in the first election after the war it obtained more votes than the Communist Party, proved a weak and divided force; within the CGIL, the Socialist position was considerably handicapped by the death of Bruno Buozzi, captured and shot by the Germans in the summer of 1943.[54] In France, the Socialists supported the reunification of the CGT in 1943 largely for ideological reasons. Non-Communists joined with those around Robert Bothereau's journal *Résistance Ouvrière*, which appeared from the middle of 1943, forming an internal faction, from December 1945 onward, called *Force Ouvrière*.[55] *Force Ouvrière*, however, proved to be no match for the Communist-dominated CGT apparatus.

In Belgium and the Netherlands, things turned out differently. In both countries, because of their weakness after the war, Socialists were reluctant to merge with the new Communist-dominated militant unitary trade unions, the Comité de lutte syndicale and the EVC. Nevertheless, Social Democrats saw some advantages in unification, too. A unitary confederation could neutralize the Christian trade unions, which in both countries constituted a strong social power. In Belgium, the Socialists did eventually merge with the Comité de lutte syndicale and the MSU. Although the membership balance was only very slightly to their advantage—in Wallonia, the newcomers held the majority—the Socialists managed to dominate the new confederation, for the Communist strongholds were limited to certain regions and industries.[56]

In the Netherlands, talks about a merger between the Socialist (NVV) and unitary (EVC) unions were held from the moment of liberation onward; the Christian unions—as was the case in Belgium—rejected an organizational merger with any of them.[57] The NVV leadership was likewise very reluctant to agree to a merger and tried to preserve the good prewar relations with the two confessional confederations, even if it publicly spoke out in favor of the principle of labor unity. Yet here nominal support for unity was translated into practice solely in the sense that the NVV opened its ranks to all political tendencies. At the same time, significantly, the NVV opposed propaganda for a unitary federation and embarked on a confrontational course vis-à-vis the Dutch Communists. Moreover, on 17 May 1945, the Socialist, Catholic, and Protestant unions concluded a cooperation pact with the employers and the state. This was a symbolic expression of the institutional recognition of these three trade union movements by the new, postwar political system; it would lead to the creation of the Stichting van de Arbeid, the "Magna Carta" of Dutch labor relations. Notwithstanding its rapid growth—its numerical strength equaled that of the NVV and exceeded that of both Christian unions—and despite the presence of the Communist Party in the Dutch government, the EVC was kept out of this agreement. Undoubtedly, the then-minister of labor, Socialist Bert Drees, acted as the ally of the NVV in this respect. The EVC remained unsuccessful in obtaining official recognition as a collective bargaining partner.

This exclusion of the EVC from the Dutch postwar tripartite (state–employers–unions) cooperative scheme had the immediate effect of strengthening the position of the NVV in the merger talks. But these negotiations also deepened inner divisions within the EVC and thus ultimately weakened it in more ways than one. In the end, the exclusion of the EVC from the postwar tripartite "concertation" scheme considerably contributed to its rapid disappearance, following closely the trajectory of the Dutch Communist Party, then in rapid decline.

THE POSITION OF THE CHRISTIAN TRADE UNIONISTS[58]

In the discussions about postwar trade union unity, Christian workers became a primary target, on both the international and the national levels and for both Socialists and Communists. Socialists in particular looked toward Christian workers to broaden the base of their movement. This attitude could be traced to the 1930s,[59] but it became more prominent after the war when Socialists retreated from the virulent hostility toward institutionalized religion that had characterized continental Western European socialism since the mid–nineteenth century.

The attitude of the Christian trade unions, which in interwar Europe had been important only in some particular regions (Flanders, the Netherlands, the Ruhr area, and the Rhineland), toward trade union unity was radically different in the Axis countries compared to the Allied Western European countries. Of course, the political situation after the war played its part in this configuration. In Eastern Europe, liberated and occupied by the Soviets, any attempt to re-create Christian unions was doomed. Likewise, in West Germany the occupation authorities prevented any attempts to restore the former Richtungsgewerkschaften. However, it is very unlikely that a more compliant Allied policy would have provoked a comeback of the prewar Christian trade unions; there is enough evidence to argue that, if a strong demand for Christian unions had existed, the authorities would not have been able to oppose it effectively.[60] In Austria and Italy, Catholics worked within the unitary trade union federation as well; these countries were not subject to the same kind of strict occupation regime as was Germany, and unfettered political life had returned there much earlier.

In the Axis countries, the surviving Christian labor leaders largely shared the desire for unity. They reflected the wishes of the occupiers and responded to the perceived weaknesses of a divided labor response to the rise of fascism in the 1920s and early 1930s. Material barriers to the restoration of the former Christian trade unions (i.e., the lack of necessary staff) also played a role. Above all, though, Christians in the Axis countries gave priority to the formation of Christian Democratic parties and to political and economic reconstruction; most Christian union leaders agreed with and joined these efforts.[61]

Incidentally, for Catholic militants, trade union unity was an option only if there remained possibilities for Catholic politics and education within the unitary organizations. To protect Catholic workers from Socialist influence within unitary federations, the Catholic Church relied on collateral organizations, such as the Catholic Workers' Movement in Germany and the newly created Christian Association of Italian Workers (ACLI) in Italy, to promote Catholic social doctrine and religious training.[62] In addition, in Germany specific factory-based ancillary organizations were set up with the express purpose of familiarizing workers with Catholic social teaching and counteracting the Communist presence, such as the Catholic *Betriebsmännerwerke*.[63] To guarantee that Catholic workers in the unitary unions would vote in favor of Christian Democratic parties—thereby obviously undermining claims of absence of confessional ties—Christian Democrat–sponsored political associations were formed within the unitary federations in Italy, Austria, and, to a lesser extent, Germany. The Christian trade union activists in the Austrian People's Party (ÖVP) organized the Austrian Manual and Office Workers Federation, which operated as an informal faction for the Catholics within the ÖGB and, simultaneously, as a trade union watchdog for the ÖVP.[64] In Germany, the idea of a labor caucus within the Christian Democratic Party (CDU) was initially raised in December 1945, but it materialized only two years later, in November 1947. As a reaction to the weak and diminishing influence and position of the "Christian Socials" within the DGB, "social committees" (*Sozialausschüsse*) were created within the CDU, in effect constituting a separate Christian workers' faction.[65]

The idea that Christians and Socialists together could contain the Communists in a united trade union federation was a major argument in favor of trade union unity, for there can be no doubt about the anticommunism of the Christian Democrats. This raises the question of why anticommunism did not induce Christian trade unionists in the Allied countries to follow the same reasoning as their comrades in Germany, Italy, and Austria. Essentially, the former believed that, in the end, an autonomous position offered more guarantees in the fight against communism, compared to the risk of always getting "the short end of the stick" in a unified federation.[66]

In France, Belgium, the Netherlands, Luxembourg, and Switzerland—the only countries where a Christian labor movement still existed in 1945—unity with Socialists and Communists in unitary trade unions was not really an issue, even if there was certainly a greater openness for collaboration with the Socialists. In some regions, as in Liège and the coal mines of Dutch Limburg, Christian trade unionists nevertheless succumbed to the siren calls of unified trade unions. Most Christian unions (apart from the Dutch, who declined even close collaboration), however, agreed with "unity of action" but not with "unity of organization."

They indeed mustered many arguments against organizational unity. The Christian unions usually found their principles strengthened by their experiences during war and occupation. The "unified" structures imposed by the fascists offered an easy argument against unity. More important, Christian trade unionists for the most part felt that they could enter the postliberation period with their heads held up high, uncompromised and, indeed, even strengthened. This was especially so in France and the Netherlands. The postwar leaders of the French CFTC, especially Gaston Tessier and Jules Zirnheld, notwithstanding their close collaboration with other political tendencies in the French resistance, strongly opposed a merger with the CGT. In the Netherlands, the Christian trade unions compared their "firm" stance to that of the NVV. The situation is a bit more complex in Belgium, but, in their own eyes, even those who had joined the UTMI believed they had done nothing wrong.[67] And the Belgian Socialist war record certainly was not better, even if most Socialists had not followed De Man's collaborationist path. In Germany, their persecution and occasional resistance activism apparently helped the memory of the Christian labor movement's initially weak and ambiguous opposition to the Nazis at the end of the Weimar Republic to fade.[68] Similarly, in Austria, the persecution of the Christian labor leaders after 1936 seemed to have eliminated the memory of their collaboration with the fascist regime of Engelbert Dollfuß after February 1934.[69]

In both Belgium and the Netherlands, finally, the Catholic hierarchy itself supported separate Catholic trade unions. The Dutch episcopacy even explicitly repeated that Catholics could not join non-Catholic trade unions.[70] Elsewhere, however, the Christian unions could not necessarily count on the support of the Catholic hierarchy. Lutheran church authorities, meanwhile, never spoke out in their favor.[71]

The choice to continue autonomously at the national level also explains why the Christian trade unions, which in any case reestablished the prewar International Confederation of Christian Trade Unions, refused to join the WFTU in 1945. Although, in particular, the French and the Belgians were interested in close collaboration, the WFTU's policy of accepting only one affiliated union federation per country would have necessitated that Christian confederations merge with the Socialist and Communist unions. In the end, all Christian confederations refused to affiliate with the WFTU.[72]

CONCLUSION

The myth of labor unity was very powerful in 1945. The drama of the times appealed for unity, and in working-class communities this was easily materialized via pleas for labor unity. This inspired many workers and labor activists in large parts of the continent, and it was one expression of the hope for renewal, or even just a release of emotions, an outburst of the desire to put an end to the nightmare that was World War II. It was truly a transnational "utopian ideal" for many, and it was concretized and symbolized by the WFTU, functioning as a beacon for both advocates and opponents.

However, the concept of labor unity was elusive and encompassed many meanings. It had a strongly appealing character in certain industries and regions (mostly overlapping), but—what is often overlooked—not for everyone and everywhere. For too many contemporaries, it often came down to an unacceptable loss of the identity and dignity, or perhaps status, that they had managed to preserve in the long night of occupation and war. And, last but not least, the practical implementation of the dream of labor unity was often related to tactical maneuvers of a political nature.

This article argues against the assumption that trade union unity was mainly a demand from the rank and file, which was successfully restrained by bureaucratic trade union structures and leaders, or—inasmuch as this needs special mention—that it fell victim to the Cold War after 1947. To be sure, the appeal was heard most clearly at the grassroots level, particularly in the mining and metalworking industries. However, this "aristocracy of labor" did not represent the entirety of the working class, and many workers were never seduced at all. Moreover, the war not only enhanced unity and solidarity, but it also created new divisions and strengthened old enmities. The unitary trade union federation was often mainly an instrument for political objectives. That was obviously the case for the Communists but also for the Allied forces, as it indeed tended to be so for Socialists and Christian Democrats, who hoped for postwar stability as a condition for economic recovery. In this context, it is worth noting that, in Germany, an independent Catholic trade union, which eventually arose in opposition to unity within the DGB, drew its support primarily from the younger generation and not from the older activists who had experienced the events of 1933.[73]

Was the cry for labor unity a realistic opportunity for radical change—as it was widely believed to have been the case in the 1970s, when this problematic preoccupied most authors writing on the subject? In fact, it was not. One reason was that it was the Communists, and in particular those closest to Moscow, who managed to dominate and control most of the unitary movements and who appointed themselves as the spearhead of the unitary movement, forcing other tendencies onto the defensive. And even if contemporaries perceived the Communist unions as quite radical, the basic Communist strategy in the postwar years was to ensure Communist participation in democratic governments. On that altar, many a revolutionary dream was sacrificed.

One last observation about the relationship between trade union unity and the idea of pluralism, which appear to be two sides of the same coin: Trade union fragmentation in interwar Europe, which is sometimes labeled pluralism, was in a certain sense exactly the opposite, namely the expression of a lack of democratic respect for the other. In this sense interwar Europe lacked pluralism; nowhere was mutual intolerance within the labor movement more apparent than in Austria. It can therefore be argued that it was not so much trade union pluralism and the existence of a divided labor movement that explained the weakness of labor's response toward fascism, but on the contrary that the lack of real pluralism, especially in a context of underdeveloped liberal democracy as in Germany and Austria, contributed to the breakthrough of fascism.[74] After the war, however, a new leaf was turned, and prewar opposition that hampered mutual respect and tolerance, such as the Socialist rejection of religion in continental Western Europe or the virulent antisocialism of the Christians, was considerably diminished. Paradoxically, thus, the unity achieved in the Axis countries illustrates the depth of pluralism and tolerance that had come into its own. The relative degree of unity in the former Axis countries is a far stronger manifestation of pluralism than the maintenance of a segmented trade union landscape in the rest of continental Western Europe. Labor unity in the postwar years was a myth as well as a trompe l'oeil, but the result was all to the better.

NOTES

I wish to thank Gerd-Rainer Horn, Padraic Kenney, and Paul Misner for their suggestions and linguistic revisions of an earlier version of this text.

1. In this period, the reference to labor unity within all-encompassing industrial unions also had other meanings, in particular the unification of white- and blue-collar workers as well as, to a lesser extent, civil servants. The term also referred to the centralization of unions at the national level. See Denis MacShane, *International Labor and the Origins of the Cold War* (Oxford: Clarendon, 1992).

2. "Le Syndicalisme chrétien," *Les Dossiers de l'Action Sociale Catholique* 21, nos. 5–6 (1944): 341.

3. Lutz Niethammer, "Structural Reform and a Compact for Growth: Conditions for a United Labor Union Movement in Western Europe after the Collapse of Fascism," in *The Origins of the Cold War and Contemporary Europe*, ed. Charles S. Maier (New York: New Viewpoints, 1978), 201–43. For Belgium, see Rik Hemmerijckx, Wouter Steenhout, and Luc Peiren, "De socialistische vakbeweging tijdens de Tweede Wereldoorlog," in *Een eeuw solidariteit 1898–1998: Geschiedenis van de socialistische vakbeweging*, ed. Luc Peiren and Jean-Jacques Messiaen (Brussels: Ludion, 1997), 63–72.

4. Alya Aglan, "Des syndicalistes dans la Résistance," *Vingtième Siècle* 67 (July–September 2000): 119–27; Jean-Pierre Le Crom, "Syndicalisme et Résistance," in *La Résistance et les Français: Villes, centres et logiques de décision*, ed. Laurent Douzou, Robert Frank, Denis Peschanski, and Dominique Veillon (Paris: Institut d'Histoire du Temps Présent, 1995), 397–415, 254; George Ross, *Workers and Communists in France: From Popular Front to Eurocommunism* (Berkeley: University of California Press, 1982); Michel Dreyfus, *Histoire de la CGT: Cent ans de syndicalisme en France* (Brussels: Complexe, 1995), 191–233; Bernard Comte, *L'honneur et la conscience: Catholiques français en résistance (1940–1944)* (Paris: L'Atelier, 1998).

5. Gino Bedani, *Politics and Ideology in the Italian Workers' Movement: Union Development and the Changing Role of the Catholic and Communist Subcultures in Postwar Italy* (Oxford: Berg, 1995), 7–8.

6. Wolfgang Schroeder, *Katholizismus und Einheitsgewerkschaft: Der Streit um den DGB und der Niedergang des Sozialkatholizismus in der Bundesrepublik bis 1960* (Bonn: Dietz, 1992), 75–76, 79. On the process of "recuperation" of the resistance in Belgium, France and the Netherlands, see Pieter Lagrou, *The Legacy of Nazi Occupation: Patriotic Memory and National Recovery in Western Europe, 1945–1965* (Cambridge: Cambridge University Press, 2000).

7. Anton Pelinka, *Gewerkschaften im Parteienstaat: Ein Vergleich zwischen dem Deutschen und dem Österreichischen Gewerkschaftsbund* (Berlin: Duncker & Humblot, 1980), 28; Josef Hindels, *Österreichs Gewerkschaften im Widerstand* (Vienna: Europaverlag, 1976); Ludwig Reichhold, *Geschichte der christlichen Gewerkschaften Österreichs* (Vienna: Österreichischer Gewerkschaftsbund, 1987), 576–86; William Patch, "Fascism, Catholic Corporatism, and the Christian Trade Unions of Germany, Austria and France," in *Between Cross and Class: A Transnational History of the Christian Labor Movement in Europe*, ed. Jan de Maeyer, Lex Heerma van Voss, and Patrick Pasture (Bern: Lang, forthcoming).

8. Anthony Carew, "A False Dawn: The World Federation of Trade Unions," in *The International Confederation of Free Trade Unions*, ed. Anthony Carew, Michel Dreyfus, Geert Van Goethem, Rebecca Gumbrell-McCormick, and Marcel van der Linden (Bern: Lang, 2000), 165–99; Horst Lademacher, Jürgen C. Hess, Herman J. Langeveld, and Henk Reitsma, "Der Weltgewerkschaftsbund im Spannungsfeld des Ost-West-Konflikts: Zur Gründung, Tätigkeit und Spaltung der Gewerkschaftsinternationale," *Archiv für Sozialgeschichte* 18 (1978): 119–215.

9. Pelinka, *Gewerkschaften*, 32. For Germany, see Helga Grebing, *Geschichte der Deutschen Arbeiterbewegung: Ein Überblick* (Munich: Deutscher Taschenbuch Verlag, 1966), 269–84. Reichhold, *Geschichte*, 575, points to contacts between German and Austrian trade union leaders.

10. Paul Ginsborg, *A History of Contemporary Italy: Society and Politics 1943–1988* (London: Penguin, 1990), 79–88; Donald Sassoon, *One Hundred Years of Socialism: The West European Left in the Twentieth Century* (London: Fontana, 1997), 88–89.

11. The impact of Allied policies on the reconstruction of German trade unionism has been seriously questioned by MacShane, *International Labor*, 187–97. See, in more detail, Horst Lademacher and Walter Mühlhausen, "Die deutschen Westzonen: Wiederaufbau und Intervention: Bemerkungen zur Gewerkschafts- und Strukturpolitik der Besatzungsmächte," in *Zwischen Wunsch und Wirklichkeit: Die belgischen, niederländischen und westzonalen deutschen Gewerkschaften in der Phase des Wiederaufbaus 1945–1951*, ed. Horst Lademacher, Herman Langeveld, and Gjalt Zondergeld (Münster: Lit, 1994), 431–550; Michael Fichter, *Besatzungsmacht und Gewerkschaften: Zur Entwicklung und Anwendung der US-Gewerkschaftspolitik in Deutschland 1944–1948* (Opladen: Westdeutscher Verlag, 1982); Carolyn Eisenberg, "Working Class Politics and the Cold War: American Intervention in the German Labor Movement 1945–1949," *Diplomatic History* 7, no. 3 (Autumn 1983): 283–306; Rolf Steininger, "England und die deutsche Gewerkschaftsbewegung 1945–1946," *Archiv für Sozialgeschichte* 18 (1978): 41–118; Siegfried Mielke, "Die Neugründung der Gewerkschaften in den Westlichen Besatzungszonen 1945 bis 1949," in *Geschichte*

der Gewerkschaften in der Bundesrepublik Deutschland: Von den Anfängen bis heute, ed. Hans-Otto Hemmer and Kurt Thomas Schmitz (Cologne: Bund, 1990), 19–83, especially 28–35; Schroeder, *Katholizismus*, especially 81–83.

12. Schroeder, *Katholizismus*, 78.

13. Andreas Kohl, "Gewerkschaften in Österreich," in *Gewerkschaften in den Demokratien Westeuropas*, vol. 2: *Grossbrittannien, Niederlande, Österreich, Schweden, Dänemark*, ed. Hans Rühle and Hans-Joachim Van Veen (Paderborn: Schöningh, 1983), 239–326, especially 252–54; Reichhold, *Geschichte*, 569–71; Patch, "Fascism."

14. See Detlev Brunner, *Sozialdemokraten im FDGB: Von der Gewerkschaft zur Massenorganisation, 1945 bis in die frühen 1950er Jahre* (Essen: Klartext, 2000), 27, note 2; Lademacher and Mühlhausen, "Westzonen," 431–550; Mielke, "Neugründung," 33; Niethammer, "Reform," 220–22.

15. Hemmerijckx et al., "Socialistische vakbeweging"; Wouter Steenhout, "De Unie van Hand- en Geestesarbeiders," in *België 1940: Een maatschappij in crisis en oorlog* (Brussels: Navorsings- en Studiecentrum voor de Geschiedenis van de Tweede Wereldoorlog, 1993), 277–84; Rik Hemmerijckx, "De Belgische socialisten tegen de Unie van Hand- en Geestesarbeiders," in *België 1940*, 481–96; Jozef Mampuys, "Le syndicalisme chrétien," in *Histoire du mouvement ouvrier chrétien en Belgique*, ed. Emmanuel Gerard and Paul Wynants (Leuven: Leuven University Press, 1994), vol. 2, 151–277, especially 216–27.

16. Hermann J. Langeveld, "Niederlande: Reform und Kooperation," in *Zwischen Wunsch und Wirklichkeit*, 57–277, especially 98–105 and 124–41; Ernest Hueting, Frits de Jong Edz., and Rob Neij, *Naar groter eenheid: De geschiedenis van het Nederlands Verbond van Vakverenigingen 1906–1981* (Amsterdam: Van Gennep, 1983), 115–28, especially 122–23; Ger Harmsen, "Vakorganisaties in de eerste jaren van de Duitse bezetting: Doorgaan of stoppen," *Zeggenschap*, 3 (May–June 1990): 28–37; Jan-Jacob Van Dijk and Paul Werkman, *Door geweld gedwongen: Het CNV in oorlogstijd* (Utrecht: Christelijk Nationaal Vakverbond, 1995); Ger Harmsen and Bob Reinalda, *Voor de bevrijding van de arbeid: Beknopte geschiedenis van de vakbeweging in Nederland* (Nijmegen: SUN, 1975), 220.

17. Patrick Pasture, "Belgium: Pragmatism in Pluralism," in *The Lost Perspective? Trade Unions between Ideology and Social Action in the New Europe*, ed. Patrick Pasture, Johan Verberckmoes, and Hans De Witte (Aldershot: Avebury, 1996), 1: 91–135.

18. See note 16.

19. Jean-Pierre Le Crom, *Syndicats, nous-voilà! Vichy et le corporatisme* (Paris: L'Atelier, 1995); *Les ouvriers en France pendant la Seconde Guerre Mondiale*, ed. Denis Peschanski and Jean-Louis Robert (Paris: Institut d'Histoire du Temps Présent, 1992); *Syndicalismes sous Vichy*, ed. Jean-Louis Robert, special issue of *Le Mouvement Social* 158 (January–March 1992); Michel Dreyfus, *Histoire de la CGT* (Brussels: Complexe, 1995), 195–202; Marc Sadoun, *Les socialistes sous l'Occupation, Résistance et collaboration* (Paris: Fondation Nationale des Sciences Politiques, 1982).

20. Niethammer, "Reform." For Belgium, see, in English, Patrick Pasture, "The April 1944 'Social Pact' in Belgium and Its Significance for the Post-War Welfare State," *Journal of Contemporary History* 28, no. 3 (1993): 695–714, and, in greater detail, *Het sociaal pact van 1944: Oorsprong, betekenis en gevolgen*, ed. Dirk Luyten and Guy Vanthemsche (Brussels: Vrije Universiteit Brussel Press, 1995). For the Netherlands, see Langeveld, "Niederlande," 105–16; Maarten van Bottenburg, *"Aan den Arbeid!" In de wandelgangen van de Stichting van de Arbeid 1945–1995* (Amsterdam: Bakker, 1995). Compare this, however, to German plans referred to earlier (see note 16).

21. Niethammer, "Structural Reform," 208–12; Daniel L. Horowitz, *The Italian Labor Movement* (Cambridge, Mass.: Harvard University Press, 1963), 181–243.

22. Hans Mommsen, "Der 20. Juli 1944 und die deutsche Arbeiterbewegung," in *Sozialismus und Kommunismus im Wandel: Hermann Weber zum 65. Geburtstag*, ed. Klaus Schönhoven and Dietrich Staritz (Cologne: Bund, 1993), 236–60. One may note the influence of fascist antiparty thinking in such views.

23. See Emiel Lamberts, ed., *Christian Democracy in the European Union (1945–1995)* (Leuven: Leuven University Press, 1997); Michael Gehler, Wolfram Kaiser and Herman Wohnout, eds., *Christian Democracy in 20th Century Europe* (Vienna: Böhlau, 2001); and Gerd-Rainer Horn and Emmanuel Gerard, eds., *Left Catholicism: Politics and Society in Western Europe at the Point of Liberation: 1943–1955* (Leuven: Leuven University Press, 2001).

24. Hugh McLeod, *Religion and the People of Western Europe 1789–1989* (Oxford: Oxford University Press, 1997), 132. See also Martin Conway and Tom Buchanan, eds., *Political Catholicism in Europe 1918–1965* (Oxford: Clarendon, 1996); Lamberts, ed., *Christian Democracy in the European Union*; and Gehler et al., eds., *Christian Democracy in 20th Century Europe*.

25. See Gerd-Rainer Horn, *European Socialists Respond to Fascism: Ideology, Activism and Contingency in the 1930s* (New York: Oxford University Press, 1996).

26. Niethammer, "Reform"; MacShane, *International Labor*. Such strategic considerations, for example, made the Communists in Germany abandon the strategy of the "revolutionary trade union opposition" that had caused their total isolation in the last days of the Weimar Republic.

Some recent studies, however, deny the existence of such a common strategy; see, for example, José Gotovitch, Pascal Delwit, and Jean-Louis De Waele, *L'Europe des Communistes* (Brussels: Complexe, 1992), 157–62. See also Sassoon, *One Hundred Years of Socialism*, 98–112 and chapter 1 by Aldo Agosti in this volume.

27. Peter-Jan Knegtmans, "De jaren 1919–1946," in *Honderd jaar sociaal-democratie in Nederland 1894–1994*, ed. Jos Perry, Peter Jan Knegtmans, D. F. J. Bosscher, Maarten Brinkman, and Louis Zweers (Amsterdam: Bakker, 1994), 114–17; Jan Bank, *Opkomst en ondergang van de Nederlandse Volksbeweging (NVB)* (Deventer: Kluwer, 1978).

28. Stefan Berger, "Germany," in *The Force of Labor: The Western European Labor Movement and the Working Class in the Twentieth Century*, ed. Stefan Berger and David Broughton (Oxford: Berg, 1995), 71–105, 83.

29. See Annemieke Klijn, *Arbeiders- of volkspartij: Een vergelijkende studie van het Belgisch en Nederlands Socialisme 1933–1946* (Maastricht: Universitaire Pers Maastricht, 1990).

30. Alain Bergounioux and Gérard Grunberg, *Le long remords du pouvoir: Le Parti socialiste français 1905–1992* (Paris: Fayard, 1992), 165.

31. Reichhold, *Geschichte,* 579–86; Federico Romero, *The United States and the European Trade Union Movement* (Raleigh: University of North Carolina Press, 1992), 31–77, especially 36.

32. See note 40.

33. Pelinka, *Gewerkschaften*; Lademacher and Mühlhausen, "Westzonen"; Schönhoven, *Gewerkschaften*, 198–216.

34. Schroeder, *Katholizismus*, 76; Theo Pirker, *Die blinde Macht: Die Gewerkschaftsbewegung in Deutschland* (Berlin: Olle & Wolter, 1979), 1: 55; Andrea Ciampani and Massimiliano Valente, "Christian Workers and Unitary Unions in

Democratic Countries: Political and Catholic Dynamics in Italy and Germany, 1944–1974," in *Between Cross and Class*, ed. de Maeyer et al.

35. Paul Coomans, Truike De Jonge, and Erik Nijhof, *De Eenheidsvakcentrale (EVC) 1943–1948* (Groningen: Tjeenk Willink, 1976); Hueting et al., *Naar groter eenheid*; Rik Hemmerijckx, *Van Verzet tot Koude Oorlog, 1940–1949: Machtstrijd om het ABVV* (Brussels: Vrije Universiteit Brussel Press, 2003); Rik Hemmerijckx, "The Belgian Communist Party and the Socialist Unions, 1940–1960," *Journal of Communist Studies* 6, no. 4 (December 1990): 124–42; José Gotovitch, *Du rouge au tricolore: Les Communistes belges de 1939 à 1944: Un aspect de l'histoire de la Résistance en Belgique* (Brussels: Labor, 1992).

36. On the MSU, see Hemmerijckx, *Van Verzet*; Rik Hemmerijckx, *Le Mouvement syndical unifié et la naissance du renardisme*, Courrier hebdomadaire du Crisp No. 1119-1120 (Brussels: Centre de recherche et d'information socio-politique, 1986).

37. Coomans et al., *Eenheidsvakcentrale*, 490. See also Hueting et al., *Naar groter eenheid*, 159–245; Langeveld, "Niederlande."

38. Hemmerijckx, *Van Verzet*.

39. Coomans et al., *Eenheidsvakcentrale*, 488–94; Hemmerijckx, *Van Verzet*.

40. MacShane, *International Labor*, 205–13, citations on 206–7. See also Brunner, *Sozialdemokraten*, 152–301; and Pelinka, *Gewerkschaften*, 34.

41. Niethammer, "Reform," 213. See, furthermore, George Ross, *Workers and Communists in France: From Popular Front to Eurocommunism* (Berkeley: University of California Press, 1982); Dreyfus, *Histoire*, 191–232; Edward Mortimer, *The Rise of the French Communist Party 1920–1947* (London: Faber, 1984); MacShane, *International Labor*; Philippe Buton, "Les ouvriers et le Parti Communiste (1936–1947)," in *Les ouvriers en France*, ed. Peschanski and Robert, 307–25.

42. Bergounioux and Grunberg, *Remords*, 165. See also Robert Verdier, *PS-PC: Une lutte pour l'entente* (Paris: Seghers, 1976); and Philippe Buton, *Les lendemains qui déchantent: Le PCF à la Libération* (Paris: Fondation Nationale des Sciences Politiques, 1993).

43. See also Patrick Hassenteufel, "Partis socialistes et syndicats: L'autonomisation réciproque," in *La Gauche en Europe depuis 1945: Invariants et mutations du socialisme européen*, ed. Marc Lazar (Paris: Presses Universitaires de France, 1996), 513–33.

44. Pelinka, *Gewerkschaften*, 43; Reichhold, *Geschichte*, 579–648.

45. MacShane, *International Labor*, 204.

46. Ginsborg, *A History of Contemporary Italy*, 87.

47. Dreyfus, *Histoire*, 331.

48. Dreyfus, *Histoire*, passim; Ross, *Workers*, 26 and passim, but in particular 19–47; Bergounioux and Grunberg, *Remords*, 162–67; Sadoun, *Socialistes*, 277–83.

49. Hemmerijckx, *Van Verzet*.

50. Lange, "Niederlande," 142–50.

51. Sassoon, *One Hundred Years of Socialism*, 83–112.

52. See, for Germany, Fichter, *Besatzungsmacht*; Lademacher and Mühlhausen, "Westzonen"; Michael Fichter, *Einheit und Organisation: Der Deutsche Gewerkschaftsbund im Aufbau 1945–1949* (Cologne: Bund, 1990); Klaus Schönhoven, "Kalter Krieg in den Gewerkschaften: Zur Gewerkschaftspolitik von KPD und SPD nach 1945," in *Sozialismus*, 261–80; and, for Italy, Romero, *United States*, 231–77.

53. See, for example, the results of the elections for the *Kammern für Arbeiter und Angestellte* in 1949: Socialist faction, 64.4 percent; Catholic faction, 14.2 percent; Communists and extreme left, 9.7 percent; Independents, 11.7 percent. Pelinka, *Gewerkschaften*, 197.

54. Horowitz, *Italian Labor*, 181–243 and 253–60.

55. *Force Ouvrière* 2, no. 1 (20 December 1945); MacShane, *International Labor*, 255–57. In 1947, Force Ouvrière separated from the CGT to create the independent trade union federation CGT–Force Ouvrière (FO).

56. Hemmerijckx, *Van Verzet*.

57. For the following, see Hueting et al., *Naar groter eenheid*, 159–245; Langeveld, "Niederlande," 124–74; Van Bottenburg, *Arbeid*, 65–68; Coomans et al., *Eenheidsvakcentrale*.

58. On this whole paragraph, see Patrick Pasture, *La difficile recherche d'une troisième voie: Histoire du syndicalisme chrétien international* (Paris: L'Harmattan, 1999).

59. Stefan Berger, "European Labor Movements and the European Working Class in Comparative Perspective," in *The Force of Labor*, 245–61.

60. Compare Schroeder, *Katholizismus*; Rudolf Uertz, *Christentum und Sozialismus in der frühen CDU: Grundlagen und Wirkungen der christlich-sozialen Ideen in der Union 1945–1949* (Stuttgart: Deutsche Verlags–Anstalt, 1982).

61. Schroeder, *Katholizismus*, 81, 84–96. Among the former Christian trade union leaders who opted for a political career, one may note Karl Arnold, Jacob Kaiser, Johannes Albers, and Karl Schmitz, among others.

62. See Ciampani and Valente, "Christian Workers," for a comparison of these organizations.

63. Schroeder, *Katholizismus*, 84–86.

64. Reichhold, *Geschichte*, 587–607.

65. Uertz, *Christentum*, 65–67; Schroeder, *Katholizismus*, 285–99.

66. See also Patrick Pasture, "Diverging Paths: The Development of Catholic Labor Organisations in France, the Netherlands and Belgium since 1945," *Revue d'Histoire Ecclésiastique* 87, no. 1 (1994): 54–90.

67. Some of them even tried to be recognized as "heroes of the resistance." See Lagrou, *Legacy*, 57–58.

68. See William L. Patch Jr., *Christian Trade Unions in the Weimar Republic, 1918–1933: The Failure of "Corporate Pluralism"* (New Haven, Conn.: Yale University Press, 1985); Michael Schneider, *Die christlichen Gewerkschaften 1894–1933* (Bonn: Neue Gesellschaft, 1982); Patch, "Fascism."

69. Reichhold, *Geschichte*, is most instructive on selective memory in Austria.

70. About the clerical character of the Dutch Katholieke Arbeidersbeweging (KAB), see Pasture, "Paths."

71. See Pasture, *Recherche*, passim.

72. Pasture, *Recherche*, 209–12.

73. Pasture, *Recherche*, 248–49.

74. Compare Pelinka, *Gewerkschaften*, 28–31. This short discussion is inspired by Carl Strikwerda's penetrating study, *A House Divided: Mass Politics and the Origins of Pluralism: Catholicism, Socialism and Flemish Nationalism in Nineteenth Century Belgium* (Lanham, Md.: Rowman & Littlefield, 1997), especially 415–16.

3

Liberated Zones in Northern Italy and Southeastern France

The Cases of the Alto Tortonese and the Vercors

Anna Balzarro

Resistance movements were a political and military phenomenon that linked the fate of the populations of European countries occupied by Nazi troops. Although each country had its own history, the occupying power was the same. A clash of civilizations took place in the whole of Europe.[1] The war was not just a traditional military conflict; contemporaries witnessed the contrast between two opposite visions of the world. One idea of Europe was reflected in the Nazi *Weltanschauung*: a Europe under the complete authority of Germany and purified of all those political, racial, and cultural elements that were not part of their project. Its very opposite was the hope of a Europe with free populations, where everybody would be treated with dignity and would enjoy the same rights.

A factor common to those occupied nations was the totality of the war, which had an extraordinary impact on their entire populations. In World War II, civilians were involved more than in any other previous conflict. Bombs over built-up areas, racial deportations, and starvation affected both men and women, adults and children, young and old, indiscriminately along an imaginary front line that included a good part of Europe. Another common factor was the characteristic of "civil war" in its double meaning: On the one hand, it was a conflict that divided nations between collaborators and partisans; on the other hand, it was the second of two wars that devastated Europe in the space of thirty years.[2]

As I have just mentioned, the conflict split individual nations transversely and put some European countries against others. At the same time, however, it rebuilt a sense of national identity on different foundations and created an affinity of purpose based on a common vision of the world. I think, for example, of the collaboration between partisans of different countries and the

Anglo-American troops: A relationship cemented by common ideals of freedom and democracy and by the firm belief that the defeat of some fellow countrymen (I have the Italian events especially in mind) could be advantageous for the common good of the whole population. Study of the phenomenon across more than one country is therefore useful, not only because it helps us to better understand individual national events, but also because it allows us to put a national movement into the wider context in which it occurred. One particularly interesting area for such study is the "free" or "liberated" zones that came into existence in various European countries.

THE FREE ZONES: A EUROPEAN PHENOMENON

The free zones were territories of limited extent (one or more valleys, some towns, a plateau) that the partisans managed to conquer from enemy occupation and to hold temporarily during the course of the war. These areas of free territory were totally surrounded by the Nazi army; in this sense, it is possible to see the free zones as "islands" of freedom. In these territories, the partisans faced problems connected with the defense of the liberated zones (the German troops would make all possible efforts to reoccupy these zones and would treat both partisans and civilians brutally) as well as with the territories' administration, attempting to ensure the organization of essential services, such as the arrival of supplies and the running of hospitals and schools. One is dealing, therefore, with the projection into wartime of political and administrative problems that pertain to peacetime reconstruction but where it is impossible to ignore the dramatic reality of that very special historical context.

Free zones came into existence in many countries. The most significant examples occurred in Bulgaria, Yugoslavia, Greece, the Soviet Union, France, and Italy. The introduction to the proceedings of a meeting on this aspect of the European resistance, collectively authored by the Istituto Storico della Resistenza in Provincia di Novara e in Valsesia, emphasizes that the free zones reflected the peculiarities of the liberation movement of the country, in particular "all the military, political and social components of our war of liberation and the war of other populations, the ratio between moderate and revolutionary forces, the level of maturity of the populations and of the partisan groups, and the relationship between spontaneous behaviour and organization."[3] The free zones were thus a "mirror" of the nature of national liberation movements; however, another fundamental interpretation of the free zones lies in their transnational features. Emerging independently but at roughly the same time, they exhibit great affinities that connect the histories of the various free zones: the problem of control and military defense of the liberated territories, their administrative control, and the relationship between the political and the administrative aspects of such control and the repression that normally brought to an end this type of experience.[4]

In my opinion, the transnational features of the free zones can be best showcased if we analyze two specific cases pertaining to two different nations. I will therefore concentrate on two free zones, one occurring during the French resistance (in the Vercors), the other during the Italian resistance (in the Alto Tortonese).

Italy and France had different historical experiences during the 1930s, they played different roles during World War II (one was an aggressor, the other was a victim), and the duration of their resistance movements was not the same. On the other hand, they are neighboring countries with many points in common. In the 1920s and 1930s, many Italian antifascists found refuge in France; during the war, some French partisans took part in the Italian resistance and vice versa; and, at the end of the war, the two most important Communist parties of Western Europe developed in France and in Italy.

The Vercors is certainly the most conspicuous example of a French free zone and has historical and political implications extending beyond the end of the war, concerning not only the internal equilibrium of the French resistance but also its relationship with the Allied forces. Hence, it is appropriate to use the vicissitudes of the French mountainous plateau of the Vercors as one of the two examples of free zones. I would like to show the remarkable similarities between the experience of the Vercors and that of the Alto Tortonese; even taking into account the specific characteristics of both cases, an affinity can be noticed both in the historical events themselves and in the memoirs of those who witnessed and took part in them.

VERCORS AND ALTO TORTONESE: A COMPARISON OF TWO HISTORIES

The Vercors is a high plateau shared between the departments of the Drôme and the Isère. It is a place that, because of its experiences in the summer of 1944, has become a key element in the construction of the collective memory of the French resistance. During the German occupation, in accordance with a plan drawn up by two civilians (Pierre Dalloz and the writer Jean Prévost) and submitted for the attention of the representatives of France Libre, it was established that the Vercors had to play a decisive role at the time of the Allied landing in the south of France. It was thought that, thanks to its geography, a great number of armed men, ready to go into action at the right moment and to join the troops already ashore on the Mediterranean coast, could be hidden on the plateau. In fact, because of a series of misunderstandings, the mobilization in the Vercors was premature (June 1944). At the time of the Normandy landings, the radio had broadcast the passwords concerning the mobilization of the resistance in many parts of the country, including the Vercors, in order not to reveal to the enemy where the landing was to take place. Hearing these orders, those responsible for the Vercors resistance believed that their moment had come and proceeded to mobilize volunteers in the area, who poured in en masse from 9 June onward.

During June and July, much frenetic activity took place on the plateau. There was an intense exchange of telegrams between Algiers and resistance forces asking for airborne reinforcements and arms; and the numerous volunteers who had reached the Vercors experienced "freedom" inside occupied France. The French flag was flown on the plateau, the restoration of the republic was proclaimed, and the decrees of Vichy were publicly abrogated. But brutal repression by German troops subsequently put an end to this experience.[5]

The story of the Alto Tortonese, in turn, offers an example of the organizational skill reached by the partisans' movement in Italy in September 1944. At the beginning of September, the whole area, which includes Val Borbera, Val Grue, and Val Curone as far as Brignano Frascata, passed under the control and administration of the partisan brigades. Between September and December, town councils, elected by the heads of each family, took office. Administrative activity was based on uniform criteria, although this was not always strictly adhered to; in theory, the town councils had to follow the directions of the partisans' headquarters. In October, the enemy attack interrupted this experience of self-government for the winter months. Self-administration resumed in the spring, after the end of the round-ups (i.e., after the temporary Nazi reconquest of the Alto Tortonese in the winter of 1944–1945).

The cases of the Vercors and the Alto Tortonese have been selected for the main reasons detailed in the following five sections.

The Geographic and Social Context

The comparatively close geographic position of the two areas—one in southeastern France, one in northwest Italy (see map on page 55)—is one of their points in common, together with other aspects of the physical environment and socioeconomic organization. The villages of the Vercors are about one thousand meters above sea level. In 1944, the economy of the zone was based mostly on cattle breeding, especially of milk cows. Such activity had an influence also on other elements of the local economy, as small-scale industry was in fact mostly related to dairy farming. Because of the mountain climate, agricultural production was not geared toward large-scale cereal production for the market; cereals were distributed locally and were used mostly for animal feed.[6]

The Alto Tortonese is a hilly area, where the economy is concentrated mostly in the hands of peasant smallholders. Wheat production has always

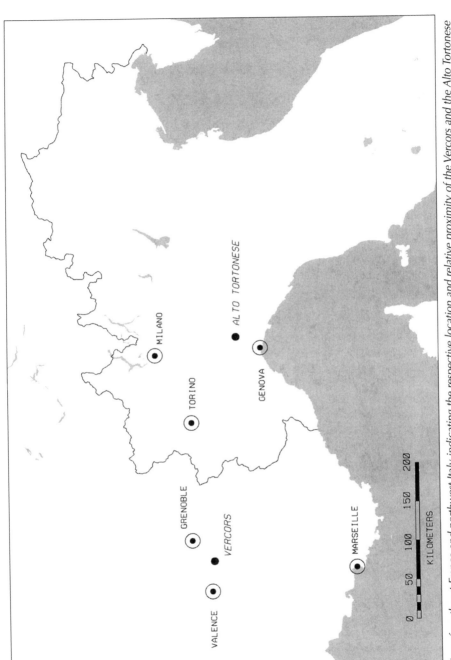

Map of southeast France and northwest Italy indicating the respective location and relative proximity of the Vercors and the Alto Tortonese

been pronounced, but a significant percentage of the working population was also involved in animal husbandry, in particular the raising of cows and pigs. The possession of animals was, among other things, very important for trade, as the owners of the cattle could exchange cattle for other goods they needed.

The Islandlike Characteristics

The physical characteristics of the Vercors (a plateau surrounded by steep rocks) evoke "separation" from the surrounding territory. This characteristic was particularly important after the great mobilization of 9 June. On that date, many young volunteers climbed the plateau, thinking that the time had come for the national insurrection and that they had the duty to protect the Vercors as a rampart where Franco-American troops would be parachuted in. Volunteers therefore mined tunnels and blocked roads in order to make the plateau inaccessible to German troops. All these actions, of course, stressed the "island of freedom" nature of the plateau, a characteristic typical of the free zones. The days of isolation, in fact, coincided with the administration of the territory by the resistance forces and with the proclamation, on 3 July, of the Republic of the Vercors.

In the Alto Tortonese, the need for good defenses also emphasized the islandlike characteristic of the liberated valleys. The area occupied by the partisans was in fact linked with the plain by one bridge only, the bridge of Pertuso. On 6 October, during the first period of the free zone (September–December 1944), the partisans blew this bridge up in order to defend those valleys from German attacks. Therefore, in both areas, steps taken to render the liberated territory more easily defensible had made the separation between the free zone and the territory occupied by the Germans much clearer.

The Repression

Most free zones, as mentioned earlier, did not last indefinitely, since German repression usually put an end to these experiences or, in some cases, temporarily interrupted their free development. In the Vercors, the casualty figures due to enemy counterinsurgency were particularly dramatic (dozens of partisans and civilians were killed in many villages)[7] and are well-known. My studies, however, have brought to light another type of violence that is seldom mentioned and that underlines the similarities between the vicissitudes of the French plateau and those of the Alto Tortonese: rapes. In both these areas, Soviet prisoners of war, including many soldiers from the Central Asian republics, participated in the attacks under the command of German officers. In the Vercors, the presence was noted, among others, of Kalmyks and Tartars, and in the Alto Tortonese of Turkmens and Uzbeks.

These troops raped women of all ages in both regions. Despite their various origins, their foreign characteristics meant that the local populations in both areas referred to them as "the Mongols." It is difficult to establish exactly the number of rapes that occurred. In general, it is possible to ascertain the names of the villages that suffered most but not the number of victims. Sources of information with regard to these villages of the Vercors where the rapes took place are mostly articles published after the end of the war; for the Alto Tortonese we also have more recent witnesses. As we shall see, study of the memoirs of the members of the resistance reveals some further interesting points of similarity.

Italians in the Resistance of the Vercors and French Partisans in the Alto Tortonese

Because of their geographic vicinity, the presence in France of immigrant workers, and the activity of antifascist militants (i.e., Giuliano Pajetta in the Var, Aladino Bibolotti in Grenoble, Francesco Leone in Lyon, and Emilio Sereni in Nice), the participation of Italians in the resistance of southeastern France was, according to Jean-Marie Guillon,[8] much more important than French historians and memoirs are inclined to mention. In spite of this "silence," it is fair to note that more than thirty years ago, Fernand Rude quoted the Italian political refugee, Carlo Marchisio, who was already active in 1942 in the socialist resistance movement, Franc Tireur, as one of the instigators of the resistance in the Vercors. The exchange between the two countries, however, was not unidirectional only, in spite of the obviously greater presence of Italians in France compared with the French in Italy. Giambattista Lazagna, vice commander of the Divisione Pinan-Cichero, the partisan force operating in the Alto Tortonese, not only had spent part of his early youth in France but also remembered well that five or six Frenchmen (one of them was the Parisian Foucher, who fell in action and received a medal posthumously) fought with them in the valleys of the Alto Tortonese.[9]

There is a further point in common between the Vercors and the Piedmont. According to Paul Dreyfus, some resistance fighters in the Vercors later on also participated in the April 1945 alpine campaigns, fighting in the Savoy and Delfinato valleys and pushing on over the frontier. Dreyfus also notes that on 28 April 1945, in Turin, liberated following a successful uprising by Italian partisans, some French battalions participated in the victory parade, including the Sixième Bataillon de Chasseurs Alpins from the Vercors.[10]

Civilians and the Military

The resistance in the Vercors began on the initiative of socialist militants (already active in the early 1940s) and professional officers. Their relationship was not always easy; however, especially during the months of the free zone, in June and July 1944, two centers of command coexisted: the military leadership, entrusted to the officer François Huet, and the civilian center, under the leadership of the socialist militant Eugène Chavant. Both were assisted by two officers, one responsible for the northern part and one for the southern part of the plateau, and by two civilians with similar territorial jurisdiction.

The resistance of the Alto Tortonese also originated with collaboration between a political nucleus (consisting of the *comitato di liberazione nazionale* of Tortona and some Communists from Genoa) and some disbanded components of the demobilized army; the presence of professional officers is not so frequent, and participation in the resistance movement is mostly due to single individuals' initiatives. In any case, even if in the free zone of the Alto Tortonese many military commanders had been civilians prior to the war, there were still problems resulting from the simultaneous presence of different ideas and ways of thinking and a lack of mutual comprehension.

In the Vercors, these different ways of thinking were more striking than in the Alto Tortonese and particularly influenced the way in which the partisan experience was taken into account, as we can see from the memoirs of those involved, written after the end of the war. The analysis of the "transnational" connections between the memoirs from the two zones thus calls for the extension of the comparison not only to the way of thinking of individuals but also to their way of remembering the resistance in the years following the liberation.

TRANSNATIONAL ASPECTS OF MEMORY: PARTICIPANTS' ACCOUNTS

The comparison between the published memoirs of those involved in the events in question[11] allows one to note the interconnection between the public and the private aspects of memory. The importance given to the memory of the two free zones within their respective national contexts is rather different, but, if we focus on the accounts that the protagonists themselves decided to give of their own experience, such differences are considerably reduced.

In a study of the recollections of the Vercors experience, Gilles Vergnon has identified two trends: the *légende dorée* (i.e., the positive myth of that experience) and the *légende noire*, concerning the opposite myth of the "betrayal" of the Vercors by the Allies and France Libre.[12] The légende dorée includes two distinct but correlated "memory currents," one closely linked to the memory of military aspects (*Vercors militaire*), the other more sensitive to the aspects of fraternity and resistance as a community experience (*Vercors des gueux*).[13] From the study of these memoirs, it becomes clear that there are significant points in common between the "less military" memoirs of the Vercors (Vercors des gueux) and those of the Alto Tortonese. To show this convergence, I shall concentrate on three particular topics of research: (1) aspects of partisan life, (2) the ideals and the actual experience of anticipated freedom, and (3) the violence of the enemy.

Aspects of Partisan Life

Pierre Tanant's book[14] epitomizes the "military spirit" of the Vercors. One notices a certain amount of mythologizing of the war and, in particular, of risk as an element which makes life worth living. This love for action is accompanied by a vision of the experience of the Vercors in the light of the criteria and values of a traditional army. Tanant conceptualizes this military spirit as a code of moral behavior. But, how do those memoirs not profoundly influenced by the "military spirit" represent the partisan experience? In the memoirs by "Lieutenant Stephen" (André Valot),[15] a forest engineer who took part in the resistance in the Vercors from the very beginning and who is a significant exponent of the Vercors des gueux genre, the "spirit" of the Vercors was not the same as that of a traditional army but was instead characterized by "camaraderie" and fraternity.

In the books on the Tortonese, we find many characteristics that resemble the accounts of the Vercors des gueux. In *Ponte rotto*, the memoirs of Giambattista "Carlo" Lazagna, the political aspects are interconnected and often superimposed on the military aspects together with particular attention given to the human and moral aspects of the experience.[16] In the foreground is the love for freedom: freedom from Nazi oppression and inner freedom. Furthermore, as we can see when reading the memoirs of Giambattista "Marzo" Canepa, the partisan experience is considered as a moment of fraternity and solidarity and is likewise important from a "moral development" point of view.[17]

Another common feature between the two cases is one of the favorite subjects for analysis in the memoirs: the prominence of the young and the very young, who had chosen to undertake the "adventure" of the resistance. It is not by chance that the book of photographs by Marcel Jansen (which, in my opinion, can be included among the memoirs of the resistance in the Vercors since it represents a sort of photographic memory of Jansen's experience on the plateau) is dedicated to "All the partisans who were less than 20 years old."[18] *La Repubblica a Torriglia*, one of the books of memoirs written by Canepa, appears particularly concerned with the teenagers who joined the resistance and who became heroes, sacrificing their lives and participating in that common experience of fraternity and solidarity. Tender attention for the dead teenagers is accompanied by an effort to find space for feelings in general.

These memoirs, as they deal with sentiments and dramas like the death of many very young partisans, do not, however, assume a rhetorical or heroic tone. On the contrary, it is the very antiheroic structure of the story that makes them special. Indeed, they often deal with dramatic episodes without forgetting some comic details.

The Experience of Anticipated Freedom

If we take into account the memoirs of the Vercors, where the military spirit is generally stronger, we see that this spirit is present even when the story deals with the experience of the free zone. In Tanant's memoirs, his love for freedom is linked to old national traditions and to an exaltation of the spirit of sacrifice. According to Tanant, France must earn its freedom fighting, attempting to forget the most recent events, even if this means great bloodshed, since its history has always required this sacrifice. Tanant considers the "Free Republic of the Vercors" as an image of the future liberated France, although he never forgets its strategic role as a fortress.[19] In other memoirs of the Vercors, the feeling of freedom prevails over the military spirit.

We find a different perspective, for example, in Albert Darier, another author whom we can place into the Vercors des gueux genre of memoirs, who considers the defense of one's life to the bitter end of great value.[20] The main character of Darier's book "believes earnestly in this free Republic of the Vercors. And all his companions have the same belief."[21] The value of the partisan experience lies in its concept of individual choice, of voluntary action. Freedom is the greatest of values, for which it was well worth risking one's life. The Vercors is seen as the beginning of their world ("*le commencement de leur monde à eux*")[22] and is called "*le pays de la liberté*," the country of freedom.[23]

In the books by both Darier and "Lieutenant Stephen," the historical roots to which they refer are those of the French Revolution. One can see the connection with the events of revolutionary France, the pride for the actions of the poorly dressed and ill-fed volunteers who fight against a well-organized army, a pride very similar to that found in the memoirs of Italian partisans. Lazagna in fact emphasizes how the Germans must submit to an insurgent population, and in particular he remembers the dismay of a German colonel, himself incorporating the "quintessential spirit of Prussian militarism," who, after roughly thirty years as a military career officer, is obliged to surrender to a group of "boys."[24] The reference to the free zone as an island of freedom ("this land, which is free as an island in a sea of oppression and violence")[25] is also present in the memoirs of Lazagna, even though the author frequently refers to the more rational aspects connected with the construction of the "partisan state," such as the organization and defense of the liberated territory. The feeling of freedom is common to both experiences and finds a similar expression in the memoirs of the Vercors des gueux and in those of the Alto Tortonese. These writers stress the characteristics of equality and fraternity that make the war different from the war of a "regular" army, even if in the Alto Tortonese the sentiment of freedom is also accompanied by particular attention to the organization and management of the free zone, set up by the partisan command, strongly aiming toward a real democracy to be established after the war.

In books by the principal characters of the Vercors resistance, we find a strong bond between freedom and the mountains. There are remarkable similarities among memoirs of partisans who fought on the Vercors plateau. Tanant describes the Vercors as a fortress but also as a beautiful plateau that, on account of its altitude, imparts a feeling of freedom. The beauty of nature and the relationship between mountains and freedom are likewise present in the Italian memoirs. Franco Castelli has written that the mountain includes "a whole web of myths and symbols, both traditional and new."[26] Castelli recalls the dichotomy between the mountains and the plains, corresponding to a distinction between two choices: the partisan choice, identified with the mountain, and the fascist choice, identified with the plain.[27] In the memories of the Alto Tortonese, we can sometimes find a direct parallel with the Vercors narrative of "mountain-freedom," giving expression to a "longing for the life in the mountains," although in the writings of both Lazagna and Canepa there is ample space for the openly political aspects implicit in the creation of a partisan "state." When Lazagna recounts the arrival at Ramaceto along a stony path, for example, he lingers over a description of nature. Sometimes an admiration for the beauty of nature exists side by side with the awareness that those areas are territories where the partisans must fight and perhaps die: the theater of war from which some of them will never return.

The Violence of the Enemy

The burden of enemy violence, especially hard in the Vercors, is manifest in all the books and is also quite evident if one takes a trip across the plateau, scattered with plaques and monuments. How is this violence described in the memoirs? How is the memory of the massacres correlated to the memory of the rapes? With regard to sexual violence, is it true that there is a tendency to "sanitize written life stories," as suggested by Marlene Epp?[28] Was there a tendency to avoid giving an exact account of what happened in one's country, perhaps to the women of one's own family?

If we consider the memoirs of the Vercors, the echo of the sacrifice is inevitably strong. Tanant devotes a whole chapter to "*le martyre*" (martyrdom), a quasi-religious word also used to describe the sufferings of Christians in the distant past; this is similar to other writings on the Vercors that emphasize the military aspect. André Valot, in contrast, does not avoid graphic expressions, presenting a realistic picture of the dramatic violence suffered by the inhabitants of Vassieux. Here we do not find, as in Tanant's book, a veneration of the violence conceived as an almost religious aspect of martyrdom, but Valot lingers over the details of what happened. From these often terrifying accounts emerges the moral indignation of the author. In "Lieutenant Stephen's" memoirs, the notion of a more secret violence, one usually not very evident in the memoirs of the Vercors, emerges: the rapes by "the Mongols."

If we turn our attention from the Vercors to the Alto Tortonese, we wonder which form memory takes with regard to the enemy's violence. What space is given to the rapes in the memoirs? Examining, for example, Lazagna's *Ponte rotto* we find an account of the violence suffered by both the fighters and the civilians. Mention of crimes against property is made ("the Mongols" were frequently associated with robbery), but more serious violence, in particular rape, is not forgotten. The image of sexual violence as a terrible impending threat more than as a real tragedy, hitting the villages of the Alto Tortonese and those of neighboring areas, also appears in Canepa's memoirs, although some phrases reveal that in those villages some rapes had in fact occurred.[29] Concrete references to "the Mongols'" behavior appear in the memoirs of another partisan, Rodolfo Maggiolo;[30] in the writings of the physician of Rocchetta;[31] and in the oral testimony of the partisan Giuseppe Balduzzi given to Daniele Borioli and Roberto Botta.[32] Balduzzi remembers, among other things, his friendly discussion with a gynecologist evacuated from Genoa; the doctor mentioned the problem of having to deal with undesired pregnancies of many raped women and wondered whether it was right for a Catholic like himself to defy not only the law but the precepts of the Catholic Church and assist these women in an abortion.

CONCLUSION

Parallels between the Vercors and the Alto Tortonese show the importance of studying similar phenomena in different national contexts. Employing a transnational approach may aid in bringing into prominence previously neglected aspects of the German occupation in Europe (e.g., sexual violence) that, for various reasons, may have appeared as incidental phenomena when looked at in one particular, isolated region only. When speaking of "free zones," we are addressing an aspect of European resistance movements that has many common traits, from a strategic-military point of view and from the perspective of a collective consciousness and its influence on memory.

In particular, in spite of some significant differences (to cite but two examples, the greater importance of the story of the Vercors in the collective memory of the French and the more specifically political characterization of the experience of the Alto Tortonese), we have noticed that the Republic of the Vercors and the free zone of the Alto Tortonese showcase many significant common traits: the comparatively proximate geographic position, the socio-geographic context, the aspect of serving as an "island" of freedom, the presence of "Mongol" troops who fought against the partisans and the populations of the two zones, and, last but not least, the rapes. If we consider the memoirs of the ex-partisans, we find several similarities between particularly those accounts of the Vercors that are less influenced by the "military spirit" and the books on the Alto Tortonese. In these two cases, in fact, the partisan experience is remembered above all for its aspects of fraternity and community life, with ample space for sentiments of tenderness toward the young fighters. With regard to style, moreover, in both the memoirs of the Vercors *des gueux* genre and those of the Alto Tortonese, the authors never descend to mere rhetoric, not even when they deal with the victims of the violence.

Finally, in both groups of memoirs, there is a common way of experiencing the free zone, most clearly visible in the portrayal of the elation of a person who has succeeded in "anticipating" the future and, in spite of the dangers, has been able to enjoy a short season of freedom.

NOTES

1. Guido Quazza, "Introduzione," in *Guerra, guerra di liberazione, guerra civile*, ed. Massimo Legnani and Ferruccio Vendramini (Milan: Angeli, 1990), 13–36.

2. Claudio Pavone, "La seconda guerra mondiale: Una guerra civile europea?" in *Guerre fratricide: Le guerre civili in età contemporanea*, ed. Gabriele Ranzato (Turin: Bollati Boringhieri, 1994), 86–128.

3. Istituto Storico della Resistenza in Provincia di Novara e in Valsesia, ed., *Le zone libere nella Resistenza italiana ed europea*, presentations and communications at the international meeting of Domodossola (Novara: Tipografia San Gaudenzio, 1969), vi.

4. Massimo Sani, unpublished presentation at the seminar on the resistance in Europe, "Repubblica e Resistenza," Rome, 30 March–30 April 1995.

5. Because of these characteristics of "land liberated from the enemy," the story of the Vercors was the subject of a paper presented by Fernand Rude at the meeting on the free zones of the European resistance (Domodossola, 1969) mentioned earlier; see Fernand Rude, "Politici e militari nella repubblica del Vercors," in *Le zone libere*, 239–60.

6. Jean-Claude Duclos and Michel Wullschleger, *Le Vercors* (Grenoble: Glénat, 1990), 11–20. I refer also to the interviews cited in Anna Balzarro, *Le Vercors et la zone libre de l'Alto Tortonese: Récits, mémoire, histoire* (Paris: L'Harmattan, 2002), 22.

7. Vassieux-en-Vercors, seventy-six civilians and one hundred *maquisards* killed; Saint-Nazaire-en-Royans, thirty-seven maquisards shot; La-Chapelle-en-Vercors, sixteen men shot; Villards-de-Lans, seventy people killed; Mallevall, thirty-nine people killed; in the cave of La Luire (Saint-Agnan-en-Vercors), patients and health officers from Saint-Martin-en-Vercors' hospital were either shot or rounded up and deported.

8. Jean-Marie Guillon, "Italiens et Espagnols dans la Résistance du Sud-Est," in *Italiens et Espagnols en France 1938–1946*, ed. Pierre Milza and Denis Peschanski (Paris: Centre National de la Recherche Scientifique, 1991), 556–65.

9. Giambattista Lazagna briefly recalled the figure of Foucher in a meeting among scholars and protagonists of the resistance in the Alto Tortonese that was held at Rocchetta Ligure on 16 September 2000. The tape recording and the transcription of

these contributions have been edited by the Associazione Nazionale Partigiani d'Italia (ANPI), Sezione Valborbera "Pinan," *Valborbera 1943–1945: Cronache e testimonianze di libertà e di solidarietà internazionale* (Paderno Dugnano: Colibrì, 2001). The presence of Foucher is cited by Lazagna on 82.

10. Paul Dreyfus, *Histoire de la Résistance en Vercors* (Paris: Arthaud, 1984), 288–89. On the Turin uprising, see Roberto Battaglia, *Storia della Resistenza italiana* (Turin: Einaudi, 1979), 649–54.

11. For further details on this subject, see Balzarro, *Le Vercors et la zone libre de l'Alto Tortonese*, 149–205, and Anna Balzarro, "La Resistenza del Vercors e la zona libera dell'Alto Tortonese nelle memorie edite dei protagonisti: Alcuni appunti per una ricerca," *Quaderno di Storia Contemporanea* 27 (2000): 31–59.

12. Gilles Vergnon, "L'évolution des représentations du maquis du Vercors," in *Résistants et Résistance*, ed. Jean-Yves Boursier (Paris: L'Harmattan, 1997), 253–68.

13. In this case, I also refer to expressions used by Vergnon, "L'évolutions des représentations du maquis," 259.

14. Pierre Tanant, *Vercors: Haut lieu de France* (Grenoble: Arthaud, 1947).

15. André Valot ("Lieutenant Stephen"), *Vercors, premier maquis de France* (Valence: Association Nationale des Pionniers et Combattants Volontaires du Vercors, 1991).

16. Giambattista Lazagna, *Ponte rotto: Storia della Divisione Garibaldina Pinan-Cichero* (Genoa: Partigiano, 1946).

17. Giambattista Canepa, *La Repubblica a Torriglia* (Genoa: Di Stefano, 1975); Giambattista Canepa, *Storia della Cichero* (n.p.: Associazione Nazionale Partigiani d'Italia, n.d.).

18. Marcel Jansen, *Reporter au maquis* (Valence: Peuple Libre, 1994).

19. Tanant, *Vercors*, 86.

20. Albert Darier, *Tu prendras les armes* (Grenoble: Imprimerie Veyret-Picot, 1974), 239–40.

21. Darier, *Tu prendras les armes*, 199.

22. Darier, *Tu prendras les armes*, 206.

23. Darier, *Tu prendras les armes*, 210.

24. Lazagna, *Ponte rotto*, 254.

25. Lazagna, *Ponte rotto*, 141.

26. Franco Castelli, "La montagna nell'immaginario partigiano," *Protagonisti* 62 (January–March 1996): 26.

27. Castelli, "La montagna nell'immaginario partigiano," 29–30. See also Claudio Pavone, *Una guerra civile: Saggio storico sulla moralità nella Resistenza* (Turin: Bollati Boringhieri, 1991), 32.

28. Marlene Epp, "The Memory of Violence: Soviet and East European Refugees and Rape in the Second World War," *Journal of Women's History* 9, no. 1 (Spring 1997): 61.

29. Canepa, *Torriglia*, 88.

30. Rodolfo Maggiolo ("Rodolfo"), *Val Borbera 1944: Diario di un partigiano* (n.p.: Tolozzi, 1977).

31. Tito Tosonotti, *L'ospedale Val Borbera in Rocchetta Ligure: Attività e vicende partigiane* (Pegli: n.p., 1967), 17.

32. Passage of the interview of Giuseppe Balduzzi quoted in Daniele Borioli and Roberto Botta, *I giorni della montagna: Otto saggi sui partigiani della Pinan-Cichero* (Alessandria: Wr, 1990), 27–28.

4

The Influence of Socialist Realism in Italy during the Immediate Postwar Period

Juan José Gómez Gutiérrez

The main outlines of socialist realism were formulated at the First Congress of Soviet Writers held in Moscow in 1934. However, socialist realism arrived in Italy only in the wake of World War II. By that time, the country had passed through twenty years of fascist dictatorship, defeat in the war, German occupation, and the partisan movement. All sectors of Italian society felt that a refoundation of the nation at all levels was on the agenda. According to the art critic Giuseppe Marchiori, "it looked as if everybody wanted to start again, without a past, and find a rationale for work in human solidarity, which had been denied and betrayed for so many years."[1]

As the result of its determined opposition to Mussolini's regime, the Communist Party enjoyed great prestige in Italy, which increased after the party renounced revolutionary politics and proposed, instead, a "new democracy" based on a wide antifascist social alliance.[2] The Italian Communist Party's (PCI) cultural policy was tailored to this end, intending to act as a bridge between socialist realism and the Italian modernist tradition. As a result, a large number of intellectuals willing to collaborate in the reconstruction of the country joined the Communist ranks.

Nevertheless, the composite character of Italian Communist culture became evident after 1947 with the outbreak of the Cold War. Earlier, the PCI had backed broad associations of intellectuals on a diffuse left-wing political basis. However, in 1947 the antifascist alliance of parties broke up, and the Communists were expelled from the government of national unity, headed by the Christian Democrats. As a result, the Communist Party hardened its line in all fields, including cultural policy, and party officials all too often relied on Communist beliefs rather than independent inquiry, the latter being the traditional practice of the Italian intelligentsia.

For Stalinist intellectuals and artists, the case of the Soviet Union appeared to prove that socialism marched unhesitatingly toward its self-realization. Therefore, if artists wanted to represent reality accurately, they could not be critical but had to be celebratory. The most they could do was to indicate to the workers the means by which society would improve further. Hence, to describe it in an idealized way, to depict it even more beautifully, was not to falsify it but to represent it as the point of departure of future development. In practice, this amounted to a rhapsodic, unadventurous, and illustration-like kind of art for the consumption of the masses, which limited its subject matter to conventional representations of healthy muscular workers, Red Army heroes, and charismatic politicians.

In contrast with socialist realism, the different versions of modernism that dominated the Italian scene before the fascist period had stressed the values of imagination and originality in artists above all other considerations. After World War II, some of its representatives asked the Communists to pursue a cultural policy according to these same values. However, the political dynamic of modernist culture seemed exhausted in Italy in the late 1940s. Members of diverse realist tendencies had taken up the intellectuals' political opposition since the late 1930s, while Benedetto Croce's[3] mixture of liberalism and modernism was accused of not having opposed fascism strongly enough. For its part, futurism was paying for the sin of its support of fascism. Furthermore, neither the French nor the German avant-garde could serve left-wing intellectuals as an example to be followed, having lost their polemical and antibourgeois character when leading representatives and institutions moved to the United States.

How, then, was socialist realism received in Italy? The doctrine became a powerful stimulus for intellectuals because it proposed a new art for the masses. It declared the end of modern individualism, formulated a new notion of personal responsibility, and intended to democratize the production and consumption of cultural products. Inspired by this project, many artists and writers rushed to praise the struggle of workers. As the art historian Giulio Carlo Argan writes, "They understood that the artists' genius had lost its validity, . . . and that to re-insert themselves in society, . . . they should accept the sacrifice of their absolute individualism."[4]

Nevertheless, Soviet intellectuals went even further, actively condemning the whole avant-garde, which they regarded as the expression of capitalist individualism. This, and their almost complete subordination to the party, was unacceptable for those Italian left-wing intellectuals who still thought "bourgeois" modern culture could be revolutionary, precisely because of its incorporation of a critical element based on the notion of personal freedom. For the writer Elio Vittorini, an unorthodox PCI member:

> In 1941, when the adhesion of our intellectuals to communism began, fascism had been in power in Italy for nineteen years. The social disadvantages of capitalism appeared to them terribly worsened by the absolute abolition of civil and

political freedom. . . . Capitalism and liberalism were not, for them, the same thing. . . . The totalitarian reality in which they lived brought them to discover the individual greatness of the man who is born alone, who dies alone, and who is not free if he cannot count, above all, on individual freedom.[5]

Furthermore, by the 1940s, and despite the struggle against the Nazis, the Soviet Union was clearly a dictatorship for a large number of intellectuals. According to the art historian Vittorio Strada, some progressive intellectuals regarded socialist realism as "Stalin's invention to keep Soviet and communist writers in ignorance, and thus easier to control."[6] Vittorini reports that these intellectuals "joined communism . . . only in the realm of history: valuing it according to the historical aspects of the USSR and her associate parties as long as they fought fascism. In the realm of ideology, . . . they don't think, 'communism isn't what we thought.' They think, on the contrary, that 'communism didn't become what history demanded of it.'"[7]

Vittorini meant that, with Stalinism, the "historic possibility that communism and liberalism become the same thing"[8] had been lost. In fact, however, several interpretations of communism existed in Italy, and it was the task of the party to hold them together. In Russia, the intellectuals could be "kept in ignorance," because of the formidable propaganda apparatus. Reprisals against dissidents and even state terrorism accompanied the theory of socialist realism. This was unthinkable in Italy. Yet Soviet thought influenced large numbers of artists and intellectuals in the period after the war. And they focused their research on overcoming the two problems afflicting the avant-garde from a Communist point of view: the problem of its roots in individualist thought, and the problem of its failure to relate to a proletarian, uneducated audience.

However, as Strada writes, in its 1934 Soviet version, "socialist realism . . . became a rigorous border that cut off the links . . . with the larger world's complex literary life and with the Soviet literary experience of the 1920s itself."[9] For that reason, the partial alignment with official Soviet culture brought the PCI a number of problems that were never completely solved. Unlike in the USSR, Italian Communist politicians could state an opinion, but they could not, nor indeed did they want to, impose it. Instead, despite their repeated calls to order, they devoted themselves to creating a sufficiently broad space to ensure the coexistence of modernist and socialist realist intellectuals within the PCI. To achieve these ends, the party rejected the formulation of a clear artistic and aesthetic policy. It was not unusual when Palmiro Togliatti, the party leader, asserted that "the defects of our intellectuals are based on their tendency to isolate themselves and their manner to approach problems in a way that makes their products appear incomprehensible for the masses, all under the influence of degenerated forms of bourgeois culture."[10] Nevertheless, if somebody complained, a new statement was often issued, making it clear that "no Marxist aesthetic has been formulated, neither in *Rinascita* nor in *L'Unità*. Every one of us just expressed his personal opinion."[11]

However, Communist politicians were in a complicated situation in this respect, as many progressive intellectuals opposed socialist realism as aggressively as others opposed modern culture. For example, Massimo Milla, an independent musical critic of the *Belfagor* review and the Turinese edition of *L'Unità*, had called the 1949 Congress of Soviet Musicians, presided over by Andrei Zhdanov, "a sad spectacle of incompetence." Milla regarded Zhdanov himself as "ignorant in musical matters" because he had condemned Shostakovich's music as "formalist."[12] A quarrel started when Togliatti answered from the pages of *Rinascita* that Milla himself was the ignorant one, and he claimed the right of a Leningrad soldier to prefer "a little pop song instead of the *Seventh* of Shostakovich."[13]

For Togliatti, Zhdanov intended not to teach music to the musicians but to give an opinion about contemporary art:

> Together with the voice of the technicians, of the specialists, of the virtuosi, we heard a voice that understands art as the expression of social life and presents the artists with the exigencies of that life, calling on them to carry out the duty that art always carried out, when it was truly art, and not an exercise of intellectualist decomposition. Who says that artistic problems are only a matter for *competent people* who, in this case, would be initiates in the cabalistic jargon that small groups of composers, critics or philosophers have introduced into their circles?[14]

Milla answered in *Rinascita* equating Zhdanov's criticism with the Nazi distinction between healthy and degenerate art. He also argued, "Today, if we love the arts and esteem the people, we must be honest and tell the people that the arts are difficult and require devotion, humility and sacrifice."[15]

However, in response to Togliatti's arguments, other intellectuals, like the film critic Luigi Anderlini, were coming to the opposite conclusion from Milla and reinforced their commitment to socialist realism as the postwar period went on. Anderlini stressed that the right criterion in art criticism was not the quality, expressive richness, or formal originality of the work but, rather, the range of its social basis in terms of both producers and audience.

Analyzing the relationship between the artistic avant-garde and socialist realism, Anderlini focused on the contending social classes to which each concept was, in his view, organically attached, in the belief that the characteristic worldview of each social class generated a specific aesthetics. Furthermore, he asserted that the working class carried the elements of a new and, even in comparison with modernism, more advanced culture, precisely because it was the new revolutionary class: "When speaking of popular culture, we frequently mean different and even contradictory things: Popular culture can be the 'magic,' 'primitive,' 'barbaric' culture of the subaltern world. . . . However, it can also be the culture of the masses in a wider sense, or the culture of the working class as such."[16]

Culture was meant to give a meaningful role to progressive bourgeois intellectuals insofar as, to quote the British art historian John Berger, they "have realised that they are nothing unless they become the voice of the people."[17] However, other left-wing writers, such as Giuseppe Petronio, disagreed with this thesis, thinking that intellectuals like Anderlini "let themselves be seduced by the romantic myth of an autonomous culture of the subaltern class" while, in fact, the proletariat was "degraded by misery and ignorance."[18] Petronio stressed, instead, the need for an intellectual avant-garde that would take up the task of leading the masses toward socialism by diffusing modern culture among them.

THE CULTURAL POLITICS OF THE PCI

To reconcile these perspectives, the PCI sought to soften the image of socialist realism in Italy by raising the question of its relationship with the avant-garde, not in terms of an unresolvable contradiction but, rather, as one step in an evolution from modernism to a new kind of socialist culture that coincided only partially with the Russian model. In fact, no Soviet writer published a single article in *Rinascita* during the late 1940s and early 1950s. The journal preferred Louis Aragon's French version of socialist realism, because it was formulated in a manner more congenial for Italian intellectuals, conceiving communist militancy in a vaguely mythical way, in the form of a new religion of converted cultivated people:

> My party has given me back the epic sense
> My party has given me the colours of France
> My party, my party thanks to your lessons
> For since then everything reaches me in songs
> Anger and love, joy and suffering.[19]

Aragon's "party lyricism," as Alberto Moravia called it,[20] claimed to be the inheritor of the progressive French cultural tradition, incarnated in Zola, Victor Hugo, and Rimbaud, and to derive his accommodation with the masses from a process of intellectual development and not from a mere conversion to the Communist creed. The Frenchman explained his position in *Rinascita* as follows:

> I have an idea of the art of the novel that is not compatible with the imitation of literary models. . . . The realist looks for his models in life and not in books. . . . Very many people, particularly writers, confuse realism and naturalist painting. . . . They do not think, like me, that realism is first of all a perspective from the point of view of the spirit of the writer. . . . If his worldview is socialist, it is completely natural to call "socialist realism" the realism of the artists I am mentioning. . . . It is very

significant that socialist realism in Russia has honoured the study of Tolstoy, Dostoyevsky, Gogol, and Pushkin. In France, it looks back at other masters. That is why it is understandable when I say that one only arrives at socialist realism on the national road. . . . Socialist realism will find its universal values in each country only if it deeply penetrates into the national reality of the soil in which it arises.[21]

In reality, this was not different from what Stalin had said back in 1925 in his speech "On the Political Duties of the University in the Eastern Nations": "We are building a proletarian culture. This is perfectly true. However, it is also true that proletarian culture, socialist in content, assumes different forms and ways of expression amongst the different peoples attracted to socialist unity."[22] Likewise, in the late 1940s, an artwork made under Aragon's premises could equally well be a product of a Soviet painter or Picasso. Aragon was looking for a wide definition of the term that could reconcile widely differing perspectives, arguing that "the systematic rejection of everything that is not figuration, delivered with academic authority, diminishes realism."[23]

The example of Picasso was, of course, paradigmatic because his Communist commitment was then beyond dispute. Although his realism was different from that of Balzac or Tolstoi, Aragon argued, Picasso should not be excluded from the proletarian pantheon of fame. On the contrary, in the light of his work, it was necessary both to broaden the meaning of socialist realism in the present and to search for new aspects in Picasso that could underscore his direct links to the realism of the past. Another Frenchman, the painter André Fougeon, wrote in *Rinascita* in 1947 that, in order "to develop the new realism, there exist new technical means. I believe in the superiority of modern language, which takes into consideration the technical revolution that has occurred in painting, for example impressionism, fauvism and cubism . . . , to call the people to action and to celebrate their struggle and their victory."[24]

Nevertheless, PCI representatives stressed that the need to maintain the relationship with a mass audience imposed limits with regard to the application of these technical advances. Most intellectuals agreed that culture had a duty vis-à-vis the working class. However, many intellectuals viewed the dogmatic insistence on idealizations of the average person as retrograde as, for them, the core of the communist cultural program should consist in the transformation of that *average* person into a subtle and highly differentiated one, as well as in the recomposition of the balance between individual and collective experience.

THE *REALISTI* ARTISTS

The *realisti* were the most fully developed Italian expression of an art committed to socialist ideology. These artists deemphasized the values of form and aesthetics in order to concentrate on the clarity and the communicative strength of the depicted subject. This led many commentators to describe them as backward and as propagandists.[25] Nevertheless, the problem the realisti were addressing was not in and of itself an aesthetic or formal one. For the realisti, to foreground aesthetic problems was a feature of European avant-garde art, which they rejected as outmoded. Their approach, according to the painter Renato Guttuso, consisted in bypassing the bourgeois avant-garde and in "seeing the modern from a more modern point of view."[26]

For the realisti, modernism was not contemporary. Rather it was already a historic product to be superseded by realism. After all, what was there left to invent, after fifty years of the avant-garde? The realisti did not intend to make art for art's sake as the modernists had done but rather to use art for their own ends of political action and social communication.

The group portrayed its work simultaneously as a further evolution of modernism and as a differentiated version of socialist realism. They never severed their links with the traditional exhibition circuits, although they developed alternative networks with the help of the PCI apparatus and local left-wing governments. An example was the Suzzara Prize, organized from 1948 onward by the village council of Suzzara, a Communist stronghold in Lombardy, under the motto "Labour and Workers in Art." The prize was the brainchild of the village's Communist major, Tebe Mignoni, the Suzzarese cultural entrepreneur Dino Villani, and the filmmaker Cesare Zavattini, who came from the nearby village of Luzzara. Together with experts, a white-collar worker, a blue-collar worker, and a peasant composed the jury. The prizes consisted in local products like a calf, a colt, or a Parmesan cheese. Regular participants were Guttuso, Aldo Borgonzoni, Giulio Turcato, Gabriele Mucchi, and Armando Pizzinato.

All these artists had evolved from different avant-garde backgrounds. In the late 1940s, Guttuso tempered his earlier aggressive cubist syntax and fauvist coloring by adopting a less schematic style, inspired by nineteenth-century trends and the Italian Renaissance; Borgonzoni converted the antifascist iconography of Picasso's *Guernica* into explicit Communist emblems; Mucchi put broadly expressionistic resources at the service of his social protest; Turcato's painting combined constructivism, fauvism, and cubism to produce works occupying a midway position between the poster and the easel painting. Finally, Armando Pizzinato's cubist, futurist, and expressionist influences were put at the service of his calls to political action.

Another distinctive feature of the realisti was their interest in finding visual means that could serve best to reach a mass public. The size of Guttuso's painting tended to increase in the early 1950s; Borgonzoni and Pizzinato produced frescoes in, respectively, a trade union office building in Medicina (Bologna) and the Council Palace of the Province of Parma. Mucchi and Guttuso also illustrated several left-wing publications, such as *L'Unità* and the magazine *Il Calendario del popolo*.

Pizzinato's *Un fantasma percorre l'Europa* (A Specter Haunts Europe; see page 73) is one of the most representative paintings of the movement. It is a 2.6 by 3–meter canvas made in 1948 to commemorate the centenary of the *Communist Manifesto* and then exhibited in the 1950 Venice Biennale. The scene does not depict a specific historic episode but rather is an allegory of the alliance between the working class and the peasantry. The depth of the space is only suggested by the scaffold, and the figures are reduced to geometric elements. However, Pizzinato reconciles his spirit of inventiveness and the impetus of the composition with a clear rhythm and the possibility of easy reading by an uneducated audience. As Ballo puts it, the Italian realists "attempted to avoid the self-indulgence of formal sophistication and, instead, they wanted to bring the masses a new lay gospel."[27]

However, it must also be recognized that, from 1947 onward, the PCI began to tighten its views on matters of "artistic policy" for several years. For example, the abstract painter Ennio Morlotti, who had called himself in 1944 "a worker of the arts in the socialist factory of the future,"[28] later complained that Emilio Sereni, the Stalinist chairman of the party's cultural commission, once asked him to follow the example of the Vatican: "Don't you see Pius XII's followers invading Italy with their little saints? Why don't you too make an effort to create figures understandable for everybody?"[29] Sereni promoted a simplified version of *realismo*, which put the stress on mass communicability and openly political subject matter. This policy enjoyed great support among the party's ranks but, of course, eventually tended to further muddy the waters in the relationship with the most vehement defenders of avant-garde art.[30] As those observers critical of both Sereni and the realisti argued, viable left-wing cultural politics could not be produced solely in relation to the desire for a mass public because this meant, in Morlotti's words of 1975, "to put painting at the service of the slogan."[31]

The risk of further breaking the broad alliance that the PCI intended to forge in the end induced the party, from 1951 onward, to move away from open advocacy of socialist realism, gradually to abandon even the model of the realisti, and Communist officials were instructed altogether to cease making statements on aesthetics. Instead, Togliatti now began to advocate, for party leaders in general, "an ability to shut up, to listen to what others say and to profit from it for their own work and for the direction of others' work."[32] In 1952, Sereni was replaced as head of the party's cultural commission by Carlo Salinari, a professor of Italian, who strongly criticized the former's attempts to liquidate "the whole tradition of Italian bourgeois avantgarde thought, in opposition to the objective social and economic situation."[33]

Regarding the artists themselves, the end of any type of realismo became clear after the "Quadriennale of Contemporary Art" held in Rome in 1955. At this occasion, the art historian Antonello Negri highlighted "the recuperation of feelings, themes, and interests that, earlier on, had been sacrificed in

Armando Pizzinato, *Un fantasma percorre l'Europa* (*A Specter Haunts Europe*), 1948, oil on canvas, 260×300 cm. Cà Pesaro Modern Art Gallery, Venice.

favor of an overly restricted conception of the militant content of realist work,"[34] while Guttuso admitted that their earlier criticism of the avant-garde meant that they had, at times, "sacrificed an artistic tradition of considerable significance. It was our exclusionist point of view that made us unintentionally travel along too easy a road, and [caused us to] be satisfied with a vague populism, *returns* [to tradition] . . . and stylistic analogies. We ignored genuine artistic arguments on purpose."[35]

SOCIALIST REALISM, MODERNISM, AND PCI CULTURAL POLICY

Italian culture of the immediate postwar period was largely characterized by the encounter between Soviet socialist realism and Western avant-garde art. Under the auspices of the PCI, Soviet culture was widely discussed in the country, and some postwar developments were decisively influenced by it. However, its emphasis on the universal communicability of the artwork, above all other considerations, left a feeling among many modernist intellectuals (who were nevertheless close to the Communists in other fields) that, in the sphere of art, quality was being sacrificed for quantity. These critics regarded socialist realism as mere propaganda for action, as a revolutionary catechism unable to lay the foundations of a real culture. For them the problem of the discrepancy between the taste of the intelligentsia and that of the majority of the working class (or, in other words, the problem of the disjuncture between the aesthetically valuable and the socially progressive) was articulated too crudely by the proponents of socialist realism.

As a result, the commitment to the PCI of artists such as Vittorini or Morlotti weakened over time. Clearly, their criticism of Soviet cultural policy, Soviet repression of freedom, and the overwhelming domination of politics over culture was justified. But, despite the ultimate "thaw" in PCI cultural policies, these artists eventually abandoned the party, although Vittorini continued to gravitate around the Italian left. Still, it would be an exaggeration to consider their break with the party as a direct response to authoritarian political tendencies. In reality, Vittorini and Morlotti quit not because they stood for cultural freedom from politics but because they were proposing an alternative cultural politics that went beyond what even the "reformed" post-1951 PCI could accept. The Communists could renounce a policy of forcing intellectuals in a given cultural direction. They could be ideologically permissive. But, in the controversy over socialist realism, they could not issue an official aesthetic based on an open acceptance of modernist tenets, as this would have torn apart the party, given that it stood, after all, in a very distinct political tradition.[36] The PCI could and did accept neutrality in cultural matters, but they could never openly advocate a modernist approach. Whatever might have been the case in artistic debates, to abandon the emphasis on the need for art to be comprehensible to a mass audience would have been *politically* unacceptable to the PCI's broader constituency, which was then deeply influenced by Stalinist cultural precepts.

Still, to say, "I like this" was not the same as to say, "You must write or depict this." The Communist leaders certainly made their point, maybe arrogantly, sometimes with a superficial knowledge of the subject, and, at other times, acting unfairly in confrontation with minority positions. Even so, unlike the case of the Soviet party, the PCI leadership never tried to impose an official cultural model, not even in the hardest years of the Cold War. The Italian Communists, however, recognized that the problem of the reappropriation of aesthetic taste by the masses and the problem of democratizing art, which Soviet debates foregrounded, did indeed have to be addressed by intellectuals.

NOTES

1. Giuseppe Marchiori, "Sale XXX, IX and XL, il Fronte nuovo delle arti," in *Catalogo XXIV esposizione arti visive: Biennale di Venezia*, 2 vols. (Venice: Ente Autonomo Biennale di Venezia, 1948), I: 166–67.

2. Such "new democracy" was defined in opposition to both fascist dictatorship and the prefascist liberal state, the latter having failed, according to the Communists, to deeply penetrate the fabric of the country and to organize the masses against fascism. With this program in mind, the PCI gained almost two million members and 20 percent of the vote in 1946. On this topic, see also chapter 1 by Aldo Agosti in this volume.

3. The neoidealist philosopher Benedetto Croce was the Liberal Party chair. He participated in an antifascist cabinet of antifascist national unity in 1944, which was composed of Communists, socialists, Christian Democrats, liberals, and smaller, short-lived center-left parties such as the Action Party and Democratic Labour.

4. Giulio Carlo Argan, *L'arte moderna 1770/1970* (Florence: Sonsoni, 1970), 605.

5. Elio Vittorini, "Il comunismo come continuazione della rivoluzione liberale," *La Stampa*, 6 October 1951.

6. Vittorio Strada, "Introduzione," in *Rivoluzione e letteratura, in dibatitto al I Congresso degli scrittori sovietici*, ed. Giorgio Kraiski (Bari: Laterza, 1967), xliii. Marco Romani expressed the ambiguous feeling of certain intellectuals in the face of the Communists' calls for political engagement: "I still remember my uneasiness when I came into the room of a colleague of lively intelligence, a very cultured man, and saw a Togliatti poster behind his desk with the finger pointing out to the viewer. It almost looked like that old image of Uncle Sam saying, 'I want you,' or the punishing god of counterreformation iconography." Romani, "Togliatti, questo sconosciuto," *La Rinascita della Sinistra* (Rome), 10 October 1997, xviii.

7. Vittorini, "Il comunismo."

8. Vittorini, "Il comunismo."

9. Vittorio Strada, "Introduzione," lviii.

10. Palmiro Togliatti, "Intervento al VI Congresso," cited in Nello Ajello, *Intellettuali e PCI, 1944/1958* (Rome: Laterza, 1997), 143.

11. Renato Guttuso, "Pitture di Mario Mafai," *Rinascita* 2, no. 11 (1945): 254. *Rinascita* and *L'Unità* were, respectively, the PCI cultural and political mouthpieces.

12. Massimo Milla, in *La rassegna musicale* (Turin) 3 (July 1949): 247–49, quoted in Ajello, *Intellettuali e PCI*, 225.

13. Roderigo di Castiglia (pseudonym of Palmiro Togliatti), "Direzione ideologica," *Rinascita* 5, no. 10 (1948): 453–54.

14. Roderigo di Castiglia, "Orientamento dell'arte," *Rinascita* 6, no. 10 (1949), in Palmiro Togliatti, *Opere*, 6 vols. (Rome: Riuniti, 1979), 5: 523.

15. Massimo Milla, "Disorientamento dell'arte," *Rinascita* 6, no. 11 (1949): 500–1.

16. Luigi Anderlini, "Marxismo e cultura popolare," *Avanti!* 12 March 1950, reprinted in *Antropologia culturale e questione meridionale: Ernesto De Martino e il dibattito sul mondo popolare subalterno negli anni 1948–1955*, ed. Carla Pasquinelli (Florence: La Nuova Italia, 1977), 101.

17. John Berger, "La colonna," quoted in James Hyman, "A 'Pioneer Painter': Renato Guttuso and Realism in Britain," in *Catalogue for the Guttuso Exhibition at the Whitechapel Art Gallery, 17 May–7 July 1996* (Palermo: Novecento and Thames & Hudson, 1996), 45.

18. Giuseppe Petronio, "La creazione di una società solidale," in *Antropologia culturale*, ed. Pasquinelli, 106.

19. Louis Aragon, "Du poète à son parti," *Rinascita* 2, no. 1 (1945): 17. I thank Bernard A. Evans for translating the poem from the French original.

20. Alberto Moravia, "Il cuculo comunista," *Il Mondo*, 4 February 1950, cited in Ajello, *Intellettuali e PCI*, 52.

21. Louis Aragon, "Realismo Socialista e realismo francese," *Rinascita* 6, no. 2 (1949): 483–85.

22. Quoted in Strada, "Introduzione," xli.

23. Louis Aragon, "Introducción," in Roger Garaudy, *Hacia un realismo sin fronteras: Picasso, Kafka, St. John Perse* (Buenos Aires: Lautaro, 1964), 11.

24. André Fougeon, "Un saluto di Fougeon," *Rinascita* 4, no. 6 (1947): 164–65.

25. For example, Guido Ballo writes, "At this point, we must distinguish between realism and naturalism. Realism, in fact, does not have to be imitative. What it really does is to reconstruct or to invent nature according to its own laws—not to imitate the superficial appearance of nature. . . . The problem of the neorealists is that they have succumbed too often to naturalism." See Guido Ballo, *Modern Italian Painting, from Futurism to the Present Day* (London: Thames & Hudson, 1958), 165.

26. Renato Guttuso, "Del realismo del presente e d'altro," quoted in Antonello Negri, *Il realismo degli anni trenta agli anni ottanta* (Rome: Laterza, 1994), 114.

27. Ballo, *Modern Italian Painting*, 165.

28. Ennio Morlotti and ErnestoTreccani, "Secondo manifesto di pittori e scultori," 1944, reprinted in *Storia moderna dell'arte in Italia*, ed. Paola Barrochi (Turin: Einaudi, 1992), 42.

29. Ennio Morlotti, "Morlotti spiega la crisi dei pittori," interview with Marco Fini in *L'Europeo*, 17 April 1975, quoted in Ajello, *Intellettuali e PCI*, 249.

30. In his first year in office, Sereni developed a network of at least thirty-three local cultural commissions that mainly existed in Tuscany and the Emilia Romagna. See

the folder containing the records of the meeting of the Central Committee's Cultural Commission on 19 October 1949 in the Fondo Partito Comunista Italiano, Fondazione Istituto Gramsci, Rome. PCI membership was particularly pronounced in these two regions as, by the late 1940s, one-third of all PCI members, or about seven hundred thousand people, lived in Tuscany and the Emilia Romagna. However, the number of professional intellectuals, including teachers, technicians, professionals, and students, was extremely low here: 970 in Bologna in 1948 and 204 in Modena during 1950. See Stephen Gundle, *Between Hollywood and Moscow: The Italian Communists and the Challenge of Mass Culture* (Durham, N.C.: Duke University Press, 2000), 56.

31. Ennio Morlotti, "Morlotti spiega la crisi dei pittori," quoted in Ajello, *Intellettuali e PCI*, 249.

32. Palmiro Togliatti, speech at the PCI Central Committee Cultural Commission on 3 April 1954 in Togliatti, *Opere*, 5: 823.

33. See Nicola D'Antonio's introduction to "Intervento di Carlo Salinari alla reunione del comitato centrale del PCI, 10 November 1951," in Carlo Salinari, *Due interventi di politica culturale* (Montecaglioso: Amministrazione Comunale di Montecaglioso and Rocco Fontana Editore, 1988), 11.

34. Antonello Negri, *Il realismo degli anni trenta agli anni ottanta* (Rome: Laterza, 1994), 112.

35. Renato Guttuso, "Il coraggio dell'errore," *Il Contemporaneo* (13 June 1955), italics in the original.

36. When Vittorini quit, Togliatti argued that he "came with us because he thought that we were liberals. However, we are communists." Roderigo de Castiglia, "Vittorini se n'è giuto: E soli li ha lasciato . . . ," *Rinascita* 8, no. 8 (1951), in Togliatti, *Opere*, 5: 616.

II

1968

5

"1968" and the Cultural Revolution of the Long Sixties (c. 1958–c. 1974)

Arthur Marwick

A popular perception of historical truth is encapsulated in the phrase "The Swinging Sixties," and there is now quite widespread agreement among historians that some truly portentous developments did take place in Western Europe (as also in North America) between the late 1950s and the mid-1970s. Economic historians had envisioned the period as extending back to the end of the war, as with Eric Hobsbawm's "Golden Age" (1945–1973) or Jean Fourastié's "Thirty Glorious Years" (1946–1975), while Henri Mendras moved it forward, his "Second French Revolution" running from 1965 to 1984. *Dynamische Zeiten: Die 60er Jahre in den beiden deutschen Gesellschaften* (edited by Axel Schildt, Detlef Siegfried, and Karl Christian Lammers) sticks pretty strictly to the actual decade of the sixties, with the main chapters ending rigorously in 1969.[1] The French tend to be obsessed with their own "revolutions" and with the potent national associations of certain single years: 1789, 1848, 1936 (the year of the Popular Front government and sit-in strikes), and 1968. However, the year 1968 continues to have international resonance; one of the most recent of the very many books on *that* single year, *1968: The World Transformed*, was edited by Carole Fink, Philip Gassert, and Detlef Junker for the German Historical Institute in Washington, D.C. The latest scholarly French collection tries to combine a continuing assertion of the special significance of the single year with a recognition that noteworthy developments had occurred in the immediately preceding years, by adopting the rather odd formulation *Les Années 68* (with the subtitle "The Years of Contestation").[2]

The central argument of this chapter is that, if we are looking for a precise and clearly defined period of multiple and enduring social and cultural change, and not just for a period of economic recovery and growth (with regard to

Hobsbawm's and Fourastié's periodization, it is worth reflecting that no one ever speaks of "The Swinging Fifties"), then that period fell between circa 1958 and circa 1974. (I say "circa" because there are never sudden beginnings or abrupt endings—people do not lament on 31 December 1957, "We can't go to bed with each other because that's against current mores," and rejoice on 1 January 1958, "Let's do it—the moral climate has changed"; nor, on 31 December 1974, do they say, "Gosh, hasn't this period of change been great!" while on 1 January 1975 lamenting, "Oh dear, back to the dullness of the fifties!")

My claim is that what transpired between the two dates may properly be designated "The Cultural Revolution of the Long Sixties." Change is already perceptible in the late fifties, while ratification of some of the most crucial transformations—divorce and abortion reform in Catholic Europe, for example—only came in the midseventies. The word *revolution* may seem inappropriate or hackneyed, when one could more precisely speak of "transformation" or, following the German example, of "dynamic years." "Years of contestation," however, is too narrowly focused, suggesting that everything of significance took place on the streets, thus ignoring the positive, long-term, society-wide changes. Actually, now that we recognize that revolutions on the Marxist model simply don't (and never will) happen, we do speak freely of "educational revolutions," "paperback revolutions," "welfare revolutions," "youth revolutions," and "sexual revolutions"; one key to "The Cultural Revolution of the Long Sixties" is that it entailed a multiplicity of such single-topic "revolutions," taking place *simultaneously* and reacting and interacting with each other. My main purpose is to compare the impact and consequences of the Cultural Revolution with those of "1968," taken to signify both the highly concentrated events of May and June 1968 in France and the analogous but more diffuse events of 1967–1969 in the other European countries (I focus on Italy and West Germany).

If our concern is with "transnational moments of change," we have to ask, How long is a moment (even if our metaphor is based on the fulcrum, not the clock!), and how do we define "transnational"? Certain single years—say, 1789 (or should it be 1793?), 1830, 1848, 1918—would probably be widely accepted as "transnational moments of change," *transnational* being employed as a descriptive term, applicable (or not) to certain specific historical phenomena. In my own work, I have spoken of "The *International* Cultural Revolution." I accept that "transnational" is the more apposite "descriptive" adjective, while continuing to insist that my approach, being "analytical," is most appropriately described as "comparative."[3] In any event, a cultural revolution spread over a period of about sixteen years can scarcely be termed a "moment"; "1968" certainly can, but whether it was one of significant change is a matter for discussion in this chapter.

1968

Over the photograph of a blazing car, *Der Spiegel* on 27 May 1968 starkly declared, "Französische Revolution." Similar headlines appeared across Europe. Many commentators recalled the words of the nineteenth-century Austrian archconservative Metternich: "When Paris sneezes, the rest of Europe catches cold." Yet, in March and April, the French newspapers had been congratulating themselves that while student rebellion had been seriously afflicting West Germany and Italy throughout 1967 and on into 1968, France had remained immune.[4] France, partly because of its special political geography and heavy concentration of vital institutions in Paris, partly because of a history punctuated by popular risings that had helped to topple governments, really was different. That is why in France "1968" stands for the dramas of May and June when, along with extreme violence on the streets of Paris and other cities, government, industry, public services, education, television, radio, and newspapers were in a state of near-paralysis; in the other Western European countries, as I have remarked, "1968" stands for events that were actually spread over the years 1967 to 1969 (in West Germany a number of commemorative books were issued in 1977, celebrating 1967 as the crucial year of revolt;[5] Italy's "Hot Autumn" of intensive working-class action was the autumn of 1969). In Paris, the setting up of alternative structures in industry, in the professions, in the public services, in broadcasting, in the Sorbonne, in the Beaux Arts, and in the Odéon was more organized and more tangible than their analogues elsewhere in Western Europe. But they operated very much as parallel "talking shops," never in fact taking over from the traditional institutions, which were expected just to disappear. The violent confrontations taking place almost continuously seemed more menacing to central political power than the widely scattered confrontations in other countries, but, in the end, they had a somewhat ritualistic quality about them. The revolution, the theorists held, would simply happen, without the need for precise actions, such as assassinating Charles de Gaulle, blowing up the Chamber of Deputies, or taking proactive control of the television stations. Paris, perhaps, coughed, but it failed to sneeze. Universally, it was a case not of "revolution that failed" or "revolution betrayed" but "revolution that never was."

The events, whether dramatically concentrated into a couple of months or spread over three years, shared two fundamental strands—one involving the student movements, which, being relatively well organized across countries, can appropriately be described as "transnational," and the other one involving a variety of actions by the workers, usually related to specific local situations and, accordingly, less "transnational." In addition, the further qualification has to be made that, perhaps because workers' conditions were already relatively satisfactory in West Germany, the same intensive working-class agitation was not present there. In both France and Italy, the student movements were very eager to become involved in the industrial actions, while trade union leaders generally did not welcome student intervention. Behind student protests certainly was one broad, transnational pattern of grievances, though each country exhibited particular national variations. General hostility to the policy of nuclear deterrence and to what was perceived as Western "neo-colonialism" became focused in campaigns against American military involvement in Vietnam (the International Vietnam Conference in West Berlin, 17–18 February 1968, is particularly worthy of note). General criticisms of consumer society were reinforced by a sense that universities were conformist and authoritarian and too closely integrated with that society. In West Germany, the case was made that the formation of the Grand Coalition government in 1966 entailed the suppression of all genuine possibilities of democratic opposition, impelling the Sozialistischen Deutscher Studentenbund (SDS) to create the uniquely German organization, the Ausserparlamentarische Opposition (APO) in December of that year. The proposals of the Grand Coalition to arm itself with special powers in the face of the perceived Communist threat intensified the conviction of student protesters that governmental authority was still dominated by National Socialist ideology.

The most effective student demonstrations in all countries were those with a single focal point, such as government attempts to restrict university entry, or the visit of some foreign dignitary with (in the eyes of student radicals) unclean hands, or some new twist in the Vietnam War. At the end of May 1967, the shah of Persia visited West Berlin. He was seen as a puppet of the West and a suppressor of Iranian nationalism, and he had with him his own cohort of thugs, members of the Iranian secret police, the SAVAK. On 2 June, Benno Ohnesorg, a nonactivist student taking part in his first demonstration, was shot dead by a plainclothes police officer.[6] His killing, together with the massive funeral march that followed, initiated the intense phase of student marches and sit-ins in West Germany as, in a process that became a crucial phenomenon in every country, moderate students felt bound to join with the activists.

In Italy, the three spheres of militant action, apparent early in 1967 and intensive from November (the beginning of the new university year) onward, were the universities, the factories, and the secondary schools. The universities' fundamental grievance was the proposed Gui Law, designed to limit intake into grossly overcrowded universities. The wave of industrial action was provoked by the way the rise in the abysmally low living standards of the postwar years, enjoyed for over a decade, was slowing down considerably. By February 1968, a number of universities were under occupation. The rector of Rome University, Professor Pietro Agostino D'Avack, was an extreme reactionary, and his actions in repudiating reforms (which more liberal-minded professors were prepared to concede to the student occupiers) and in calling in the police on 29 February 1968 to expel the students led directly to the most notorious event of Italy's "1968." Following a mass march on Friday, 1 March, to the Architecture Faculty, high above the Valle Giulia that runs through the Villa Borghese park, radical students attempted to storm up two flights of steps to occupy the building, implacably defended by members of the special police, the Celere. "The Battle of Valle Giulia" began around 11 A.M. and lasted for just over two hours. Throughout that time, all of Rome could hear the constant sound of police and ambulance sirens. Smoke and flames from burning vehicles could be seen from miles away. A police van very nearly ran down a group of students carrying a wounded colleague; at the same moment, a police officer raised his automatic rifle. Actually, in the whole encounter, firearms were not used, save for the case of one police officer who fired one shot in the air. But those taken into custody were beaten up and in some cases had pistols held to their foreheads. Injuries among students and passersby were recorded at only fifty-three, but this was because students wished at all costs to avoid falling into the hands of the police; injuries, in fact, amounted to several hundred. However—a matter for satisfaction among some students—the police had also, for the first time, suffered quite heavily: 160 were injured. By evening, word of the Battle of Valle Giulia had reached all other Italian universities and touched off a new phase of violence across the country, often deliberate and highly organized, with student *servizi d'ordine* (paramilitary defense units) becoming more and more prominent.[7]

In France, the analogue of the Gui Law was the proposed Fouchet Law, also aimed at imposing restrictions on university entry. At the bleak Nanterre campus on the outskirts of Paris, the liberal administration under Dean Pierre Grappin had been relaxing regulations, particularly in regard to visits by male students to female dormitories, but a group led by Daniel Cohn-Bendit, a sociology student and German citizen, was determined on a policy of no compromise with the authorities. Rumors spread that he was to be forcibly repatriated to Germany and that the university was compiling a blacklist of militant students. On 6 January, an occupation was staged in the sociology building. Grappin (unwisely) called in the police, who acted with considerable brutality. At the same time, the Vietcong had launched their Tet Offensive; in Paris this was celebrated with an intense bout of attacks on various American buildings. The police picked up demonstrators in the streets, raided homes, and invaded certain campuses, including that at Nanterre. On 22 March, Cohn-Bendit, with a greatly swollen following, led a band of protesters into the Nanterre conference chamber. Taking the name Movement of 22 March, the Cohn-Bendit group planned a teach-in (an American innovation) on the evils of imperialism for 29 March. Just as Grappin (perhaps again unwisely, though certainly his student opponents were irreconcilable) declared the campus closed, news came through of the assassination attempt

on the German student leader Rudi Dutschke. Meanwhile, eight members of
the Movement of 22 March had been ordered to appear before a university
disciplinary committee at the Sorbonne on 6 May. This, together with the
closing of Nanterre, provided the motivation for the Sorbonne demonstration of Friday, 3 May. About five hundred, drawn from all the main student
organizations, took part. So also, provocatively, did the fascist organization,
Occident. Police forces were massed outside. It was the rector, Paul Roche,
who eventually called the police in to remove the demonstrators.

The "events" had begun. Militants who had escaped the attention of the
police sprang into immediate action; many other students with no previous
history of violence joined them. The first weapons to be called into action
were cobblestones, many being ready to hand where street repairs were being carried out. The police responded with truncheons and tear gas, their attacks spilling over onto passersby and local residents.

By Friday, 10 May, moderate students had become sufficiently radicalized,
the wider public sufficiently scandalized, and the militants and ideological
extremists sufficiently organized for the students to go onto a systematic offensive. The night of 10–11 May was the first night of the barricades. The
general attitude held by the National Union of French Students (UNEF),
probably shared by a majority of students, was that the university quarter belonged to students and should not be "invaded" by the police.[8] At 2:15 on the
morning of 11 May, the police went on the offensive, using a variety of
grenades, viciously attacking students, passersby, and residents.[9] It was obvious to almost everyone that the force was excessive, crossing into the
realm of the sadistic. The French trade union leaders, though, as I said, not
at all keen to become involved with the students, called for a twenty-four-
hour general strike to be held on 13 May. That same morning, on the initiative of Prime Minister Pompidou, the Sorbonne was reopened to students.
The consequence was not quite what the authorities had hoped for: Students
poured in, declaring the ancient heart of the university to be under occupation. The general strike was supported by 30 to 40 percent of the workers.
Younger workers enthusiastically took up the idea of occupying their factories: Within a week, about seven million were engaged in this particularly
evocative form of strike action. Similar action was taken by a large number
of middle-class people, who carried out strikes and sit-ins in the name of
greater independence and a reorganization of their professions.

Ordinary life was coming to a standstill, in a manner completely different
from what was happening in other countries. Only the police were in over-
drive. After a day of demonstrations on 23 May, Paris suffered the most extreme violence on the third of the "Black Fridays," 24 May (the other two
were 3 May and 10 May); the students had by now perfected their barricades,
their communications, and their offensive weaponry. The near-paralysis
(unique, I must stress again, to France) lasted well into June. Broadcasting

was closed down for five weeks, gasoline queues began appearing on 21 May, and shortly thereafter petrol ration coupons were issued for priority occupations. There were a number of arson attacks, including a spectacular one of 24 May on the stock exchange.

While opposition politicians seemed incapable of concerted action, de Gaulle produced a *coup de théâtre*. He "disappeared," thus distracting attention from events in Paris; although the story was that he was simply relaxing at his home in Colombey-les-Deux-Églises, in fact he visited General Jacques Massu, commander of the French armed forces stationed in Baden-Baden, to ensure that he could call on the support of the military, if *necessary* (the critical point, demonstrating that this "revolution" was more illusion than reality, is that it never became necessary). On his return the following day (30 May), the president announced an immediate election—first round on 23 June, second on 30 June. On 10 June, police charged strikers at the Rénault car factory at Flins and on 11 June at the Peugeot factory at Sochaux. Fleeing at Flins from the special police force, the CRS, twelve secondary school students found themselves surrounded, jumped into the Seine, became entrapped in the mud, and were attacked with truncheons; one, Gilles Tautin, was drowned. At Sochaux, two workers were killed. Inevitably these tragedies were the occasion for further protests, held on 11 June in Paris and elsewhere—Toulouse had a night of barricades and street fires. On 14 June, the police took decisive action against the talking shops, clearing out the Odéon, the Beaux Arts, and then the Sorbonne, now rat infested and showing the depredations of hippie culture, rather than high culture.[10]

Altogether, between the beginning of May and the end of July, there were eight deaths directly arising from the incidents between protesters and police. No student was killed in any of the big-city demonstrations, the only person killed in central Paris being a young male bystander at a barricade on 24 May. On that same day, a police commissioner was killed in Lyon by a truck whose brakes students had released. The remaining five dead (in addition to Tautin) were all workers. The total of those injured seriously enough to be hospitalized (and this did include a considerable number of police) amounted to 1,798, of whom 953 were in the Paris region.[11] Other vital statistics: In the election there was a 3 percent swing to the government, giving them, in the second round, a crushing majority of 358 seats out of 485; the proportion of students consistently participating in the full range of protest activities was about 12 percent.

In West Berlin, the only demonstration fully comparable to those in Paris or to the Battle of Valle Giulia was the "Battle of Tegeler Weg" on 4 November 1968, where the main student weapon, as in Paris, was the cobblestone: 130 police and 21 students were injured.[12] In Italy, deaths remained in single figures until November 1969, rising sharply thereafter as Italy joined with Germany in moving into a distinctive new phase marked by terrorist activity (in

Germany, the SDS dissolved itself in the spring of 1970, the APO having already evaporated into nothing).

If we put aside the Cultural Revolution and focus solely on the events of May–June 1968 (in France) or 1967–1969 (elsewhere), we can identify two distinct types of direct consequences. First, there was the powerful sense of shock administered to the authorities, resulting in some immediate reforms affecting both workers and students. Second, there was the way in which young people who had hitherto stood aloof from student protests (which occurred sporadically throughout the sixties) found themselves irresistibly drawn into experiences that were uniquely intense and all-encompassing. The factor of intensified *participation* was an important one in maximizing the immediate impact of the events, and from the participation of female students, portentous repercussions ensued.

As early as 25 May 1968, Pompidou entered into three days of negotiations with unions and employers. The Grenelle Agreements offered the workers respectable gains: a general wage increase of 10 percent, a 35 percent rise in minimum wages, an agreement in principle on shorter work weeks, a 5 percent increase in the proportion of medical expenses reimbursed by social security, strike pay at 50 percent of normal wages, and legislation giving unions greater shop floor rights. On 14 November 1969, the Italian government agreed to official union demands for a forty-hour week within three years, progress toward parity between manual and clerical workers, elimination of differentials for those under twenty, and a guarantee of union rights; a further innovation was the introduction of educational classes within the work week.[13]

Workers' rights, we saw, was not such a pressing issue in Germany; but here, as in France and Italy, there was relaxation in the authoritarian regimes in both schools and universities and an acceptance of student rights to consultation and participation.[14] Female participation in the protests and demonstrations amounted to a concentrated dose of consciousness-raising, made all the more potent by the chauvinistic attitudes women constantly encountered from their male "comrades," who took it for granted that females make the coffee, type the flyers, and slip readily into bed. The new wave of feminism, rising in 1968–1969 and reaching high flood point in the early seventies, was fed by other tributaries as well, but there can be no question about the extent to which it was a direct outcome of things that happened in 1968.[15]

THE CULTURAL REVOLUTION OF THE LONG SIXTIES (c. 1958–c. 1974)

The emergence and dynamic escalation of the Cultural Revolution were due, fundamentally, to the convergence of certain structural, ideological, and institutional circumstances and then, secondarily, to the simultaneous occurrences of specific events (the Algerian war, first, and then the all-pervasive Vietnam War crystallized anti-imperial sentiment). Most critical of the structural factors were the working through of the baby boom of the 1940s, resulting in a notably high proportion of young people in all countries; economic growth (giving young people an unprecedented security and self-confidence—and their elders the opportunity to support the boom in consumer goods); and a range of technological developments, relating to transport and communication, production and diffusion of popular music, and the manufacture of these same consumer goods. *Discussion* of the contraceptive pill contributed to the spread of permissiveness, and its wide availability from the early 1970s onward consolidated that spread, but the sexual revolution itself began *before* the pill was in wide use. Key ideological circumstances were a revival of wartime aspirations as recovery gave way to affluence and some aspects of the Cold War faded; strong reactions, particularly, but not exclusively among young people, against the conformist practices and taboos of the fifties; new developments in Marxism, especially those combining Marx with Freud; yet, at the same time, a revived emphasis on the liberal principles of democratic rights and due process. Insofar as many institutions were conservative and, indeed, reactionary—the churches, the universities, and, above all, the police—they played a major part in provoking the conflict and violence, which are a component of the Cultural Revolution that must never be ignored (though one with few important long-term consequences). At the same time, some institutions were changing, including state broadcasting authorities, not excluding the Catholic Church, which was given an inspiring lead by Pope John XXIII (1958–1963).

Elsewhere I have listed sixteen distinctive features as characterizing the Cultural Revolution.[16] In this short chapter, I shall condense these into four.

First, an enormous proliferation of movements (New Left, environmental, feminist, etc.) and institutions (experimental theaters, arts labs, etc.) arose that were generally critical of, or in opposition to, one or more aspects of established society. Young people, and the youth culture they (with the usual commercial interests panting at their elbows) created, had an unprecedented prominence, though it is important to note that frequently the middle-aged and the middle class were involved as well. The respect traditionally accorded to age and experience now mutated into enthusiasm for everything youthful and energetic. Key features of what began as a distinctive youth culture (pop/rock music, convention-defying fashion) were welcomed into the wider culture. Many of the new initiatives had a pronounced entrepreneurial character, there being a constant emphasis on "doing your own thing." The many different developments expanded and interacted with each other, bringing about a condition of constantly accelerating change.

With respect to both the importance of young people and the question of their relationship to established society, particular attention must be given to the legislation that in all countries, in the final stages of the Cultural Revolution, gave the vote to eighteen-year-olds. This legislation—1968 in the United Kingdom, 1972 in West Germany, and 1974 in France and Italy—scarcely betokens implacable hostility on the part of the older generation toward the younger. Some elements in the New Left took the view that, if their own violent actions could provoke an extreme "capitalist" response, this would bring an end to "bourgeois" society; in the short term, these individuals contributed greatly to the destructive aspects of the Cultural Revolution but were of least long-term historical significance.

Second, infinitely more important than that (misconceived) political program was the spread of sexual freedoms and the upheavals in relationships between men and women and adults and children, entailing a general emancipation from the stuffy conventions of the fifties. To take but one piece of evidence, a survey in 1968 of Italian women married in the late fifties and early sixties showed that, during the early years of marriage (i.e., during the sixties), they developed highly liberated sexual attitudes, among other things putting sex as the most important element in a marriage—their mothers, interviewed in the same survey, put this last.[17]

With respect to still younger women and girls, the transformations in their outlook can be seen in a number of other surveys, including one conducted in France toward the end of the decade. Fernande, a chemistry student, said that she would have no wish at all to give up a job she herself had chosen and liked, even for the sake of a husband and children: "I do not conceive of marriage as a form of slavery and I believe that every woman has the right to do what she likes doing." Agnès, a college student and future nursery nurse, declared that "a job is the means to personal freedom." In her opinion, a job was just as important to a girl as to a boy, and she had no intention of giving up work if she married.[18] A survey of Italian teenage girls conducted between February 1964 and August 1965 had revealed similar independence of mind and also indicated rational and relatively emancipated attitudes toward sexual matters.[19]

With respect to young children and their relations with their parents and teachers, the testimony of the American diplomat Lawrence Wylie, who, over twenty-odd years, conducted three surveys in the village of Peyrane in the Vaucluse, is illuminating. He compared the situation of the five-year-old Dédou Faire, whom he had known at the beginning of the 1950s, with that of another youngster, whom he encountered in 1972.

Twenty years ago the five-year-old Dédou Faire . . . expected to obey his elders. . . . In the single classroom for two dozen 4- to 6-year olds, the discipline was stern. . . . This year I saw Dédou's nephew, another Dédou Faire, having a tantrum in the street in front of his house; his mother seemed completely indifferent to what in the past would have been a neighborhood scandal. In school, children now speak more freely, just as at home they take part in adult conversations without being regularly silenced.

For what is a crucial component of the Cultural Revolution Wylie's own conclusions very much tally with my own, derived from wide research in several countries. He perceived that greater tolerance, greater permissiveness, did not necessarily undermine the family and could, indeed, strengthen it. He noted that parents and teachers were often puzzled and uncertain, but added that "at home people have learned to tolerate—even to enjoy—a less authoritarian social atmosphere; . . . the belief in hierarchy has given way to concern for each individual's will, a mutual respect, a tolerance of differences that I would never have thought possible."[20]

Third is what I term "measured judgment," the product of the growth of tolerance among those in authority and respect for due process and for difference and innovation. By the end of the sixties, film censorship had all but disappeared, and that of television was greatly loosened. In France, Jacques Balland, a highly representative figure, appointed in January 1966 by the Gaullist government as director of the main University of Paris student residences at Antony, not only abolished the rules designed to prevent malefemale cohabitation but took to mixing with student activists in the university refectory.[21] Where lower courts were often bigoted, higher courts tended to be measured in their judgments. In West Germany, it was ruled that the SDS files seized by the police in January 1967 must be returned; on Easter Sunday 1968, then–minister of justice Gustav Heinemann made his famous call for "tolerance in view of a better future."[22]

Finally, the truly vital feature of the Cultural Revolution was not the antics of privileged minorities but the transformation in the lives of majorities. Wage rises would not have been nearly as important without the ready supply of consumer goods and modern domestic conveniences to spend them on. It is fashionable these days to trace the history of consumerism back for several centuries,[23] but one has only to consult the detailed statistics to see how crucial (and how unique) developments over the sixties were.[24] The same statistics bring out the way in which formerly irredeemably backward territories (such as the Italian south) were beginning to share in the amenities of contemporary civilization. Revisiting a family in a village sixty-five miles south of Rome in 1969 when an inside bathroom had been installed—previously family members and guests had had to take to the fields—a Roman sociology professor was told, "I feel like a human being, like other people, not like an animal as I felt before."[25] Those who railed against the consumer society of the sixties could not grasp how welcome it was to those who were only in the process of joining it.

"1968" AND THE CULTURAL REVOLUTION: RELATIONSHIP AND COMPARISON

Without the Cultural Revolution—fostering self-confidence and a spirit of irreverence among young people and, in particular, students—there could have been no events of 1968 but, being in essence political, these events were not really representative of the historically most significant aspects of the Cultural Revolution. Certain specific demands were met and certain new voices were heard (first of radical women, then of gay men).[26] Shocking occurrences do have impact; some people drew wrong conclusions (e.g., about the imminence of revolution), but the dramatic events also provoked, or crystallized, responses from those in positions of authority more quickly than would otherwise have happened.

A particularly valuable document with regard to this notion of "crystallization" is the special edition that the French women's magazine *Elle* managed to bring out on 17 June 1968, skinny and without advertisements. The editor, Helen Gordon-Lazareff, spoke directly to her readers, saying that, without taking one side or the other in the political debate, she understood how *traumatic* (my italics) their experiences had been. In addition to noting how parents had become involved through their children, she remarked on the large part played by girls and young women in the protests in which they had shown "an amazing courage." She referred to "the new epoch which has now begun and which has shaken the foundations of our lives." She recognized how parents often had difficulty in understanding children who participated in the lycée protests but also how some came to understand the rightness of their children's actions.[27]

Absolutely direct testimony of that process of dawning understanding is to be found in the hand-typed diary of an Italian widowed schoolteacher, Anna Avallone, who, after at first being shocked by her student son and his miniskirted, feminist girlfriend, both activists in 1968–1969, eventually came to sympathize with both of them.[28] It may be that because West Germany had remained the most conservative and conventional of major European societies throughout most of the sixties, it was here that the impact of the challenges of 1968 was greatest, giving an immediate impetus to the development of a more open, participatory democracy, seen in the *Bürgerinitiativen* (citizens' initiatives), and to the widening of educational opportunity. Important early examples of Bürgerinitiativen were the Rote Punkt Aktion in Hanover in 1969 (resisting local transport fare increases), Aktion Kinderspielplatz (calling for children's playgrounds) in Munich in 1972, and the housewives' boycott against high meat prices in Northrhine-Westphalia in 1973. Two important education acts were passed in 1970 and 1971.[29] But such developments obviously had their origins in changes taking place throughout the sixties.

So we come to the inescapable conclusion: The moment of "1968" was a moment of high drama but not of significant long-term change; the transformations still affecting the lives of ordinary people at the beginning of the twenty-first century must be attributed to the entire Cultural Revolution of the Long Sixties.

NOTES

1. Eric Hobsbawm, *The Age of Extremes: The Short Twentieth Century, 1914–1991* (London: Hamilton, 1994); Jean Fourastié, *Les Trente Glorieuses ou la révolution invisible de 1946 à 1975* (Paris: Fayard, 1979); Henri Mendras, *La Seconde Révolution française* (Paris: Gallimard, 1994); Axel Schildt, Detlef Siegfried, and Karl Christian Lammers, eds., *Dynamische Zeiten: Die 60er Jahre in den beiden deutschen Gesellschaften* (Hamburg: Christians, 2000).

2. Carole Fink, Philip Gassert, and Detlef Junker, eds., *1968: The World Transformed* (Cambridge: Cambridge University Press, 1998); Geneviève Dreyfus-Armand, Robert Frank, Marie-Françoise Lévy, and Michelle Zancarini-Fournel, eds., *Les Années 68: Le temps de la contestation* (Brussels: Complexe, 2000).

3. For comparative history, see Arthur Marwick, *The New Nature of History: Knowledge, Evidence, Language* (Basingstoke, U.K.: Palgrave, 2001), 213–14.

4. *L'Express*, 18–24 March 1968.

5. Peter Mosler, *Was wir wollten, was wir wurden* (Reinbek: Rowohlt, 1977); Tilman Fichter and Siegward Lönnendonker, *Kleine Geschichte des SDS* (Berlin: Rotbuch, 1977); Frank Wolff and Eberhard Windaus, eds., *Studentenbewegung 1967–69* (Frankfurt/Main: Roter Stern, 1977).

6. See Claus-Dieter Krohn, "Die westdeutsche Studentenbewegung und das 'andere Deutschland,'" in *Dynamische Zeiten: Die 60er Jahre in den beiden deutschen Gesellschaften*, ed. Axel Schildt, Detlef Siegfried, and Karl Christian Lammers (Hamburg: Christians, 2000), 695–718.

7. My account of Valle Giulia is based on articles in *Epoca* and *l'Espresso*, 10 March 1968. For Italian developments, I have made extensive use of the Archivio Movimento Studentesco Italiano in the Fondazione Giangiacomo Feltrinelli, Milan, Italy.

8. UNEF, "La vérité sur les événements de la nuit de 10 au 11 mai," 11 May 1968, in *Journal de la commune étudiante: Textes et documents novembre 1967–juin 1968*, ed. Alain Schnapp and Pierre Vidal-Nacquet (Paris: Seuil, 1969). For French developments, I have used the documents in the collection "Mai 1968 (brochures et tracts)," 14 AS 238 and 250, in the Archives Nationales, Paris, and the collection "Archive 1968" in the Centre d'Histoire Sociale du XXème Siècle, Paris, along with published collections such as Geneviève Dreyfus-Armand and Laurent Gervereau, eds., *Mai 68: Les mouvements étudiants en France et dans le monde* (Paris: Bibliothèque de documentation internationale contemporaine, 1988).

9. Arthur Marwick, *The Sixties: Cultural Revolution in Britain, France, Italy and the United States, c. 1958–c. 1974* (Oxford: Oxford University Press, 1998), 605–17, and the sources cited there.

10. David Caute, *Sixty Eight: The Year of the Barricades* (London: Hamilton, 1988), 224.

11. Marwick, *The Sixties*, 617.

12. Wolfgang Kraushaar, *1968: Das Jahr das alles verändert hat* (Munich: Piper, 1998), 277–79.

13. Marwick, *The Sixties*, 615, 623–24, and sources cited there.

14. For a firsthand account of "reforms" in an Italian secondary school, see Adriano Guerini, *La rivoluzione al liceo* (Florence: Protagon, 1971).

15. Marwick, *The Sixties*, 692–724; Eva Maleck-Levy and Bernhard Maleck, "The Women's Movement in East and West Germany," in *1968*, 373–95.

16. Marwick, *The Sixties*, 17–20.

17. Lieta Harrison, *La donna sposata: Mille mogli accusano* (Milan: Mondadori, 1972), 17–79, 207–32.

18. Jacqueline Chabaud, Evelyne Sullerot, and Claude Ullin, *Un métier pour quoi faire?* (Paris: Hachard, 1969), 9–13.

19. Lieta Harrison, *L'iniziazione: Come le adolescenti diventano donne* (Milan: Mondadori, 1966), 1, 39–132.

20. Lawrence Wylie, *Village in Vaucluse* (New York: Norton, 1974), 583.

21. See the excellent article by Michael Seidman, "The Pre–May 1968 Sexual Revolution," *Contemporary French Civilization* 25, no. 1 (2001): 20–41, especially 28.

22. Klaus Hildebrand, *Von Erhard zur Grossen Koalition 1963–1969* (Wiesbaden: Brockhaus, 1994), 381.

23. The latest example is Peter N. Stearns, *Consumerism in World History: The Global Transformation of Desire* (London: Routledge, 2001).

24. Augusto Graziani, ed., *L'economia italiana dal 1945 al oggi* (Bologna: Mulino, 1972); Gisèle Podbielski, *Twenty-five Years of Special Action for the Development of Southern Italy* (Milan: Giuffrè, 1978); André Gauron, *Histoire économique et sociale de la cinquième république*, 1: *Le temps des modernistes* (Paris: Maspero, 1983).

25. Feliks Gross, *Il Paese: Values and Social Change in an Italian Village* (Westport, Conn.: Greenwood, 1974), 137.

26. Marwick, *The Sixties*, 727–32, and sources cited there.

27. *Elle*, special issue, 17 June 1968, in "Mai 1968 (brochures et tracts)," 14 AS 238, Archives Nationales, Paris.

28. Anna Avallone, "Il mio sessantotto: Ricordi di una 'madre' e 'insegnante,'" in Istituto Archivio Diaristico, Pieve Santo Stefano, Italy. See Marwick, *The Sixties*, 627–31.

29. Fred Karl, *Die Bürgerinitiativen, soziale und politische Aspekte einer neuen sozialen Bewegung* (Frankfurt/Main: Institut für Marxistische Studien and Forschungen, 1981); Karl Dietrich Bracher, Wolfgang Jäger, and Werner Link, *Republik im Wandel, 1969–1974: Die Ära Brandt* (Wiesbaden: Brockhaus, 1986), 127–55.

6

The Working-Class Dimension of 1968

Gerd-Rainer Horn

The year 1968, whether understood as that single year or as a metaphor for the larger mobilization cycle of 1965–1967 to 1975–1977, is one of those "moments of madness," like 1848, that has left an indelible imprint on—and changed the direction of—the modern societies we live in. Though most studies of 1968 focus on one state or region, virtually no serious author disputes the inherently transnational character of the contestations of that year/decade. Such apparent unanimity is rare and testifies to the immediate and long-term effects of the events of that period. The recognition of the landmark status of 1968 as an unmistakable international and, indeed, transnational moment, however, has not prevented the emergence of powerful myths. Indeed, it is safe to say that precisely this sudden appearance of a major paradigm shift in what to contemporaries appeared as the middle of an unprecedented boom period has given rise to, if not actually promoted, a whole industry of interpretations of the sixties.

Indeed, a useful point of departure for any assessment of the academic and popular reception of 1968 may be precisely the preferred choice of "the sixties" as the most prevalent descriptor for a period that far outlasted the end of that decade. Indeed, though the years prior to 1968 often witnessed turbulent moments of great importance to the later period, in the vast majority of affected states the years *after* 1968 saw a much more deep-going radicalization of society and politics than the earlier period. In virtually every single country on the European continent, but not only on the continent, where 1968 played a significant role, the first half of the 1970s saw far larger numbers of individuals and far more widespread sectors of society at large actively involved than was the case in the entire decade of the 1960s.

Indeed, leaving aside the case of France and Czechoslovakia, where the calendar year of 1968 indeed coincided with the high point of open activism (though not necessarily with the maximum depth and spread of oppositional attitudes), only the United States is a likely point of support for the view that the decade of the 1960s should be regarded as the high point of organized efforts to redirect society and politics along alternative and less inhumane pathways. And even in the United States, the peak of antiwar activism and radical challenges to the status quo occurred in the early 1970s (i.e., after the invasion of Cambodia).

The partially misguided focus on the sixties as the classic decade of anti-establishment activism, which, for the most part, took place in the 1970s, may be regarded as a reflection of the powerful grip American culture effects on all of us today. The fact that most commentators today classify the rebellious mood of 1968 primarily as a cultural revolt is likewise in part a product of this fixation on the United States. Indeed, the choice of "the sixties" as the preferred term for the phenomenon of 1968 powerfully reinforces this image of this mobilization cycle being primarily all about a cultural revolt. In North America, after all, the moment of 1968, however defined, was most visible and pervasive on the cultural terrain, resulting in a fundamental paradigm shift in popular attitudes toward interpersonal relationships in the private and the public sphere.

Of course, as is admirably demonstrated by Arthur Marwick in chapter 5, a similar sea change of opinion affected European societies as well. And there is no contest that the tier of northern European states—Great Britain, the Netherlands, West Germany, Switzerland, Austria, and Scandinavia—has good reason primarily to remember 1968 as a period of cultural and/or generational revolt. Yet, all too often, the wholly justifiable view of 1968 as cultural critique and paradigm shift serves to obscure other challenges that were frequently regarded by the powers that be as clear and present dangers to the status quo. The radical and incisive political dimension of 1968, giving rise—in its most uncompromising manifestation—to a powerful far left, serving as the backbone to many central organizational features of the sixties, not the least important one being the United States antiwar movement, is one contemporaneously prominent feature today frequently absent from academic and/or nostalgic reappropriations of 1968.

Surprisingly, another central feature of 1968 in the southern half of Europe is largely absent from the most widely distributed and most praised studies of that time: the working-class dimension of 1968. Any contemporaneous participant-observer in the contestations of the mobilization cycle of 1965–1967 to 1975–1977 in the southern tier of European states would be wholly surprised by the large-scale absence of attention to working-class concerns in much of the relevant literature on 1968 as a global phenomenon. Of course, local, regional, and national studies of 1968 in Belgium, France,

Spain, Italy, or Czechoslovakia do pay some attention to the proletarian dimension of 1968. Yet the larger the net is cast, the more prominent become the features of 1968 as youth rebellion and/or cultural revolt at the expense of any serious discussion of radical politics or, even more so, the element of working-class revolt. This chapter is designed to provide a corrective to this dominant trend in the historical literature and the memoir industry on 1968.

Cross-border history becomes possible in part as local, regional, and national studies accumulate a wealth of insights that permit the drawing of larger conclusions and inferences ranging beyond geographic, cultural, or national boundaries, ultimately inspiring historians to strike out on their own and to investigate cross-border phenomena. As the historians' gaze begins to stray beyond conventional limits, comparisons are made, differences noted, and parallels observed. Thus, comparative study is often a first and necessary stage on the road to transnational studies. But transnational history itself can be subdivided into several varieties, with a first important stage often taking the shape of the recognition and observation of cross-border similarities and parallels. Only once a phenomenon has been firmly established as a transnational one may serious investigations of the factors (and connectors) between these similar phenomena get under way (though, naturally, it is not impossible for a historian to concentrate *from the very beginning* on such transnational threads).

Given the serious lack of attention to the transnational phenomenon of working-class revolt as a central feature of 1968, this essay should be understood as belonging to the category of transnational history that primarily aims to establish (and not yet to explain) the transnational nature of a given phenomenon. Unlike student activism or youth revolt, which became transnational in part as a result of ongoing international and, indeed, transcontinental university exchanges and the equally well-established near-universal (English) language of modern communications media, the transnational features of worker revolt are more complicated to explain.[1]

Last but not least, a word of caution about the place and reach of transnational history. The false image could easily take hold of transnational history as the "royal pathway" for historical investigations, with comparative or mononational histories relegated to supporting roles. The case of worker revolt in 1968 may serve as a useful corrective in this regard. In the northern tier of European states, the working-class dimension of 1968 was far less visible and noisily present than in the southern tier of states. A glance across the Atlantic, where the major working-class mobilization in the United States during the sixties was the famous march of thirty thousand construction workers in the streets of Manhattan in support of President Nixon's decision to invade Cambodia, clearly shows the limits to the reach of this phenomenon.

In other words, although transnational history of the working-class dimension of 1968 is direly needed for the southern European states, a truly continental vision of 1968 would precisely have to focus on comparison—that is, highlighting and investigating the obviously apparent differences between "north" and "south." Neither task can be said to have been carried out in the relevant historical literature to date. Let us begin with the (slightly) less daunting problem of the reconstruction of common themes, astounding similarities, and clear-cut parallels in the southern tier of European states.

CONTOURS AND SOCIETAL RELEVANCE

The mobilization cycle of the working-class dimension of 1968 began in Francoist Spain when, on 27 October 1967, a national day of protest against political repression and the loss of purchasing power led to massive demonstrations, battles with police, and large numbers of arrests in many cities throughout Spain. The mostly proletarian demonstrators thus powerfully battered the image and reality of Spain's then forty-year-old dictatorship.[2] Though Generalissimo Francisco Franco would hold on to power until his death in November 1975, in retrospect the year 1967 turned out to be a watershed year. From that year onward, solidarity strikes and work stoppages for openly political claims dominated Spanish labor relations at the expense of claims related to collective bargaining and similar primarily economic concerns.[3]

In France, 14 May 1968 became the magic date catapulting French labor into the forefront of events. Several weeks into the hot phase of student activism in Paris and elsewhere, the workforce of the Sud-Aviation aircraft factory on the outskirts of Nantes in southwestern France refused to leave the plant, effectively occupied their factory, and forbade the company manager to leave the grounds. The next day, workers at the Renault car factory in Cléon in semirural Normandy, just south of Rouen, inspired by their comrades in Nantes, likewise began an open-ended strike, occupied the factory, and refused to let the company director out of his office. A telephone call to fellow union activists at the Renault plant in Flins, also located in provincial Normandy, though closer to Paris, led to similar action there. The spark had been struck.[4]

On the evening of 16 May, seventy thousand French workers were out on strike. By 21 May, five million workers had joined the fray. And by the time the strike wave began to recede in early June, between six and eight million workers had participated in the largest shutdown ever experienced in strike-prone France, far exceeding the previous high-water mark for French strike activity, the two million strikers at the heyday of Popular Front activism in May–June 1936. And for about a half dozen years, the number of French strikes exceeded the usual post-1950 levels.[5]

The French May events, the highly unusual simultaneous eruption of student and worker unrest on an entirely unprecedented scale, constituted the most visible manifestation of the multiple challenges symbolized by the reference to that magic year of 1968. Nowhere else in the course of that year did the combined energy and power of social movements lead to a similar political regime crisis, in this case a frontal assault on the Gaullist Fifth Republic. And the weeks-long general strike must be regarded as the central factor accounting for the volatility of the political conjuncture of May–June 1968. But if the French May remains until today the reference par excellence to the transnational social movement associated with that fateful year, it is also true that this powerful outburst of the creative energy by workers and students alike was by and large concentrated within the relatively brief period of the second half of May and the first half of June.

On the other side of the Alps, Italian workers had been involved in a similar mobilization cycle, slowly increasing their strike activity from 1966 onward. In 1967, 2.24 million workers downed their tools. The numbers more than doubled in 1968. But it was not until 1969, and here particularly the last quarter, that the high point of strike activity was reached: 5.5 million workers walked off their jobs in a series of local, regional, and national strikes. On 19 November 1969, almost the entire Italian labor force participated in a one-day general strike. And, as was the case in France as well, labor–management conflicts continued at an accelerated rate for the next half dozen years or so.[6]

Another similarity to the situation one year earlier in neighboring France was the fact that the Italian "Hot Autumn" led to a fundamental political regime crisis. For some time the Italian employers' association had refused to give in to the demands of the increasingly militant and self-confident workforce. When the successful countrywide general strike of 19 November was followed by a nationwide metalworkers' strike on 29 November, tensions rose. The atmosphere came to a boiling point on 12 December when a series of bombs exploded in Milan and Rome, killing sixteen people at the Piazza Fontana in the Lombard capital. The bombings were blamed on the far left, leading to the arrest of far left militants and thousands of union activists. As was subsequently proven, the responsibility for these killings fell squarely on the far right, and their "strategy of tension" was designed to heighten the state of instability, in hopes of generating a situation where an authoritarian government would impose its control. As it happened, Italian government officials held a series of meetings with employers, and the latter, on 21 December 1969, gave in to most union demands.[7]

In the Italian case, the demands conceded by the Italian employers' association, Confindustria, included the forty-hour week, substantial and above all equal pay raises for all categories of the multiform Italian workforce, the right of assembly in the workplace, and official recognition of new forms of worker representation (discussed later).[8] The negotiations setting the stage for the French strike wave of May–June 1968 had likewise resulted in the promise of the forty-hour workweek, the right to hold workforce assemblies at the place of employment, an average salary jump of 10 percent, and a 35 percent increase in the minimum wage.[9] But ultimately the more deep-going and long-lasting radicalization of the Italian working class, compared to their French colleagues north of the Alps, can be gauged in a series of struggles entered into by Italy's equally radicalized three major trade union confederations that went beyond traditional, economistic, salary-oriented union concerns.

Already in November 1968, all three Italian trade union federations called for a general strike to demand a significant increase in pension payments for retired workers. The strike was the culmination of a yearlong campaign against the government, which controlled pension schemes, and resulted in a partial victory.[10] The second issue involved efforts to overcome the north–south salary and employment differential. Italian employers traditionally paid their southern workforce less than their core workers to the north, a powerful tool for divide and rule. Efforts to nullify such provisions began in early 1968 and culminated in an across-the-board termination of such schemes in March 1969.

But Italian workers and their unions did not relent. Thus, for instance, a series of strikes and demonstrations led to the commitment by employers to finance meaningful investments in the South to create new sources of employment.[11] In addition, Italian unions actively engaged in struggles over housing reform, going as far as lending substantive support to squatters in private and municipal housing. And unions likewise legitimized illegal forms of popular protest (*autoriduzione*), such as the refusal to pay rising transport, electricity, gas, or telephone charges. In the words of Robert Lumley, "The factories themselves were no longer isolated within their surrounding neighborhoods." By "1973–4 the unions reached the height of their influence and prestige among exploited and oppressed social groups, and among radical intellectuals. They, rather than the parties of the left, had managed to strengthen the hand of social movements and to lead them without suffocating their autonomy."[12]

If there is, then, one country where the working-class dimension of 1968, in conjunction with social movements led by students and others, led to a sustained period of political, social and cultural opportunities and crises, this country was Italy and not the generally more prominently remembered France in May 1968. Compared to the relatively brief though violent flash of May–June 1968 in France, the Italian "creeping May," as it was sometimes called, proved to be simultaneously more long-lasting and deep-going. Yet even the Italian working class and trade union left ultimately failed in their long-range goal of turning the Christian Democrat–dominated and capitalist state into a noncapitalist and egalitarian society. And even between 1968 and 1974, even within Italian unions and the working-class left, unity was far from certain and not always achieved.

Indeed, as the following pages will show, to grasp the essence of the working-class dimension of 1968, it is perhaps most useful to leave behind the world of union confederations, national campaigns, general strikes, and countrywide victories. However inspiring, even the most prominent and promising acquisitions and gains can ultimately only be explained by a profound sea change of consciousness on the level of the rank and file. Perhaps the most important contribution of this working-class dimension lay in the more than proverbial empowerment of hundreds of thousands of individual human beings, condemned to labor in the factories and offices of the late industrial First World.

NEW FORMS OF REPRESENTATION

Both the French May and the Italian Hot Autumn gave rise to a plethora of innovative and largely unprecedented (at least in recent memory) institutions incorporating the process of decentralization and democratization concerning factory and office life that came to be the true hallmark of 1968 at the point of production, distribution, and administration. Perhaps the most universal feature came to be the regular convening of a general assembly of all workers on the factory or office floor, a mass assembly designed to allow maximum mobilization and active involvement of a workforce that had not been allowed to meet on company time in earlier years, even had they wanted to do so. It became a generalized trait of the 1968 era, though it was usurped in the course of the struggle, subsequently codified and sanctioned by the various agreements that summarized the nominal gains of the French May and the Italian Hot Autumn.

For instance, in what became a bastion of militancy in ensuing months and years, the vast network of production plants belonging to FIAT, the Italian automobile giant and functional equivalent to Renault in France, factory gatherings of its workforce had been outlawed by its authoritarian management structures since the mid-1950s. When, on 11 April 1969, Francesco Morini, an activist in the Catholic Metal Workers' Union (FIM) and a member of the left socialist Italian Party of Proletarian Unity (PSIUP) jumped onto a table in the canteen of the Mirafiori Sud works and began to harangue the gathering crowd of 1,500 workers about north–south unity and conditions at their plant, he happened to light a spark that turned the complex of FIAT production plants into a hotbed of activism for more than ten years.[13] Within one month of this event, the FIAT workforce had drawn up a document establishing the contours of these new organs of factory democracy that soon became the hallmark of the Italian "creeping May," just as they had been the central feature of the French May before: "In all workshops, in all sections of the plant, we must create assemblies and choose delegates and use the force of industrial action and unity to bring about a complete change in our working conditions through workers' control."[14]

These general assemblies constituted a frontal challenge to company management. To ensure maximum participation by the ranks, they met on company time and on the factory or office floor. To procure and ensure unity, they explicitly included the entire workforce, irrespective of union membership and regardless of whether individuals were members of any union at all. They were designed to ensure the maximum and rapid flow of information. They facilitated the free and open exchange of opinion and debates. And, at least on principle, these general assemblies were the supreme decision-making authorities on the company level concerning all matters deemed to be of interest to the respective workforce.[15] General assemblies best incorporated the antihierarchical nature of the working-class dimension of 1968. They flew in the face of existing factory regulations; they constituted at least implicit challenges to existing structures of trade union bureaucracies; and they constituted at least potential mechanisms to construct a system of dual power vis-à-vis employers, the state, and, if necessary, even union bureaucracies.[16]

Not everywhere did general assemblies assume all of these characteristics. Quite frequently, they served primarily as transmission belts for information flowing from a more restricted circle of activists to the ranks and only secondarily as mechanisms enabling the membership at large to instruct their leadership. If too large, general assemblies could and did obstruct rather than facilitate the free expression of opinions and the free flow of debate.[17] To avoid these and other limitations of general assemblies, an array of additional organs of workplace democracy were created in both Italy and France. Above all, a system of worker delegations saw the light of day, representing the general workforce in structures that were small enough to work efficiently while keeping open the channels of communication to the rank and file.

In France, these representative bodies were most frequently called strike committees (*comités de grève*); in Italy, they arose as strike committees, but from 1970 onward the commonly accepted term for them became the expression "factory councils" (*consigli di fabbrica*). In Italy in particular, they were most frequently chosen by the general assembly or, in large enterprises, by rank-and-file gatherings in sections of a plant, but always via some sort of electoral mechanism. As was the case with the general assemblies themselves, delegates could be members of any union or no union at all, as long as they held the confidence of the workforce that elected them. And to enhance their antihierarchical and antibureaucratic logic and intent, workers' delegates were not only elected by the ranks but, above all in Italy, subject to recall at any time.[18] However, in practice, it appears that the right to recall delegates was rarely exercised.[19] Yet, at any rate, factory councils served as powerful mechanisms ensuring the decentralization and democratization of factory-level decision-making authority. At the same time, they served to unify the workforce of large concerns by counteracting the tendency toward the compartmentalization and fragmentation of workplace demands in large factories.[20]

French strike committees, the functional equivalent of Italian factory councils, were far more indirect expressions of the new spirit of factory democracy than their Italian homologues. The most representative study of instances of factory democracy in France is a sociological analysis of data gathered from 182 factories in the *départements* of the Nord and the Pas-de-Calais. Here, strike committees existed in 70 percent of surveyed enterprises. But less than 20 percent of these strike committees were elected, and in only four cases could a general assembly recall such delegates.[21] In the more than 80 percent of cases where the workforce had no direct role in choosing their strike committee, delegates were appointed by the relevant trade union structures on location. This was the case even in the exceptional case of the central strike committee for the city of Nantes (discussed later).[22]

Another key difference in the nature and the function of French versus Italian representative bodies of workplace democracy lies in the durability of these structures. In France, they generally vanished with the termination of a strike. In Italy, they persisted as officially recognized bodies and determined labor–management relations for years following the 1969 Hot Autumn. By 1971, without union sponsorship, 168 factory councils flourished in the province of Milan alone. Starting in 1972, all three trade union federations increasingly sought to institutionalize these structures of base democracy: "Then, negotiating power [became] centralized in the hands of the executive committee of the factory council. The delegates became important only in moments of mobilisation when an extended network of activists was required."[23] But, for the survival of the gains of the 1968 era, it was still far better to have such institutionalized factory councils than to have none at all.

Yet in Italy the wave of organizational decentralization and democratization ushered in by the Hot Autumn stopped at the respective factory gates. While there existed at times plans to extend factory councils on the territorial level, as well as plans to unify and coordinate the disparate factory council activities based on common geographic locale, none of them came to fruition.[24] In France, by contrast, the concentrated nature of working-class unrest within the space of a very few weeks in late May and early June 1968 did lead to isolated instances of suprafactory strike committees incorporating representatives from various places of employment in one specific locale. Jacques Kergoat points to a few hesitant gropings toward citywide strike committees in the heat of the battle.[25] Two such overarching, local strike committees apparently existed in the Béarn, the committee at Oloron even pressuring the local municipal council to call an extraordinary session in order to procure relief funds for local families particularly affected by the dislocations caused by the weeks-long general strike.[26]

But the most celebrated instance of a citywide strike committee operating in France was the case of Nantes. Not only did there exist a smoothly functioning central strike committee, but from 23 May to 10 June 1968 the strike committee performed an extraordinary role as the effective municipal and regional authority, superseding the functions of the mayor of Nantes and the *préfet* of Loire-Atlantique. The central strike committee literally and figuratively took over city hall, controlled all activities by the mayor, rationed the rapidly dwindling supply of gasoline, facilitated the distribution of basic food items, and generally behaved as the supreme authority of the Commune de Nantes.

> In the city, emptied of the daily traffic composed of countless private automobiles, one could not but notice the vehicles belonging to the various trade unions, criss-crossing the main arteries while frequently disregarding traffic regulations. These vehicles, filled with activists wearing red armbands, recalled in an astounding manner the revolutionary period of the immediate post-liberation era.[27]

General assemblies, rank-and-file delegates, strike committees, and factory councils were all powerful and variegated instances of what Pierre Dubois rightfully underscores as an outstanding feature of that moment: "The decentralisation of decision-making power as working class mobilisation mechanism."[28] Yet the variety of organizations exemplifying workplace activism went far beyond the institutions enumerated in the preceding sentence. For most activists, those not members of delegate bodies, the organs of factory democracy most conducive to the free expression and appropriation of ideas were not the general assembly, whose sheer size, as mentioned before, frequently rendered it unwieldy and cumbersome. Instead, a multiplicity of committees and commissions, formed to study and/or resolve specific tasks or problems, in effect subcommittees of the general assembly or the relevant strike committee or factory council, created the free space within which activist members could find maximum space for creativity and expression. Whether called into existence to provide food, drink, or entertainment at moments of acute crises such as strikes; organized to provide political education or other forms of continuing education; or simply to draw up a list of plant-specific demands for the next round of contract negotiations, an astounding welter of rank-and-file-animated commissions characterized the reality of 1968 just as much as the more prominent assemblies, committees, and councils already analyzed here.[29]

PERSONAL AND COLLECTIVE LIBERATION

In effect, the entire array of innovative organizations was designed to ensure and maintain maximum participation of the respective workforce, going far beyond the restricted circle of committed union activists of earlier years. In most respects, these new institutions were simultaneously expressions of—and not just organizations designed to evoke—new forms of mobilization and struggle.[30] The French May and the Italian Hot Autumn, however, also generated more ephemeral, though equally inspiring "forms of disruption," as Sidney Tarrow terms the vast array of tactical innovations employed by Italian workers:

> A whole new vocabulary of strike forms developed, from the *sciopero bianco* (go-slow) to the *sciopero a singhiozzo* (literally hiccup strikes) [i.e., intermediate work stoppages], the *sciopero a scacchiera* (chessboard strikes) [i.e., work stoppages affecting various departments within a factory at different times], the *corteo interno* (marches around the factory grounds to carry along undecided workers), and the *presidio al cancello* (blocking factory gates to prevent goods from entering or leaving the plant). . . . Factory workers increasingly adopted public forms of display, expressive forms of action, and traffic blockages to dramatize their demands.[31]

Many of the same observations hold true for the French May as well, though north of the Alps factory occupations as such were the most visible and commented-on symbol of the novelty of 1968,[32] suggesting that, once again, the French mobilization cycle was more brief but, within those few weeks, more openly defiant. In contrast, Italian civil society experienced a more long-lasting, social movement–oriented, less exclusively workplace-centered contestation.

Regardless of the precise strategies employed and the tactics applied, the events of 1968 did not merely set in motion, in a literal and figurative fashion, hundreds of thousands and even millions of previously disinherited blue- (and white-) collar workers.[33] They also provided the catalyst for a profound process of inner transformation of countless individual psyches, casting aside deeply instilled fears and hesitations, questioning traditional modes of deferential behavior, suddenly setting free seemingly boundless bursts of energy. And in the process of individual liberation, the proletarian May also began to shape a new collective identity, designed not to counteract and cancel out recently obtained gains of individual self-confidence, but to strengthen and constantly reinforce the latter. Most analysts, certainly those observers present on the scene, describe this process of personal and collective liberation in the most evocative terms.

At Sud-Aviation in Nantes, the site of the first factory occupation in May 1968, the decision to stay inside the plant gates and to frontally challenge not only local management but well-established labor relations techniques had come about as a surprise, a highly welcome one to be sure, to many participants. An elderly worker remembers the consultative vote on the factory floor: "I raised my hand but lowered my head and closed my eyes. Then I decided to look up and around. Numerous hesitant hands began to go up.

The decision was made. I had not believed that it would happen, so I began to cry."[34] The chronicler of the occupation at Sud-Aviation describes the atmosphere on the company site that very first night:

> And how could one go to sleep on such a most unusual night? This morning we had left our homes and there, suddenly, we were plunged in the middle of an atmosphere of heated struggle. Sitting around makeshift campfires, groups of people who did not know how to go to sleep sat around and talked to each other in lowered voices. This campsite assembly exuded an immense impression of fraternity, solidarity and power.[35]

> Time had lost all importance, and the days and nights began to merge. Watches became one of the most useless things! . . . The present. Life. Now they were filled with meals eaten together, gatherings, standing guard, a few hours of sleep as a concession to fatigue, a permanent fraternal ambience.[36]

After years, sometimes decades, even generations of having to follow instantly all directives by foremen or managers, blue- and white-collar workers were losing their fears. Management personnel were forbidden to leave the factory or to enter the factory, depending on circumstance and the whims of the workforce. Company heads were hanged in mock effigy.[37] Traditionally inarticulate workers learned to express themselves, learned how to speak in public. And in this process the host of committees, commissions, and the practice of general assemblies played a pivotal role. "What happened in those general assemblies, no one was subsequently able to reconstruct in a precise fashion. But this was not what mattered. Not what was talked about, but that people talked, constituted the innovative and unique nature of the situation."[38]

Among the multitude of innovative tactics, perhaps the *corteo interno* deserves pride of place in instilling self-confidence, facilitating personal growth on a variety of levels. Rino Brunetti, a FIAT automobile worker from southern Italy, subsequently remembered:

> [W]hen you felt the *corteo* come closer, "boom, boom, boom," even the walls were shaking. But not like they did from the noise of the machines. This must be an earthquake, for heaven's sake. What's happening? Then the *corteo* arrived. And already about one kilometer ahead of the *corteo* some people began to scatter. The bosses ran away. And in a moment I see Luciano Parlanti, Roby, Antonio il Prete, Zappalà [leading factory activists] walk in . . . , perhaps our time has come. Perhaps we can redeem ourselves, right now. We have done well to come north. I swear to you, you know how it is when you want to speak and you can't. It reminded me of those festive encounters organised by the partisans after the liberation of a town. . . . We embraced each other, and this meant everything. It could signify, "we have won," or "we have finally been pulled out of the muck," "we have redeemed our honor, our pride." You thought about your father, the life he had led, you thought about those old people who had been here.[39]

Another FIAT worker remembers:

The first *cortei* were an incredible thing. The fear of the workers to leₓ
workstation. After fifteen, twenty years, under Valletta, with that boss with that
medal who had always terrorized us, we saw those ten, fifteen, twenty workers,
shouting along the corridors, and we were fearful to leave the line. And then we
went with the flow. . . . When we left the area assigned to our team, we were
no longer just twenty, we were already fifty.[40]

Marco Revelli, who collected these interviews, highlights that the corteo
interno

became in many ways the symbol par excellence, with its constantly moving
line of people, capable of taking advantage of the homogeneity produced by
the assembly line, but having overcome the despotism of the machine. And by
means of its rhythmic march, with its accumulation of force and sometimes its
violence, it enabled the reconquest of the immense production site which otherwise separated and dissected them.[41]

Slowly but surely, pushed by these offensives, the factory began to change. The
speed of the line began to slow down. The first breaks happened. The pressure
exerted by the system of machines on human beings grew less fearsome and
cruel. Formalised mechanisms of regulating the line speed; the emergence of an
informal control mechanism by the various work teams; the appearance within
each department of another person with effective powers, challenging the boss:
the delegate; all this appeared to alleviate the pressure, facilitated mechanisms
of self-defense, limited the despotic nature of the normal command posts. And,
together with the factory, human beings transformed themselves.[42]

To let Rino Brunetti speak again: "Our atrophied brains reminded me of
those caged birds which, when we go to let them free, to let them escape, do
not know how to fly. I was overcome by sadness. I told myself: 'God made
our brains not to make us think.' Then, suddenly, in '69, they started to function again. We broke the cage, and we began to fly again."[43] And, like birds,
they soon discovered that they were not alone. What Alessandro Pizzorno
terms "the process of the formation of a new collective identity"[44] is echoed
by all serious accounts. To cite Brunetti one last time: "It was like this after the
corteo: when I walked on foot from Mirafiori to Vallette [two different locations in that vast complex of FIAT production sites] I was by myself, but I felt
as if I was walking with ten, a hundred or a thousand comrades. I was by myself but I suddenly felt so safe!"[45] Corteos soon left the factory floor and con-
quered the city, publicly displaying the workers' newly found confidence and
sense of direction and purpose.[46]

Countless pages have been penned in many languages trying to analyze
the content of striker demands, generating fine-tuned distinctions between

quantitative and qualitative demands. But the most remarkable feature of the worker revolt was not the (contestable) predominance of qualitative over quantitative demands, the presumed numerical primacy of voices preferring a better quality of life over a hefty wage increase. Regardless of the actual wording of striker demands, what emerges crystal-clear from all firsthand accounts is the frequently unstated demand of the dignity of labor and the dignity of each individual person. Clearly, the fact that, in the case study of 182 factories repeatedly referred to earlier, "in the majority of cases, no precise objective was determined in the initial phases of the strike"[47] should provide food for thought. And another study of some 120 factories on strike in France also finds that "in the majority of cases studied, the strikes appear to have lasted longer than would have been necessary to negotiate the specific demands presented."[48] Therefore, perhaps the most symbolic, representative, and eloquent of all the strikes in these waves of protest may well be a strike where no demands were raised at all. The workforce at the Atlantic Shipyards in Saint-Nazaire downed their tools and occupied their factory for ten long days. They never bothered to draw up a list of grievances, despite constant pressure from their union leadership to do so.[49]

THE DYNAMIC TOWARD SELF-MANAGEMENT

Implicit in the strong undercurrent clamoring for the dignity of labor in the course of the French May and the Italian Hot Autumn, powerfully expressed in the course of workers' demonstrations, strikes, and factory occupations, the strong desire to regain control over one's life and thereby over the conditions to ensure the sustenance and meaningful reproduction of society came to be best expressed in the movement for self-management. Itself a movement predating the making of the European and American working class in the early to mid–nineteenth century, it had periodically left its mark on industrial societies, perhaps most strongly so in the Russian Revolution of 1917 and the 1936 Catalan Revolution at the onset of the Spanish Civil War.

Historically perhaps most strongly represented in various "utopian socialist" and syndicalist tendencies, by the late 1960s, workers' control- and self-management-oriented tendencies within the mainstream Marxist European left had been occluded by the Stalinist and social democratic factions dominating the terrain of political and union activism. It therefore constituted no surprise that, in Italy for instance, it was not Social Democrats or Communists who were the most comfortable with and most open toward the notion and the practice of worker delegates, factory councils, and the whole plethora of rank-and-file commissions set up by and incorporating the spirit of 1968. Instead, activists originating in the milieu of Left Catholicism, a forceful presence on the Italian scene ever since the closing years of the fascist experience, proved to be initially most receptive to such innovative ideas. The humanist and voluntarist dimension of Left Catholicism had prepared activists within the Catholic trade union confederation (CISL) better than any other to accept and propagate means and actions leading toward the self-liberation of humanity in general and the working class in particular.[50] The proletarian May in France witnessed activists hailing from the Left Catholic milieu in a similar central position, though, due to the particular inflexibility of the Communist trade union federation (CGT), the difference in attitude toward workers' control and self-management between the key union federations remained much more pronounced than in Italy, where eventually all three major federations (Communist, socialist, and Catholic) promoted a similar course.

Workers' self-management or *autogestion* was much talked about in May–June 1968 in France. To refer once more to the most representative survey of labor struggles, the case study of 182 factories in northern France, self-management became a topic of discussion in the various commissions or assemblies in 24.5 percent of all surveyed enterprises. In 18.5 percent, autogestion indeed became the concrete goal of the strike movement in the Nord and Pas-de-Calais, and in a certain number of cases the structural prerequisites for the running of the respective enterprises were all in place, but then the strikes ended, and with the resumption of work came the end of the dream of autogestion.[51] Only in less than 2 percent of all cases was there at least a partial resumption of labor without and against the standard management team.[52]

Yet another issue casting doubt over the reality—not the rhetoric—of workers' self-management in the French May events is the degree to which workplaces listed in the relevant secondary literature as practicing self-management were actually involved in autogestionnaires' practices, or whether they were mainly continuing to provide partial services necessary for the maintenance of equipment or the retention of market outlets.[53]

Still, a number of isolated instances of worker self-management existed, in which the workforce of a given concern attempted to effect control over the running of affairs. Some were classic blue-collar factories, such as a mineral water bottling plant or a cookie factory.[54] Others took hold in a predominantly white-collar milieu. In Paris, employees of the Postal Service, which in France performs functions beyond the standard sale of stamps and mail delivery, decided to maintain certain services, but under the authority of the strike committees, not regular management. Interestingly, in a display of worker solidarity, striking workers at the Banque de France ensured that Postal Service salaries were transferred into the hands of striking postal workers, who controlled and supervised the distribution of these funds to the workforce on strike.[55]

Yet, clearly, the legacy of the French May was not so much a rich treasure trove of concrete experiences of workers' self-management but the indisputable fact that autogestion was catapulted onto the center stage of national debates and became firmly embedded within the imagination of the French and francophone working class. Here the role of the formerly Catholic trade union federation (CFDT) cannot be underestimated. Autogestionnaires' ideas had been considered and debated for a number of years. It was in the heat of battle and under the impact of student activism in Paris and elsewhere that the CFDT, for the first time ever, went public with its self-management concepts. On 16 May 1968 the CFDT leadership published its historic text culminating in the following call to action:

> To civil liberties and rights within universities must correspond the same liber-
> ties and rights within enterprises; in this demand the struggles of university stu-
> dents meet up with those which workers have fought for since the origin of the
> labor movement. We must replace industrial and administrative monarchy with
> democratic structures based on workers' self-management.[56]

The CFDT in upcoming years promoted and literally incorporated the groundswell in the direction of autogestion then gripping France.[57]

Already soon after the events of the French May, some keen observers began to notice the concrete gains in self-confidence of the French workforce
in the wake of 1968. Union membership became more widespread; union
meetings occurred more frequently; strikes were frequently accompanied by
general assemblies; and such assemblies sometimes became regular features
of workplace democracy even in times of "labor peace," similar to the more
widespread Italian practice of general assemblies being held on company
property and company time.[58] One prominent industrial sociologist noted already in 1970 a tendency for post-1968 French labor struggles to suddenly
target issues of workers' control: employment, working conditions, or work
schedules.[59] By 1973, quantity turned into quality.

On 17 April 1973, the workforce of the watch factory LIP in Besançon in
eastern France began a labor action that came to last nearly a year and that
became a symbol for the new quality of post-1968 labor struggles in France
and elsewhere. It became the cause célèbre for the autogestionnaire European (far) left and called forth countless solidarity declarations and visits.
What had caught the imagination of activists across the continent was not the
fact of a nearly yearlong strike, in and of itself no longer a novelty. It was the
decision of the workforce and the CFDT leadership on 18 June to take the
production and distribution of watches into their own hands, which seemed
to prefigure an age of autogestion. Professional and solidarity networks allowed this experiment to prosper until early 1974 when LIP reopened its
doors under the regular management and ownership on 11 March.[60] It inspired a number of similar actions in France and elsewhere, perhaps most
notably in the Belgian state, then suffering from a prolonged bout of dein-
dustrialization of its formerly flagship Walloon province.[61]

The theory, and even more so the practice, of workers' self-management no longer placed questions of property and ownership at the center of activist concern, but instead it focused on questions of power and authority. "It desired the disassembly of authorities and hierarchies, the release of workers' creativity by means of self-determination and self-administration. In short, it was a blueprint for the transformation of heteronomy into autonomy, for the construction of a democratically self-constituting new society, just as the theoreticians of the non-communist New Left had imagined it."[62] With the transformation of the theory of autogestion into practice, a new quality of convergence of worker and student activism, of old and new left, had been achieved, a concrete gain that helped bring about a situation where the moment of greatest intensity and societal presence of the spirit of 1968 was to be found in the early to mid-1970s. The combination of French-generated autogestionnaires' experiences with the quasi-organic merger of trade unions and new social movements unique to Italy created a combustible mix of ideas and practices that shaped an entire generation. Interestingly enough, perhaps underscoring the transnational nature of the processes at work in economy, society, and people's minds, the ultimately most powerful manifestations of these trends emerged neither in Italy nor in France.

SPRINGTIME IN PRAGUE AND CARNATIONS IN PORTUGAL

Already back in 1968–1969, the most promising development in the theory and practice of workers' self-management occurred not in France or Western Europe but on the western edge of the Stalinist hemisphere: in Czechoslovakia. Here, the movement termed the Prague Spring, originating in the victory of a reforming tendency within the Communist Party, by the spring of 1968 had begun to call on worker initiatives in order to circumvent the obstructionist sloth of a deeply entrenched bureaucracy. The market socialist Ota Šik, vice premier in charge of enterprise reforms, by invoking the creative energies of the Czechoslovak workforce in order to break the stranglehold of Stalinist centralist practices, let the genie out of the bottle. Statutes for the democratization of enterprises were soon drafted, and by early June 1968, the first workers' councils were formed in some flagship enterprises in Prague and Pilsen. By the summer of 1968, it became clear that what had been designed as a tactical move had taken on a dynamic of its own. Not content with playing a supportive role, workers' councils demanded a decisive role for themselves in the running of enterprises, not just the right to be consulted.

Yet before workers' councils could become an irresistible force, the Warsaw Pact invasion of 21 August decisively changed the terms and the political context of these most promising debates. Still, the idea had taken root, and for a while the number of workers' councils rose even and especially under Soviet rule. In September 1968, no more than nineteen councils existed in the entire Czechoslovak state. Between 1 October and 31 December 1968, 260 additional councils saw the light of day. On 9–10 January 1969, council delegates representing 890,000 workers, a sixth of the country's entire workforce, gathered for deliberations in Pilsen. But in the course of 1969, as could be expected, the counterrevolution easily won out.[63]

What amounted to a stillborn revolution in the Czechoslovak case erupted as an open challenge to all sorts of established hierarchies from 25 April 1974 to 25 November 1975 in Portugal. When the Armed Forces Movement (MFA) staged their successful rebellion against the fifty-year dictatorship of Salazar and Caetano, they opened up the floodgates of popular activism, thus transforming Portuguese society more profoundly than any other social movement in any other state during the mobilization cycle of 1967–1975. For nineteen long months, the Portuguese state and, more important, Portuguese society experienced a seemingly never-ending series of strikes, factory occupations, and instances of workers' self-management. Due to the dual nature of the Portuguese Revolution, an antidictatorial revolt that increasingly adopted the overtones of an anticapitalist explosion of social struggles and campaigns, its image and its reality combined key features of the worker revolts of the 1968 era with the moments of euphoria at the point of liberation from Nazi rule in 1944–1945.[64]

Strike committees and factory councils operated side by side with committees whose sole task it was to cleanse all relevant institutions and concerns of collaborators with the authoritarian regime of the past fifty years. The same creative multitude of commissions and committees exemplifying the French May and the Italian Creeping May sprang up in Portugal like mushrooms in the rain. The same effervescent combination of individual and collective initiatives characterized the revolution of the carnations. In Portugal, however, the antihierarchical radiance of strike committees and similar organs of popular power was even more profound and all-pervasive than in Italy or France. Factory democracy was paralleled by the construction of organs of rank-and-file democracy—or "popular power," in the language current at that time—in neighborhoods. If anything, neighborhood councils threw up even more frontal challenges to new authorities in the Portuguese state than factory councils. Whereas factory committees and commissions—just as in France and Italy a few years earlier—rarely began to coordinate their activities beyond the confines of each individual factory compound, neighborhood committees formed zonal and even citywide associations, a network of local organs of rank-and-file democracy going far beyond the French and Italian experiences and evoking faint echoes of the institutions of dual power in the Russian and Catalan Revolutions.

Nowhere else in postwar Europe was the left as powerful as in Portugal in 1974–1975. Nowhere else in postwar Europe was the far left as influential within the left as in Portugal. Nowhere else, except for the special case of Yugoslavia, were instances of workers' control as widespread as in Portugal, affecting cities, towns, and countryside alike. At the high point of the movement for self-management, close to 130,000 individuals were co-owners of the fields and factories that employed them; 1,200 cooperatives and self-managed firms and more than a million hectares of arable land were collective property. In a country with a total population, including children, of nine million people, their presence mattered and left an indelible stamp on individual and collective memories. Yet, once again, the movement ultimately failed.

For reasons beyond the purview of this essay, 25 November 1975, when the conservative faction in the MFA regained control, was the beginning of the end of the most boundless expression of creative energies set free by the working-class dimension of 1968. And, unbeknownst to the participants and observers at that time, the defeat of the Portuguese Revolution became the turning point for the transnational mobilisation cycle ushered in on 27 October 1967 by workers in neighboring Spain. The old left further deepened their historic compromises; the new left by now multiplied solely by division, eventually disintegrating under the combined blows of urban terrorism by isolated and desperate former comrades-in-arms and state repression; the close ties, if not the organic connection between some trade union federations and the social movements emerging at that time, became progressively unfastened. Yet the memories of these experiences lived on, ensuring that European workers would not be forced to return to ground zero when their activism resumed.

NOTES

I wish to thank Andreas Graf, in whose living room this essay saw the light of day.

1. The contemporaneous influence of the far left may very well have served as an important transmission mechanism, with closely affiliated publishing houses—such as Klaus Wagenbach in West Germany, François Maspero in France, and Giangiacomo Feltrinelli in Italy—performing a particularly crucial and seriously underinvestigated role as, simultaneously, connectors and megaphones.

2. On the 27 October 1967 national day of protest, see Sebastian Balfour, *Dictatorship, Workers and the City: Labour in Greater Barcelona since 1939* (Oxford: Clarendon, 1989), 94–95, and Max Gallo, *Spain under Franco: A History* (London: Allen & Unwin, 1973), 352.

3. This information can be gleaned from the relevant table in Walther L. Bernecker, "Die Arbeiterbewegung unter dem Franquismus," in *Die geheime Dynamik autoritärer Diktaturen*, ed. Peter Waldmann, Walther L. Bernecker, Francisco López-Casero, and H. C. Felipe (Munich: Oldenbourg, 1982), 138, and the graph in José Maravall, *Dictatorship and Political Dissent: Workers and Students in Franco's Spain* (London: Tavistock, 1978), 37.

4. There exist book-length, firsthand accounts of these three catalytic struggles, capturing the spirit of the spontaneity and the largely unparalleled nature of the proletarian May in France: François Le Madec, *L'aubépine de mai: Chronique d'une usine occupée: Sud-Aviation Nantes 1968* (Nantes: Centre de Documentation du Mouvement Ouvrier et du Travail, 1988); on Renault-Cléon, see *Notre arme c'est la grève* (Paris: Maspero, 1968); on Renault-Flins, see Jean-Philippe Talbot, ed., *La grève à Flins* (Paris: Maspero, 1968).

5. A concise and lively survey of French strike activity can be found in Ingrid Gilcher-Holtey, *"Die Phantasie an die Macht": Mai 68 in Frankreich* (Frankfurt am Main: Suhrkamp, 1995), 285–97. The two most useful attempts to compute the total number of strikers engaged in May–June 1968 are Gérard Adam, "Étude statistique des grèves de mai–juin 1968," *Revue française de science politique* 20, no. 1 (February 1970): 105–19, with his final estimate of 6 to 7.5 million strikers on 118, and Jacques Kergoat, "Sous la plage, la grève," in *Retours sur Mai*, ed. Antoine Artous (Paris: La Brèche, 1988), 61–62, with his estimate of 6 to 8 million strikers on 62. A table indicating heightened strike activity after 1968 can be found in Peter Lange, George Ross, and Maurizio Vannicelli, *Unions, Change and Crisis: French and Italian Union Strategy and the Political Economy, 1945–1980* (London: Allen & Unwin, 1982), 62. However it should be stressed that this measure of heightened militancy held true only when taking the total number of individual strikes as measure for comparison and not in regard to the total number of "days lost" due to strikes or the total number of individual strikers.

6. The figure of 5.5 million strikers during the Hot Autumn and some information on the 19 November 1969 general strike can be conveniently located in Joanne Barkan, *Visions of Emancipation: The Italian Workers' Movement since 1945* (New York: Praeger, 1984), 75–76. A table showing the total number of striking Italian workers per annum from 1955 to 1970 can be found in Dominique Grisoni and Hugues Portelli, *Les luttes ouvrières en Italie (1960–1976)* (Paris: Aubier Montaigne, 1976), 74. Grisoni and Portelli's table suggests a total number of seven million strikers in the Italian Hot Autumn.

7. The societal and regime crisis of late 1969 is conveniently analyzed in the context of labor unrest in Gino Bedani, *Politics and Ideology in the Italian Workers' Movement: Union Development and the Changing Role of the Catholic and Communist Subcultures in Postwar Italy* (Oxford: Berg, 1995), 154–55.

8. Bedani, *Politics and Ideology*, 155.

9. On the negotiations in the rue de Grenelle, see Gilcher-Holtey, *"Phantasie an die Macht,"* 328–31.

10. On the significance of the pension struggle, see Barkan, *Visions of Emancipation*, 69–70, and Grisoni and Portelli, *Les luttes ouvrières*, 98–102.

11. See Grisoni and Portelli, *Les luttes ouvrières*, 100–2, and Bedani, *Politics and Ideology*, who contends, "The period between 1968 and 1972 produced a degree of North–South labour solidarity unparalleled in the nation's history" (172–73).

12. On the unique confluence and cooperation between Italian unions and social movements at that time, see Robert Lumley, *States of Emergency: Cultures of Revolt in Italy from 1968 to 1978* (London: Verso, 1990), 257–69, citations on 262 and 265–66, but also Bedani, *Politics and Ideology*, 174–78.

13. See Marco Revelli, *Lavorare in FIAT: Da Valletta ad Agnelli a Romiti* (Milan: Garzanti, 1989), 41–42, for the 11 April 1969 episode.

14. Excerpts from this document including the citation can be found in Bedani, *Politics and Ideology*, 159.

15. A concise summary of these features can be found in Lumley, *States of Emergency*, 231.

16. The institutional challenges incorporated by general assemblies are well analyzed and thoughtfully described in Gilcher-Holtey, *"Phantasie an die Macht,"* 299–300. For a detailed account of rank-and-file democracy in the white-collar environment, see Jacques Pesquet, *Des soviets à Saclay: Premier bilan d'une experience de conseils ouvriers au commissariat à l'énergie atomique* (Paris: Maspero, 1968).

17. Pierre Dubois stresses this structural limitation of general assemblies in his "Les pratiques de mobilisation et d'opposition," in Pierre Dubois, Renaud Dulong, Claude Durand, Sabine Erbès-Seguin, and Daniel Vidal, *Grèves revendicatives ou grèves politiques? Acteurs, pratiques, sens du mouvement de mai* (Paris: Anthropos, 1978), 369.

18. Useful surveys of the theory and practice of Italian factory councils can be gleaned in Bedani, *Politics and Ideology*, 156–63, and Lumley, *States of Emergency*, 257–61.

19. Alessandro Pizzorno, "Le due logiche dell'azione di classe," in Alessandro Pizzorno, Emilio Reyneri, Marino Regini, and Ida Regalia, *Lotte operaie e sindacato: Il ciclo 1968–1972 in Italia* (Bologna: Mulino, 1978), 16, note 5.

20. The centrality of delegate structures in the Italian mobilization cycle opened by the Hot Autumn is stressed by Pizzorno, "Le due logiche," 14. The tendency toward *repartismo* (i.e., the tendency within large factories to give primary exposure to the particularist concerns of one's own workshop at the expense of the factory as a whole) is well described in Marino Regini, "Come e perchè cambiano la logica dell'organizzazione sindacale e i comportamenti della base," in Pizzorno et al, *Lotte operaie*, 162–67. For the unifying role of factory committees, countervailing centrifugal tendencies on the factory floor, see Ida Regalia, "Rappresentanza operaia e sindacato: Il mutamento di un sistema di relazioni industriali," in Pizzorno et al., *Lotte operaie*, 218.

21. For the number of existing strike committees of this sample, 128 out of 182 enterprises, see Dubois, "Les pratiques de mobilisation," 375; for the modes of election and possibilities of recall, see Dubois, "Les pratiques de mobilisation," 378.

22. A good assessment and overview of the limited reality of rank-and-file democracy in the French May is provided in Kergoat, "Sous la plage," 66–67. On the mode of election to the Nantes Central Strike Committee, see Yannick Guin, *La Commune de Nantes* (Paris: Maspero, 1969), 133. The same general observation of the primary function of French strike committees as trade union coordinating committees more than instances of genuine rank-and-file democracy is stressed by Antoine Prost, "Acteurs et terrains du mouvement social," in *1968: Exploration du mai français*, Vol. I: *Terrains*, ed. René Mouriaux, Annick Percheron, Antoine Prost, and Danielle Tartakowsky (Paris: L'Harmattan, 1992), 9.

23. Lumley, *States of Emergency*, 260–61, citation on 261.

24. Bedani, *Politics and Ideology*, 163.

25. Kergoat, "Sous la plage," 68.

26. Danielle Sindic, "Le Béarn: Insertion nationale et contingences locales," in *1968*, ed. Mouriaux et al., 213 and 213, note 60.

27. On the history and function of the Nantes Central Strike Committee, see above all Guin, *Commune de Nantes*, particularly 67–140, citation on 99, but also the cogent and insightful summary in Adrien Dansette, *Mai 1968* (Paris: Plon, 1971), 262–68.

28. This is the wording of a subtitle in his "Les pratiques de mobilisation," 333.

29. Sabine Erbès-Seguin stresses the important function as mobilization mechanism of these task-oriented commissions in her "Militants et travailleurs: Organisation des relations dans la grève," in Dubois et al., *Grèves revendicatives*, 301. A useful description of the variety of commissions of this nature in France can be found in Kergoat, "Sous la plage," 69–71. For Italy, see above all Regalia, "Rappresentanza operaia," 254–58.

30. On occasion, general assemblies, for instance, were called into existence by a relatively narrow layer of activists in order to elicit rank-and-file support. But, as the experience of Peugeot-Sochaux indicates, such an institution created from above could eventually develop its own dynamic and turn into a major forum for hotly contested debates. On the case of Sochaux, see Nicolas Hatzfeld, "Peugeot-Sochaux: De l'entreprise dans la crise à la crise dans l'entreprise," in *1968*, ed. Mouriaux et al., 58.

31. Sidney Tarrow, *Democracy and Disorder: Protest and Politics in Italy 1965–1975* (Oxford: Clarendon, 1989), 186–93, citation on 186–88. But see also Roberto Franzosi, *The Puzzle of Strikes: Class and State Strategies in Postwar Italy* (Cambridge: Cambridge University Press, 1995), 267–72, and here in particular his section entitled "The Tactics: 'Everyone Did What They Wanted,'" and the remarks on the central role of the factory by Pizzorno, "Le due logiche," 15.

32. Thus, for instance, 53 percent of the sample of factories in the Nord and Pas-de-Calais referred to earlier (i.e., 96 factories out of 182) employed this form of action in the course of their struggle; see Dubois, "Les pratiques de mobilisation," 361. And, of course, the catalyst of the French proletarian May, the action by the workforce at Sud-Aviation in Nantes, took the form of a factory occupation for the duration of one month.

33. On the societal relevance of white-collar actions in the 1968 era, see Gerd-Rainer Horn, "The Changing Nature of the European Working Class: The Rise and Fall of the 'New Working Class' (France, Italy, Spain, Czechoslovakia)," in *1968: The World Transformed*, ed. Carole Fink, Philipp Gassert, and Detlef Junker (Cambridge: Cambridge University Press, 1998), 351–71.

34. Cited in Guin, *Commune de Nantes*, 59.

35. Le Madec, *L'aubepine de mai*, 61.

36. Le Madec, *L'aubepine de mai*, 118.

37. A representative photo of such a mock execution at Citroën-Javel can be seen in Christine Fauré, *Mai 68 jour et nuit* (Paris: Gallimard, 1998), 80.

38. Gilcher-Holtey, *"Phantasie an die Macht,"* 293.

39. Revelli, *Lavorare in FIAT*, 48; first ellipses in the original.

40. Revelli, *Lavorare in FIAT*, 49.

41. Revelli, *Lavorare in FIAT*, 47.

42. Revelli, *Lavorare in FIAT*, 50.

43. Revelli, *Lavorare in FIAT*, 50.

44. Pizzorno, "Le due logiche," 15.

45. Revelli, *Lavorare in FIAT*, 50.

46. See, for instance, the analysis of extrafactory demonstrations in Emilio Reyneri, "Il 'maggio strisciante': L'inizio della mobilitazione operaia," in Pizzorno et al., *Lotte operaie*, 66–67.

47. Erbès-Seguin, "Militants et travailleurs," 307.

48. Josette Blancherie, Michèle Lefebvre, Bernard Bacquet, Bernard Bodin, Jean-Louis Bresson, Patrick Delage, and Claude Lefebvre, *Les événements de mai–juin*

1968 vus à travers cent entreprises (Paris: Centre National d'Information pour la Productivité des Entreprises, 1968), 26. Interestingly, this survey, originating in management circles, likewise emphasizes the relative futility of carefully analyzing the content of demands. The authors stress that the various grievances publicly aired "can only imperfectly reflect that which workers felt and lived" and "can only imperfectly represent their real content (*contenu réel*)" (31). A preface on p. 2 indicates that, despite the study's title, investigations were carried out in approximately 120 enterprises.

49. David Caute, *Sixty-Eight: The Year of the Barricades* (London: Hamilton, 1988), 208.

50. Gino Bedani's work, focusing, as the subtitle indicates, explicitly on "the changing role of the Catholic and Communist subcultures" is particularly useful in this regard; see, for instance, his pertinent comments on 161 of his *Politics and Ideology*. For a first assessment of the contributions of Left Catholicism to postwar European politics and civil society, see the collection of articles presented in Gerd-Rainer Horn and Emmanuel Gerard, eds., *Left Catholicism: Catholics and Society in Western Europe at the Point of Liberation, 1943–1955* (Leuven: Leuven University Press, 2001); and, for the Italian dimension in particular, the contributions to that volume by Antonio Parisella and Giorgio Vecchio.

51. Dubois, "Pratiques de mobilisation," 407–9.

52. Dubois, "Pratiques de mobilisation," 403.

53. Here Jacques Kergoat is particularly good at tempering the enthusiasm of outside observers, who claim to see workers' self-management in areas where production continued for entirely different reasons. See Kergoat, "Sous la plage," 73–74.

54. The case of the bottling plant is one of the select few cases where an attempt at a serious analysis of autogestion in May 1968 was carried out in its aftermath; see Danièle Kergoat, "Une expérience d'autogestion en mai 1968," *Sociologie du Travail* 12, no. 3 (July–September 1970): 274–92.

55. Dansette, *Mai 68*, 180.

56. Cited in Albert Detraz, "Le mouvement ouvrier, la CFDT, et l'idée d'autogestion," in Edmond Maire, Alfred Krumnow, and Albert Detraz, *La CFDT et l'autogestion* (Paris: Cerf, 1975), 77.

57. On this and other aspects of the CFDT, the two superior works are Pierre Cours-Saliès, *La CFDT: Un passé porteur d'avenir. Pratiques syndicales et débats stratégiques depuis 1946* (Paris: La Brèche, 1988), and Hervé Hamon and Patrick Rotman, *La deuxième gauche: Histoire politique et intellectuelle de la CFDT* (Paris: Ramsay, 1982).

58. Dubois, "Pratiques de mobilisation," 438.

59. Serge Mallet, "L'après-mai 1968: Grèves pour le contrôle ouvrier," *Sociologie du Travail* 12, no. 3 (July–September 1970): 309–27.

60. Among the host of publications on the LIP experiment, I have relied on Arno Münster, *Der Kampf bei LIP: Arbeiterselbstverwaltung in Frankreich* (Berlin: Rotbuch, 1974).

61. A reference to a half dozen or so Belgian experiences of workers' self-management inspired by the example of LIP can be found in Marie-Thérèse Coenen, "Les front communs syndicaux: Une pratique et un outil," in *Le Rassemblement des progressistes, 1944–1976*, ed. Marie-Thérèse Coenen and Serge Govaert (Paris: De Boeck, 1999), 228.

62. Gilcher-Holtey, *"Phantasie an die Macht,"* 304.

63. This brief synopsis of workers' councils in the Czechoslovak state is largely based on the following works: Vladimir Fišera, ed., *Workers' Councils in Czechoslovakia: Documents and Essays 1968–69* (London: Allison & Busby, 1978); Joseph and Vladimir Fišera, "Cogestion des entreprises et économie socialiste—l'expérience tchécoslovaque, 1967–1970," *Revue de l'Est* 2 (January 1971): 39–67; and Miloš Barta, "Les conseils ouvriers en tant que mouvement social," *Autogestion et Socialisme* 9–10 (September–December 1969): 3–36.

64. These and the following passages on the Portuguese Revolution rely on two key studies of the dynamics of "the revolution of the carnations," as the Portuguese Revolution came to be called: John Hammond, *Building Popular Power: Workers' and Neighborhood Movements in the Portuguese Revolution* (New York: Monthly Review Press, 1988) and, more important yet, Gérard Filoche, *Printemps portugais* (Paris: Actéon, 1984).

7

1968 East and West

Visions of Political Change and Student Protest from across the Iron Curtain

Paulina Bren

The year 1968 was one during which politics East and West became, at least temporarily, a testing ground of new ideas and discoveries. In Prague, the ideological commotion was felt keenly in the details of daily life: Previously banned books went on sale; films from the West arrived in cinemas; music clubs filled with long-haired beatniks; students packed their bags and traveled West for the first time; and the previously ignored communist newspapers turned into lively forums of debate, selling out within hours. With the gradual cessation of censorship and the growing possibility of unrestricted travel, information and ideas moved east to west and west to east in a way that was unique in the experience of a postwar divided Europe.

While Czechoslovakia experimented with its politics, new visions for the future were being formulated simultaneously in the western half of Europe. Protests in France, Germany, and Italy did not go unseen by the Czech student movement. My central concern in the following essay is how Czech students during the Prague Spring looked on antigovernment youth protests taking place elsewhere during the same year, and how we might benefit from the juxtaposition of 1968 East and West in understanding this defining year of the postwar period that, after over thirty years, still remains curiously undefined and elusive.

My main focus will be the weekly newspaper of Czech university students, *Student*. Originally a faithful organ of the official Czechoslovak Youth Union, *Student* went on to become an independent and radically outspoken publication that the Soviets themselves took note of, later citing it as a political provocation. Indeed, the development of the weekly itself—its content, the political nature of its articles, its increasing awareness of student movements to the west of Czechoslovakia's borders—moved parallel with the Czech student movement's own formation, expansion, and eventual factionalism. In the following pages, I trace how Czech students defined themselves and their politics on the pages of *Student*, particularly in relation to the simultaneous protests on the streets of Western Europe. My purpose is to expand our understanding of what happened in that pivotal year, not so much by focusing on the narrative of events in a single national context but rather on the interrelations of the political ideologies being played out East and West in 1968.

THE 1960s STUDENT GENERATION IN THE MAKING

In comparison to Hungary, Poland, and East Germany after 1953, de-Stalinization in Czechoslovakia took place only slowly, hampered by the reluctance of government leaders to expose their own collusion in the 1950s Stalinist show trials. When political liberalization did finally come to Czechoslovakia, it appeared as a relaxation of not only political but also cultural boundaries. For example, at the 1965 student springtime festivities known as the *Majáles*—more absurdist theater than political demonstration—the American beatnik poet Allen Ginsberg was crowned king.[1] The journalist Tad Szulc described the spirit of 1960s Czechoslovakia as altogether synonymous "with jazz and the big-beat sound as if in retaliation against years of Stalinist monotony and boredom. . . . Blue jeans and beards appeared in Prague and Bratislava."[2] Nevertheless, what Prague's students were expressing in their daily attire of jeans and beards, as well as their recently reinstated springtime celebrations, was not a clearly articulated political thesis but a basic discontent to which they believed they had a right unlike any other generation before them. Journalist Alan Levy encountered this attitude in conversations with a nineteen-year-old who explained, "The Stalinists of the 1950's, they wrote off our parents, but they counted on us. They shouldn't have. I've lived all my life under one system, so I have every right to criticize it."[3]

This young man's presumption was echoed in scientific surveys conducted for the Communist Party by a growing number of sociologists practicing a new field of research called "youth studies." Based on this research, a 1965 internal government report, for example, asserted that contemporary youth were politically handicapped for never having experienced World War II or "the consequent class war" that, for their parents' generation, had functioned as "the greatest school of life." The generation now reaching maturity in the 1960s instead had experienced, according to the report, "a complicated social and political development, particularly as of the year 1956." For them, socialism was no longer an idealized political notion but instead a lived experience: "In contrast to the first postwar generation of young people, for whom socialism was primarily an imagined ideal . . . for today's generation of youth, socialism is an objective reality."[4] For the 1960s generation, the outcome of this firsthand experience with "socialism" was, according to the experts, an obsessive focus on "social economics" and "a desire for independent thought and communication that is then tied in with an increased level of criticism." Like a cantankerous old man, this government report and others of its kind lamented youth's physical comforts, its ample leisure time, and its unending demands and saw warning signs in its tendency to ignore party-organized activities and instead to assemble in informal groups that "create their own norms for behavior which they then strictly hold and enforce." As government reports confirmed, this generation unflinchingly critiqued the shortcomings of socialist society. They were, unlike European youth west of the border, realists rather than dreamers.

Jiřina Šiklová, known later for her work as a political dissident but then still a sociologist and practitioner of the new youth studies, argued in 1967 in an article in *Student* that "if the West German sociologist [Hans Heinrich] Muchow states that contemporary youth have no consistent life models, it seems that this is twice so in our case."[5] Not only were Czech youth as bereft of heroes and mentors as their West German counterparts, but Czech students further felt attacked by the Communist Party for belonging to the "intelligentsia." As another editorial in *Student* explained, the party deemed studying suspicious and, therefore, to be supplemented by university students' "heightened [official] political activity and, once they'd finished studying, by as low a salary as possible." The party encouraged the impression that "work at school was not considered work."[6] This, continued the editorial's author, was the reason for the low number of young people who had any interest in Communist Party membership. As the reform Communist and head of state television Jiří Pelikán admitted, the difference between his generation and this younger generation of intelligentsia was that

> our generation had the advantage that the politics of the communist party represented the politics that a large portion of students and the intelligentsia understood as progressive politics. . . . Therefore [unlike today], it was precisely the active and elite part [of the student body] that had felt that the party and its politics belonged to them.[7]

In contrast, the student generation of the 1960s did not feel that the Communist Party belonged to them, and in fact neither they nor the party seemed sure of whether they wanted one another.

These uneasy relations were at the center of Czechoslovakia's best-known student protest, in 1967 at the Strahov dormitories located just behind the Prague castle. On the night of 31 October, the dormitory lights went out. The dormitory had been experiencing electrical outages for some time, an inconvenience that usually resulted in students cursing out loud in their dormitory rooms, floating burning slips of paper from their windows, and then congregating in small groups in the courtyard from where they usually moved on to Prague's pubs and nightclubs. On 31 October the students gathered in the courtyard and shouts of "Let's all go out!" began to be heard. According to one of the students there, they all began to march down toward the castle and then on toward Nerudová street, shouting, "We want light!" Students were quickly surrounded by police cars, and when they turned to climb back up toward the castle, the police drove their vehicles up and down the street, squeezing the students onto the sidewalks. The main infraction took place when the police followed the students inside the courtyard of the dormitory, which students had assumed was a safe zone, and there attacked them with batons and tear gas.[8] This violent confrontation between students and police did not, however, immediately prompt comparison with Western European student demonstrations. What was central to the "Strahov" affair was the show of police brutality against the students, which further indicated the deteriorating relations between the regime and the intelligentsia, who were being "handled like an enemy class."[9]

Comparisons between Western European student protests and Strahov did not immediately come to mind at the time because both the domestic and international issues at stake East and West were markedly different. This was particularly clear in the case of student protests over the Vietnam War. In February 1968, university students from Brno embarked on a seven-day, 238-kilometer march to Prague in protest of the American war in Vietnam. But, unlike similar antiwar protests in the United States, this one was obviously in line with officially held views, and it thereby lacked a certain veracity. According to one participant, the weeklong march had ended with a friendly glass of Pepsi Cola at the American Embassy, "sincere moments" at the embassy of the Vietnamese Democratic Republic, and snacks with nonreformist former Communist Party first secretary Antonín Novotný, who, while dethroned in January and replaced with Alexander Dubček, was still stubbornly clinging to the role of Czechoslovak president.

Nevertheless, the Brno students must have sensed the awkwardness of their position, for they bristled on overhearing the conclusion of one party secretary regarding their antiwar protest march: "See, students don't just take part in unannounced demonstrations [i.e., Strahov], they're even capable of nice little political actions such as this." Despite their tea with Novotný, the Brno marchers insisted that their protest was "a part of the rising wave of student political activities."[10] Yet in February 1968, this was still more a case of wishful thinking than anything else. Most Czech students remained reluctant to veer from Communist Party programs and strike out as an independent political force.

The best-known exception to this was a group of university students who had first made a name for themselves when they infiltrated the official Youth Union back in 1965 and boldly declared that, if necessary, the union should act as a potential opponent to party policy. While the "Prague radicals"—as this group of students consequently came to be known publicly—lost their group identity when the unpopular Youth Union was eventually dissolved, some of the group's original members became key student leaders during 1968 and continued to push (although never abandon) the party's boundaries.[11] Thus, while some of the Brno students might indeed have envisioned their antiwar march as part of a continuum of student protest in Europe, it was these several student Prague radicals, as they continued to be called, who actively envisioned a Czech student movement that would eventually have more in common with student protests in the West than with the reformist but still pointedly conservative Prague Spring government led by First Secretary Alexander Dubček under the banner of "socialism with a human face."

Indeed, the question of what leftist political protest meant in a state that, at least theoretically, professed to occupy just such a stand came to the fore during a mass student debate organized at the huge Prague Congress Palace. When prominent student leader and Prague radical Luboš Holeček took to the podium, he declared that the main obstacle to the formation of a Czech student movement was students' inexperience with politics. According to Holeček, Czech students first had "to learn to think politically, to learn how to put such a program together . . . [because for] twenty years we have not been given the opportunity."[12] Another well-known student leader and Prague radical, Jiří Müller, emphasized in an interview conducted around the time of the Congress Palace meeting that the reformist ethos expressed in the recent January 1968 Communist Party Plenum (which had ousted First Secretary Novotný and brought the more liberal Alexander Dubček into power) represented great hopes not only for him but also for "many people with leftist opinions from non-socialist countries." Such people, according to Müller, long had viewed socialist Czechoslovakia as the embodiment of their dreams and thus had refused to hear of its reality, "believing it [that reality] less, the more to the left they stood." "Today," however, Müller declared, "we have the chance to create a society that finally can be an attractive alternative in all respects."[13]

But what would this alternative be? As an editorial in *Student* confessed, "[t]he current situation desperately demands ideas, but they will not fall from the sky. . . . There is no one among us, friends, who is up to the task. Not even [student leaders] Holeček or Müller are the messiahs, nor do they want to be."[14] It seemed that the Czech student movement, which had begun its life in 1963 when the "Prague radicals" first infiltrated the official Youth Union, had since developed along the lines of what these students did not want. In 1968, faced with the possibility for change, students found it hard to envision what they did want, in large part because of their lack of practice in thinking about politics beyond the parameters of the Communist Party. At the same time, having experienced the application of "communism" first-hand, they were unable to imagine an idealized rosy (or "red") future as persistently as could their Western European counterparts.

"RED" RUDI DUTSCHKE IN PRAGUE

With Czech students anxious to define themselves as political beings, and with the Czech student movement still missing its crucial political platform, the Western European student movement was one of the few models available to them. Interestingly, *Student* carried little on the French demonstrations, and what it did bring to its readers about the events at Nanterre and on the streets of Paris was more informative than it was instructive or polemic. In contrast, the West German student movement, and particularly its charismatic leader Rudi Dutschke, made a more significant impact on Czech students, partly because of Germany's geographic proximity but also because of Dutschke's visit to Prague in April. Student Milan Hauner wrote about Rudi Dutschke for *Student*—first about Dutschke's visit to Prague, then about a visit by Czech students to see Dutschke in Berlin, and finally a multipart series about Dutschke's political philosophy.

In the first piece about "Red" Rudi's lecture trip to Prague, Hauner began by trying to describe the politics of the German student leader whose visit, he claimed, had been ignored by the Czechoslovak press "for unexplained reasons": "Is he a Maoist, Trotskyist, Marxist, even a Liebknechtist, or else simply an ordinary beatnik who provocatively enters into discussions . . . in the uniform of today's protesting youth: in jeans, a sweater, an overgrown shock of raven hair?" While Hauner was evidently curious as well as admiring of Dutschke, and particularly of Dutschke's command of a well-thought-out political language, Hauner also recognized that Dutschke's political interventions seemed out of context when spoken in communist Czechoslovakia: "[when he speaks,] German romanticism and revolutionary radicalism are wed. In our circumstances, he could perhaps gather only tired surprise [from his audience]." Nevertheless, it was Dutschke's charisma that had carried the day, according to Hauner, and in the end he had managed during the course of his lecture to overcome his listeners' initial apathy.[15]

Following Dutschke's formal presentation, the German student leader met with Czech students on a more informal basis, and it was here, as Hauner admitted, that a certain "embarrassing mutual schooling" took place. Dutschke was highly critical of current capitalism; on the other hand, he was excessively optimistic about its transformations under a "direct democracy." According to Hauner, "[a]mong our students, the situation was just about the opposite. And even Rudi's well-formulated phrases did not manage to convince our disillusioned ones that the future direct democracy with 'new people' will not lead to the abuse of power." In Hauner's assessment, Dutschke seemed to want to have his cake and eat it, too: "In his utopian combination he is trying to fuse the productive capacities of America with the ascetic morality of the Chinese."[16] Many of the Czech students in attendance obviously considered Dutschke naive in contrast to their "hard-won realism."

Yet Hauner remained intrigued by Dutschke and his obvious mastery of a new Marxist-based political language that, although admittedly utopian, nevertheless underscored the political provincialism lurking inside the Czechoslovak 1968 reform movement. As Hauner noted, "Dutschke long ago integrated the realities of the third world into his theories," while most Czech students remained woefully ignorant about the activities of their fellow students abroad.[17] Although the more radical Czech students had recognized this and had sworn to confront this problem through a political platform of their own, no such thing had yet happened. A short while after Dutschke's visit, a new student organization was formed to replace the previous official Youth Union. Named the Association of University Students, its members did present a "program," but one that amounted to little more than a list of demands with which the Dubček-led government could have easily agreed.[18] A week later, Karel Kovanda, the most radical of the student "Prague radicals," wrote in *Student* that "[t]oday the question apparently is not against what we're fighting, but for what we're fighting." In his opinion, any student organization that was to be "vibrant, long-term, and capable of action" would "necessarily have to be created from the bottom up."[19] While Kovanda seemed to favor some sort of Maoist-inspired student revolt (which he never clearly defined), it was becoming evident that the most that Czech students could offer was a replica of the already-established reform communist program that Dubček's government was pursuing.

Toward the end of May, news on the recent protests at the Sorbonne in Paris appeared in an article in *Student*. The conclusions drawn about the Paris events again reflected concerns about the Czech student movement itself:

> We must realize that only 8% of [French] students are from workers' families and the majority of students do not stand behind socialism or communism. . . . Here is the problem with the whole student movement. Many various groups, many various demands, many leaders, but behind it all there is little unity . . . without unity and without joining up with other layers of society, they will not win their most basic demands.[20]

Not only were Czech students keenly aware that they themselves lacked political coherence, but any earlier desire to replicate the Western European student movements was now quickly wearing off as they failed to locate a clear unity among French or German students as well.

Indeed, Milan Hauner was also sounding less positive about Rudi Dutschke after visiting him in Berlin in May with a Czech student delegation for a working seminar that had been arranged during Dutschke's earlier visit to Prague. Since then, Dutschke had been shot by an outraged German citizen and was now convalescing from the assassination attempt. At first unable to gain access to Dutschke, the Czech students were eventually contacted by his wife, who informed them that Dutschke was willing to meet; following a two-hour wait, they were brought in to see him: "He sat us around him and we immediately had to tell him how things were going. It was amazing to watch him. He was literally brimming with energy, burning with curiosity, and one could in no way tell that he was having difficulties with his memory or searching for words as the result of a dangerous injury to the brain." This almost Christ-like figure, holding court with the Czech students, proved to be increasingly fallible, however: As Hauner wrote, over the course of "two improvised discussion evenings, the deep disagreement between our group and the German interrogators visibly revealed itself."[21] Despite admiration for Dutschke, the different points of view of the Czech students versus the West German students inevitably clashed.

The crucial division between the two groups, as they saw it, centered on the German students' inability to distinguish utopia from reality, goals from the means to achieving those goals, and theory from practice: "We did not hide our deep skepticism toward any kind of perfect utopia," Hauner noted. The German students' main emphasis, he wrote, was "the creation of an ideal type socialist democracy whose main foundation had to be the control of production and decision-making by all workers based on a system of representative councils at all workplaces, for purposes of guaranteeing the growth of initiative from below." While they all agreed on this, since both sides were interested in discussing socialism, they ceased to agree the moment conversation turned to the practical application of these ideas. The Czech group insisted that the application of a theory "always rests on living people and historical conditions," making it messy and more complicated than initially anticipated. The German students, much to the annoyance of the Czech students, maintained their orthodox theories despite the Czechs offering them "an expansive palette of empirical examples based on our twenty year history." The Czech students increasingly began to feel that many among the German student group were being politically radical just for the sake of being so, and in fact willing to be so at any price.

ITALIAN "TERRORISM"

Hauner's article describing the visit to Dutschke did end on a positive note: Hauner believed that more Czech students finally were beginning to recognize the international links between student movements in industrially developed countries, be they capitalist or socialist. In other words, despite disagreement about political programs, harmony could potentially be reached on the basis of a critique of industrialized culture and its damage to democratic practices East and West. Indeed, yet another month later, in July, *Student* published an article in which the authors argued that the Strahov student demonstration in Prague had been part of the chain that recently had proven established regimes vulnerable to citizen protest. They further insisted that this generation's critique of industrialized society—the very bond, they explained, that tied Strahov to Berlin to Nanterre to Turin—was applicable across the capitalist-socialist divide; that is, the key elements of a youth-driven cultural revolution were relevant to both Eastern and Western Europe.

Yet, following this enthusiastic declaration, the two authors turned to the topic of the student revolt in Italy specifically. Here they judged the cultural revolution to have overstepped its boundaries, in the process becoming—they argued—an all-too-familiar sight to anyone who had lived through the 1950s in Czechoslovakia. It was understandable and acceptable that student protestors had brought the Cannes film festival in France to a halt; but what was not acceptable was that "the ultra-left student movement" had then proceeded to do the same at the socialist-organized and, therefore, presumably student- and worker-friendly Pesaro film festival in Italy. In their eyes, this, unlike the Cannes affair, had amounted to an unjustified act of "terrorism." The authors described how, in the name of revolutionary struggle, workers had been brought into the salon at Pesaro, and then, "as you will recall from the nineteen-fifties," a debate proceeded in which the workers were not asked their opinion, and after a while the workers simply "announced that they must return to work" and that these sorts of films did not interest them anyway.[22]

The Czech student authors concluded that "a program of absolute negation is no program at all" and that the problem with all of the student movements in Western Europe is that "they're missing any kind of practical experience with socialism." The results of this lack of experience could be seen in the current trend for "revolutionary snobbism" reminiscent of the "salon Bolshevism" of the 1930s in Czechoslovakia. Another aspect of this "revolutionary snobbism" was, according to the two authors, the Western European students' rejection of "Europeanism," and therefore also of Europe's political and cultural centrality. Czech students, in their own brand of "snobbism," found the Western student movements' rejection of Europe particularly irksome for it flew in the face of their own goals. While Italian students had taken to chanting, "Asia, Africa, Latin America, YES! Europe and North America, NO!" Czech students were trying to break away from the tutelage of the Soviet Union and openly reappropriate the label of "European."[23]

By late June 1968, the Prague radicals were polemicizing with the student officials of the recently formed Association of University Students on the pages of *Student*. Unlike the "Prague radicals," the association believed that Czech students' concerns should remain largely within the domain of student-related issues such as housing, class size, university admissions procedures, and so forth. Arguments between the two groups were audibly conducted against the backdrop of the Western European student movements about which Czech students had by now had time to learn and form an opinion. Petr Rybář, chair of the Association of University Students, discussed his views in an interview in *Student* where he explained that, to his mind, a Czech student movement did not in fact exist and was only revealed sporadically during crises such as Strahov and the days that followed. In answer to the question of why a majority of students remained politically passive, Rybář replied that this was the way it should be: "A student is a student, and his task is first and foremost to study."[24] In mid-July, Karel Kovanda replied that, on the contrary, more Czech students "are beginning to realize the similarities between our university system and that in Western Europe," both of which are breeding grounds for antiquated teaching methods and uncritical thinking. Moreover, with a new, left-thinking opposition emerging in Czechoslovakia, and with students taking trips to Western Europe for the summer, where they planned to acquire "new experiences with the student struggle," Kovanda predicted student unrest, protest, and political action in Prague in the autumn of 1968.[25]

A week later, Rostislav Pšenko, a founding member of the Association of University Students, offered a rebuttal to Kovanda and his "fellow Prague radicals." In his piece, he sardonically congratulated all Czech students on finally having achieved "all we could possibly want: a [political] right, left, and center." The political "right" had been represented recently in an article in *Kulturní Tvorba* (Cultural Production) by the Prague caucus of student-communists, whereas Kovanda, in his last article in *Student*, had put out the call for a Maoist cultural revolution come autumn, thus assuming the position of the "left." The Association of University Students (seeing itself as representing the political center) was thus far resisting both ends of the spectrum: on the one hand, holding off joining the ruling National Front until it could be sure of its reformist integrity and, on the other hand, negating calls by the Prague radicals for an immediate revolution.

What troubled Pšenko the most was Kovanda's demand that the Association of University Students not only remain outside the National Front— as they were in fact currently doing—but also that it step outside "democratic society" and exist on its more provocative margins. For whereas Pšenko agreed with Kovanda that Czechoslovakia belonged to the industrialized nations and shared many of the same problems, his concern was that the discrepancies between an industrialized Western Europe and an industrialized (but economically less successful) Eastern Europe be dealt with directly. Instead, Pšenko claimed, Kovanda was coating very real problems in Maoist or Guevara-infused language, leading Pšenko to recall the climate of 1930s Czechoslovakia when the Communist Party, instead of occupying itself with the genuine political problems facing the country, spent its time constructing Soviet-like statements. In other words, the Prague radicals were offering not solutions but mere phrases borrowed from elsewhere that were unsuitable to the experience of Czechoslovakia in 1968.

In fact, Pšenko continued, "I unfortunately believe, and many people with me, that these people [the Prague radicals] are more concerned that their colleagues in the West might laugh at them if they were to demand democratic institutions—this being such bourgeois rot."[26] In this vein, claimed Pšenko, the Prague radicals had been trying to shape the symbolism of Strahov in accordance with student protests in Western Europe when in fact Strahov had been a more politically ambiguous event. Pšenko argued that it was entirely "disorienting" for students to be told that "our 'little' Strahov demonstration" was on a par with recent Western European protests. For members of the new Association of University Students, the Western European and Czechoslovak political demonstrations had opposite purposes, appropriate to two significantly different contexts: Student protests in the West were a response to the reigning "extreme order" (represented by entrenched postwar governments) that the students wished to disturb and provoke and, thereby, ultimately challenge in the name of creating change; in Czechoslovakia, on the other hand, some sort of "order" based not on arbitrary Communist Party power but on popular demand was being created. Yet the most extreme of the Prague radicals, Karel Kovanda, in his overwhelming desire to copy his Western European student colleagues, was trying to take apart this new "order" before it had been even fully constructed.

In Pšenko's view, "[w]hat this society needs—having developed for twenty years in the opposite direction to the west—is genuine, democratic rights." To his mind, this was what he had been trying to do when he, along with the Prague radicals, first worked to shift student representation away from the monopoly of the party-led official Youth Union. But the Prague radicals then had gone further, continuing to work on the margins and resisting membership in any official organization, even if it were independent of the Communist Party, as was the newly created Association of University Students. The most powerful weapons against those who wished to halt the current democratizing process, Pšenko argued, "will be for quite some time, at least in this country, the classical weapons, such as institutions."[27] For this reason, institutions remained paramount to the political battle for "socialism with a human face."

POLAND 1968

In contrast to the Western European protests, the 1968 Polish student´ protests and the accompanying government-endorsed anti-Semitic attacks seemed more relevant to the Czechoslovak experience, filled not only with familiar episodes but also with related warnings about the volatile mixture of politics, protest, communism, and the very real possibility of Soviet or else domestic repression. The geographic as well as political proximity of the Polish case was felt in the reportage on Poland. Articles in both *Student* and *Literární Listy*, the weekly for the more established generation of the intelligentsia, nervously documented the fear felt on the streets of Warsaw and in personal encounters with Poles. Many Polish students, too—unlike some Italian students who in 1968 chanted, "We are not with Dubček. We are with Mao."[28]—felt linked to the Czechs and the Prague Spring, chanting in protest, "Bravo Czechs!" and "Poland is waiting for its Dubček!"[29]

The Polish and the Soviet Communist governments seemed also to believe that the Polish 1968 was related to the Czechoslovak Prague Spring, and vice versa. As articles in *Student* noted, journalists with the Czech press as well as Czech students had been turned away at the Polish border and not allowed to enter the country; both were viewed as agents of antistate dissent. It was reported in *Student* that in Warsaw the government had whipped up a public campaign that typecast both students and "Zionists" (read: Jews) as national traitors, claiming they were closely aligned with the antisocialist reformist forces in Czechoslovakia operating under the guidance of First Secretary Alexander Dubček.[30] In May, *Student* printed a translation of an interview in the Soviet press with Soviet minister of education V. N. Stoletov, who discussed the current "problems" in Poland: "When we're talking about individual lost sheep, it is not so hard to help them. Worse is when whole groups of them pop up and when their actions have nothing in common with the real interests of the people and the country." In the same breath, Stoletov then criticized the "Czechoslovak weekly *Student* [which], for example, recently started propagating the idea of creating a student organization that has nothing in common with the Communist Party and the *ČSM* [the official Youth Union]."[31]

When it came time to take steps against the Prague Spring, Poland's Communist leader Władysław Gomułka, afraid of the ideological penetration of the Czechoslovak-Polish border, "was one of the most ardent spokesmen in the Warsaw Pact urging [Soviet leader] Brezhnev to unleash the military action in Czechoslovakia."[32] It was perhaps the mutual recognition of both Polish and Czech students that they were not just playing with words—which, rightly or wrongly, they often assumed to be the case with student activists in the West—but in fact playing with fire, and a dangerous fire at that, which made their experiences seem more relevant to one another than did the cases of Berlin, Paris, or Turin.

CONCLUSION

Ironically, it was the Soviet-led invasion of Czechoslovakia on 21 August 1968 that politicized Czechoslovak students as never before; 30 percent of students had been politically "engaged" before August, whereas that percentage doubled in the autumn.[33] Students managed to organize a strike and issue a Ten Points manifesto in November, but the content of that manifesto revealed, as the sociologist Jiřina Šiklová would write, that there was in fact no student movement to speak of. Any student movement, as such, remained split between different ideological orientations, organizations, and locations (e.g., with Prague more radicalized than Brno); and ultimately, despite student leader Holeček's promise in March 1968 that youth would create their own alternate program, there was none, and students by and large promoted the same reformist program as Dubček's Prague Spring government.[34]

Moreover, as a result of their strike, which the students quickly saw had had no effect on the fast-disappearing reforms in a now Soviet-occupied Czechoslovakia, students split into two distinct groups: The majority of students sank back into political passivity, whereas a minority became even more radicalized. The radicalized students, influenced by the "new left" in the West, formed the "Movement of Revolutionary Youth," but its members were quickly brought to trial by the post–Prague Spring orthodox Communist government that took power in April 1969.[35] As for the passive majority, one Communist Party report from spring 1969 noted, "Among them are most of those who long for nothing other than for a satisfied, materially secured life, an idol to which they are willing to sacrifice everything, if not today then tomorrow."[36] And so the platform for post–Prague Spring "normalization" was born, with citizens encouraged to pursue the dream of materialism rather than the dream of revolution.

The claim was—and still is—frequently made that in 1968 Czech students were shaping politics, whereas Western European students were only playing politics. But an exploration of the Czech student movement suggests that the situation was far more complicated, with Czech students in fact finding themselves disoriented in the newly politicized environment of 1968. With the end of censorship came information, and as Czech students learned of their Western European counterparts, the majority of them did not in fact immediately relate Czechoslovakia's political needs to Western European students' demands. In Czechoslovakia, where the push for reforming communism had been initiated by worries over the sharply falling socialist economy, applying the ideas of Herbert Marcuse and his critique of industrialized consumerism—as some among the Prague radicals wished to do—seemed strangely out of place. Moreover, the inspiration derived by many student activists in the West from Maoist and Guevara-inspired revolution did not resonate among the majority of Czech students and, if anything, reminded them all too eerily of snapshots from their country's recent Stalinist past, a legacy with which Czechoslovakia was trying to come to terms rather than repeat.

In addition, whereas in Western Europe students attacked their governments and its affiliated institutions as purveyors of outdated hierarchies and oppressive systems, in Czechoslovakia many students argued that they needed to build up democratic institutions rather than tear them down. In this sense, they were never sure whether they were ahead of the students in the West by virtue of already having experienced the gritty realities of a revolutionary utopianism or else lagging behind their Western counterparts because they had yet to possess the sort of institutions that Western European students were already critiquing. Being "realistic" leftists, as they would argue, most Czech students tended to express opinions that converged with the Dubček-led government, rather than defied it, thereby further complicating the notion of student protest as "antigovernment" protest.

Juxtaposing the 1968 student movement in Western Europe with the Czechoslovak case offers up valuable insights. First, the "iron curtain" seems to have been less impenetrable than imagined, evidenced by the political dialogue between Eastern and Western Europeans prior to 1989. Second, the inherent difficulties of that dialogue, of finding a common political language with which to speak—a difficulty usually associated with the post-1989 period in Europe—was already present among students in 1968 when, as Milan Hauner noted, meetings between German and Czech students inevitably began with an "embarrassing mutual schooling," in which each side tried to explain their political "reality" to their impatient guests. Moreover, this "embarrassing mutual schooling" continued on into the 1980s in dialogues between Eastern European dissidents and Western European leftists: Eastern European dissidents were shocked by many of their Western colleagues' insistence on unilateral disarmament (which the Eastern European dissidents found to be entirely naive), whereas Western European leftists were horrified by the Eastern European dissidents' enthusiastic approval of Reaganite policies toward the Soviet bloc.

Third, and most interestingly, a transnational examination of the events of 1968 begins to undermine the distorted view of a Cold War discourse. Within this dominant discourse, communist Eastern Europe's economic lag is automatically extended to assume a concomitant political and cultural delay as well. But in 1968, while Czech students were certainly not politically well defined or organized, they were skilled social critics of the socialist system in which they lived. As such, they often found the hopes for a perfect socialist society—be it modeled on the ideas of Lenin, Stalin, Mao, Guevara, or Castro—unrealistic, outdated, and reminiscent of the misplaced faith of the older generation of Czech intelligentsia, students from the 1950s who, at most, had functioned as the party's "loyal opposition." From this perspective, one could say that it was the Western European students who were lagging behind.

But the 1968 Prague Spring did not only affect Czechs and Slovaks. The Warsaw Pact troops' physical intervention into Czechoslovakia, aimed solely to put an end to its political experiments, forced many Western leftists to rethink their relationship to communism. Interestingly, an Italian Communist named Avellino visited Prague in 1970 and reported that Jean-Paul Sartre's existentialism had become the "dominant ideological influence" among Czech students, just as it had been among French students in the early postwar years. This was not, he argued, a "cultural lag" but represented "the same cultural and ideological resentment. Static opposition. Existentialism as a polemical reply to normalization in the Prague of 1970."[37] Having experienced the bankruptcy of utopianism, Czech students returned to its antithesis in quiet protest.

NOTES

1. For more on the effects of Western cultural influences in communist Eastern Europe, see Paulina Bren, "Looking West: Popular Culture and the Generation Gap in Communist Czechoslovakia, 1969–1989," in *Representations and Cultural Exchanges across the Atlantic: Europe and the United States 1800–2000*, ed. Luisa Passerini (Brussels: PIE Lang, 2000).

2. Tad Szulc, *Czechoslovakia since World War II* (New York: Grosset & Dunlap, 1972), 194.

3. Alan Levy, *So Many Heroes* (New York: Second Chance Press, 1980), 66.

4. State Central Archives (Prague), Archive of the Central Committee of the Czechoslovak Communist Party; materials of the Ideological Commission (Fond 10/5); folder 6: *Problematika současné mladé generace*; materials for the seventeenth meeting of the Central Committee's Ideological Commission on 7 October 1965.

5. Jiřina Šiklová, "Ideály posluchačů Karlovy university," *Student* 49 (6 December 1967): 1.

6. Jiří Hanák, "O mostu inteligence," *Student* 13 (27 March 1968): 1.

7. "Beseda o únoru a dnešku s těmi co věděli, že svět patří jim," *Student* 8 (21 February 1968): 6.

8. "Podvědomy počit strachu hrůzy nelidkosti" [interview with Pavel Dvořák], *Student* 14 (3 April 1968): 3.

9. Document: "Záznam televizního rozhovoru šéfredaktora Televizních novin Československé televize Kamila Wintra s předsedou Svazu československých spisovatelů Eduardem Goldstückrem [4 February 1968, Prague]," in Jitka Vondrová, Jaromír Navrátil, and Jan Morvec, *Komunistická strana Československa: Pokus o reformu (říjen 1967—květen 1968)* (Brno: Doplněk, 1999), 66.

10. Ladislav Kadavý, "Válka je vůl: Pokus definici protestního pochodu," *Student* 9 (28 February 1968): 5.

11. Students associated most readily with the Prague radicals included Karel Kovanda, Jan Kavan, Jiří Müller, and Luboš Holeček. Yet the Prague radical position was never clearly defined in large part because it differed significantly from one member

to another. While Müller and Holeček had been pivotal in initiating organized student discontent, the government quickly managed to have them conscripted into the army, thereby limiting their political involvement and influence. Kavan and Kovanda thus became better known, with Kovanda emerging as the most radical of the "radicals." For more on this, see Milan Hauner, "Czechoslovakia," *Students, University and Society*, ed. Margaret Scotford Archer (London: Heinemann Education Books, 1972).

12. Open Society Archives (Budapest): Section: Czechoslovakia; subject file: Propaganda; folder: Rallies 1967–1971: Radio Transcript: "Pokračování diskuse ve Sjezdové paláci konaná 20.3.68," 170.

13. Jiří Müller, "Odmítali vnímat, co jsem jim řikal," *Student* 11 (13 March 1968): 5.

14. Ladislav Kadavý, "Co se děje mezi studenty," *Student* 16 (17 April 1968): 8.

15. Milan Hauner, "Rudý Rudi v Praze," *Student* 17 (24 April 1968): 1. At this formal gathering, Dutschke also offered his advice on the Czechoslovak Prague Spring. In his view, a "palace coup" by reactionary forces within the government existed as a real possibility. For this reason, the progressive students and others should not, Dutschke said, shy away from identifying "counter-revolutionaries" and moving against them.

16. Hauner, "Rudý Rudi v Praze," 4.

17. Hauner, "Rudý Rudi v Praze," 4.

18. These demands included the reduction of mandatory army service; the removal from government of persons responsible for past political injustices; participation in rethinking the organization and program of the ruling National Front; the cessation of phone tapping and mail intervention; the end of restrictions on travel within the country; and for those being charged with crimes, treatment according to "human principles." "Návrh programu Svazu vysokoškolských studentů," *Student* 18 (30 April 1968): 8.

19. Karel Kovanda, "Jakou chceme organizaci," *Student* 19 (7 May 1968): 7.

20. Milan Syruček, "Proč vlaje rudý a černý prapor nad Sorbonou," *Student* 22 (29 May 1968): 10.

21. Milan Hauner, "Rudi Dutschke v rekonvalescenci," *Student* 25 (19 June 1968): 4. All of the following quotations about the Czech students' visit to see Dutschke are from Hauner's article. Dutschke also informed them that the sociologist Herbert Marcuse—as Hauner explained to his readers, "considered the spiritual father of the contemporary student movement in the capitalist world"—wished to visit Czechoslovakia in the autumn to address student forums there.

22. Ivo Pondělíček and Jan Svoboda, "Dětské nemoci, Studentské moci,'" *Student* 29 (17 July 1968): 5.

23. Their *modus vivendi* was summed up by the philosopher Ivan Sviták and his "Ten Commandments for a Young Czechoslovak Intellectual." Commandment 6 read, "Don't think only as a Czech or a Slovak, think also like a European. . . . You live in Europe; you don't live in America nor in the Soviet Union." Ivan Sviták, "Desatero přikázání pro mladého intelektuála," *Student* 11 (13 March 1968): 1.

24. "Student má studovat" [interview with Petr Rybář by Ladislav Kadavý], *Student* 25 (19 June 1968): 5.

25. Karel Kovanda, "Bude v Praze studentská revolta?" *Student* 29 (17 July 1968): 1.

26. Rostislav Pšenko, "Jak 'revoltovat,'" *Student* 30 (24 July 1968): 4–7.

27. Pšenko, "Jak, revoltovat." Jiří Müller responded to Pšenko in the 14 August issue of *Student*, but his objections largely centered around Pšenko's presumption in lumping the Prague radicals together when, in fact, "they all have very different opinions."

28. Stuart J. Hilwig, "The Revolt against the Establishment: Students versus the Press in West Germany and Italy," in *1968: The World Transformed*, ed. Carole Fink, Philipp Gassert, and Detlef Junker (Cambridge: Cambridge University Press, 1998), 338.

29. Milan Kroutva, "Polsko. Varšava," *Student* 14 (3 April 1968): 4.

30. V.S., "Varšavské ticho," *Student* 22 (29 May 1968): 1.

31. Student editorial staff, "'Student' ovečka zbloudilá," *Student* 21 (22 May 1968): 7.

32. Jerzy Eisler, "March 1968 in Poland," in *1968: The World Transformed*, 250.

33. Kieran Williams, *The Prague Spring and Its Aftermath: Czechoslovak Politics, 1968–1970* (Cambridge: Cambridge University Press, 1997), 179.

34. Jiřina Šiklová, "Existuje u nás studentská 'new left'?" *Listy*, 21 November 1968.

35. For more on this see the article by one of its members: J. Suk, "Československá radikální levice," *Svědectví* 17, no. 67 (1982).

36. As quoted in Williams, *Prague Spring*, 251.

37. Open Society Archives (Budapest): Radio Free Europe Research Report, 11 November 1970; as quoted in Kevin Devlin, "Czech Youth Reject Normalization—Says Italian Communist."

8

Echoes of Provocation

1968 and the Women's Movements in France and Germany

Kristina Schulz

There is no doubt that 1968 constituted a turning point in the history of the Western world, though it is only recently that the events have become a topic of historical research. There are a variety of perspectives on the emergence of the protest movements. Scholars have interpreted the events as the expression of a general crisis of society, as the outbreak of a generational conflict,[1] as the climax of a cultural revolution,[2] as a youth revolt or—and in the following I will adhere to this approach—as a social movement.[3] More obscure than the emergence of 1968—following Detlev Claussen, I use the expression "1968" as a symbolic marker for a complex mixture of "hard" historical facts and subsequent, after-the-fact bestowal of supposed meanings—remains the question of its legacy. Whereas some commentators, often not without nostalgic undertones, insist on the influence of 1968 on individuals, groups, and institutions, others deny the catalytic effect of the protest wave.[4]

The partially contradictory nature of those positions not only results from differing ideological standpoints, interests, and values of scholars, former protagonists, and witnesses of the events but also reflects an analytical problem. Social movements[5] are by definition simultaneously cause *and* consequence of social change. Thus, it is difficult to differentiate between those changes that can be attributed to the action of protest movements and those changes that must be imputed to other factors of social transformation. The examination of one particular aspect of this question, the impact of that protest movement on subsequent social movements, is the focus of this chapter. Has 1968, as it is often stated,[6] provided the space for the emergence of the ecology movement, the peace movement, and/or the women's movement? Were those new movements a kind of "reincarnation" of the "spirit of

1968"? And, if so, was this a transnational phenomenon? Or is the relationship between 1968 and the new social movements only the result of retrospective construction, a sort of subsequently created founding myth of the new social movements? My analysis will focus on the German and French women's movements, as I take the women's movements to be emblematic for the post-1968 "new social movements."[7] To what extent have the formation processes of these movements been influenced by 1968?

I shall first focus on the campaigns in favor of the liberalization of abortion laws (Article 317 and Paragraph 218 in France and Germany, respectively).[8] The campaigns started in the spring of 1971 and were a constitutive element of both the French and the German women's movements of the 1970s, even if neither abortion campaign reached the aim of free and legalized abortion. After providing a general outline of the abortion campaign's origins, I sketch out the main features of the dynamics of mobilization. Which groups initiated the manifestos leading off the campaigns in both countries? Who supported the feminists' activism, and how did the authorities react? If this first part emphasizes the parallel development of the French and the German case, in the next section I will sketch out particularities of the mobilization processes in Germany and France. A comparison will show that one reason for the successful mobilization of the German women's movement in the abortion campaign was that in 1971 German feminists could rely on mobilization structures that had emerged in the context of 1968 to a higher degree than was the case for their French sisters. In the conclusion I argue that, despite some differences, both cases show strong similarities that are not accidental but (at least partly) due to the legacy of 1968.

THE MOVEMENT FOR ABORTION REFORM IN THE 1970s

The principle of self-determination over one's body plays an important role in Western democratic societies. For the last thirty years this is illustrated by the vigorous public discourse on, for instance, drug consumption or organ donorship. As questions of the individual's dignity and autonomy are at stake, those themes raise complex discussions in which moral, medical, and social arguments become relevant. As a regulating element of the sexual order,[9] family policies and the question of reproduction have always played an important role in the discourse on the relationship between state/law and the individual's self-determination. Women's opposition to the continued illegal status of abortion in the 1970s can be seen as a challenge to the sexual order as such. As the interdiction of abortion was based on an "official" public consensus in Western democracies, the attempt to break with this consensus immediately became an international phenomenon. In the early 1970s, abortion became a topic on the public agenda in many countries, such as the United States, the Netherlands, Belgium, and Italy.

In France and Germany, public resistance by women began with a provocation. In April 1971, one of the most important journals in France, *Le Nouvel Observateur*, published the signatures of 343 French women prominent in public life, demanding free abortion on demand and admitting that they themselves had had an abortion. German journalist Alice Schwarzer organized a similar action in Germany during the spring of that year. In June 1971, a manifesto signed by 374 German women appeared in the magazine *Stern*.[10] Schwarzer functioned as the direct intermediary between the German and the French women's movements in the take-off period, as she had been in contact with women's groups in Paris and assisted in the preparation of the action in Paris.[11] Unlike its French counterpart, the German manifesto was not signed by prominent writers, artists, and actors such as Simone de Beauvoir, Marguerite Duras, and Jeanne Moreau but by socially very heterogeneous women: housewives, academics, workers, and the like. The overwhelming majority of signatories came from Berlin, Munich, Frankfurt, Cologne, and Bonn, the centers of activities of a network called Aktion 218, which had been founded in the spring of 1971 as a sort of national coordinating committee of the diverse groups connected to the abortion struggle in Germany.

Who did these groups represent? Two types of groups can be distinguished. The first entailed informal groups that were rooted in the antiauthoritarian student movement, like the group Bread and Roses, the West Berlin League of Socialist Women (SFWB) and the Red Women of Munich. The second consisted of more institutionalized associations, such as the Humanistische Union, the social democratic and liberal political parties' youth organizations, and some adult education circles.

The French manifesto had been organized by a subcommittee specializing on the abortion issue within the overall Women's Liberation Movement (MLF) in Paris. The MLF existed since the summer of 1970. The name had been invented by journalists commenting on a French solidarity demonstration with the American women's liberation movement at the Arc de Triomphe in August 1970. The demonstration had been organized by women belonging to the first French second-wave feminist group, Feminisme, Marxisme, Action (FMA). The FMA was created in 1967 and joined in 1968 by Christine Delphy, who would soon become a popular feminist researcher,[12] as well as some others, among them the novelist Monique Wittig, who was about to separate from the Groupe de Vincennes (discussed later). Since the fall of the same year, regular meetings took place, at first in private apartments, then (as the number of women increased) in the rooms of the École des Beaux Arts in the center of Paris. Whereas abortion had been a frequently discussed subject within the MLF from the beginning, it was only in January 1971 that one group specialized on the theme and started preparing the campaign, which finally emerged in full view of the public with the manifesto "I have had an abortion."

This self-denunciation was a violation of the law and deliberately meant to challenge the authorities. The French media, which up to that moment had tended to avoid an open debate on abortion, picked up this theme. It became the object of public controversy in newspapers (*Le Monde* reprinted the whole list of women one day after *Le Nouvel Observateur*) as well as on radio and television. Were the authorities (police and courts) willing to intervene? The women feared inquiries and accusations. It was rumored that suspicious persons would be persecuted. People said that a gynecologist had been arrested when he was about to procure an abortion and that more than one hundred women would be in danger of being arrested.[13] The lawyer Gisèle Halimi[14] spontaneously promised to give legal support.[15] But despite these rumors, none of the 343 women was juridically pursued. The provocation was successful, in that the prominence of the signatories protected them from any accusation. This lack of consistency between the law and its application once again revealed, so the manifesto's initiators argued, the hypocritical character of abortion legislation.

As was the case in France, the self-denunciation of German women shocked the broader public and scandalized representatives of the church, the traditional medical profession's associations, and the conservative political parties. Even before the manifesto was published on 6 June 1971 in *Stern*, a newspaper reported that "374 women attempt to overthrow the *bürgerliche Moral*."[16] The government announced its intention to pursue each case as a violation of the law.[17] In the course of the month of June 1971, criminal investigators searched countless private apartments trying to find evidence that individuals and associations were involved in illegal practices related to abortion. Even if in the end no actual indictments occurred,[18] those threatening gestures had a dual effect on the movement. First, growing pressure on the activists provoked not only extensive expressions of solidarity within the population but also a growing awareness of the subordinate position of women (in their relations with their gynecologists, with the defenders of "law and order," and with men as such). Second, the various groups demanding free abortion moved closer together and intensified communication and organization. At a coordinating meeting in Frankfurt that June, all groups associated with Aktion 218 agreed on a common goal: the abolition of Paragraph 218.[19] The manifesto thus provided the opening shot of a nationwide mobilization of abortion rights groups that, sooner or later, separated from their masculine supporters and increasingly adopted feminist points of view. After the publication of the self-denunciation in June 1971, in almost every German town women's groups were called into being, loosely connected by Aktion 218. These groups started various projects and actions, focusing in the beginning on the abortion theme but later articulating the problem of women's oppression in multiple fields.

In France, only a part of the MLF actively supported the abortion campaign, even though all constituent groups were firmly opposed to the abortion laws then in effect. During the preparations, critical voices were raised from within the ranks of the MLF, criticizing the "reformist character" of the manifesto. Such "collaboration" with the mass media would not lead to the abolition of Article 317 but would instead strengthen the position of the established moral and sexual order.[20] This was especially the opinion of a group called Psychanalyse et Politique that, within the MLF, increasingly adopted an "antifeminist" position, struggling not in the name of "equality" (e.g., the women around Christine Delphy, the FMA[21] and the symbolic point of reference of the feminist struggle, Simone de Beauvoir) but in the name of "difference."[22] If the abortion campaign nevertheless grew rapidly, it was because other groups and organizations joined the MLF, like the French Family Planning Movement, Choisir, the main French trade unions and medical associations, especially the National Association for the Study of Abortion (ANEA) and the Health Information Group (GIS). Thus the campaign became, little by little, "professionalized" and "specialized." In 1973, the Movement for Free Abortion and Contraception (MLA) was founded as an officially registered association that brought together representatives from all groups connected to the abortion struggle. MLA members were asked to participate in a commission officially convened to study the abortion issue by the Ministry of Culture, Family, and Social Affairs in the summer of 1973. The "Berger Commission" discussed concrete propositions concerning the reform of the abortion legislation.[23] Most supporters of the abortion campaign viewed this as a great success. However, these feminists paid the price for this official recognition. The topic of abortion could no longer serve as the subject of a purely *feminist* struggle. Once absorbed by other, more powerful actors of the public domain, the theme remained only partly a "woman's question."

To recapitulate: We can say that both the German and the French women's movements of the 1970s were successful in mobilizing against the abortion legislation. To put abortion on the agenda of a public debate they had recourse to a form of action that, by its provocative character, was in the tradition of the "direct actions" of the movements of 1968. I will now examine some select aspects of the movements of 1968 in Germany and France to determine whether they may explain the dynamics of mobilization of the respective women's movements.

1968 AND WOMEN'S LIBERATION:
THE GERMAN ANTIAUTHORITARIAN MOVEMENT

After having assisted in the preparation of the publication of the *Nouvel Observateur* manifesto in Paris in spring 1971, Alice Schwarzer, as mentioned earlier, decided to search for allies in order to realize a similar action in Germany.

In contrast to her sisters in Paris, she could not rely on established organizational structures. She first addressed the SFWB, which supported Schwarzer's idea. The SFWB was indirectly the successor of the first women's group created in the context of 1968, the Women's Liberation Action Council (Aktionsrat), founded in 1968.[24]

The Aktionsrat is a good example of how micromobilization contexts have an influence on emerging activism.[25] Its initiators were women connected to the antiauthoritarian student movement, among them Helke Sander, a student at the Academy of Film and Television in Berlin; Dorothea Ridder, member of the famous Kommune I; and Sigrun Fronius, president of the Allgemeiner Studentenausschuss (AstA), the student government, at the Free University of Berlin.[26] All of them sympathized with the Socialist German Student League (SDS), which had a leading position in the nationwide student movement since 1967. In 1967–1968, the dominant fraction of the SDS defended the ideas of the Neue Linke, the German variant of a new and transnational socialist current that arose in the early 1960s in the United States and Great Britain (New Left), France (Nouvelle Gauche), Italy (Nuova Sinistra), and Germany (Neue Linke) and that crucially influenced the social movements of 1968.[27] The intellectual current of the New Left tried to make Marxist theory receptive toward existentialist and psychoanalytic argumentations and approaches, expanding beyond the sphere of production to include equally the sphere of reproduction. The New Left conception of organization was based on decentralized groups *resulting* from emancipatory processes, in contradistinction to traditional modes of operation where tightly structured political parties were to lead and guide emancipatory processes. The defenders of New Left thought believed that provocative and direct actions would have a greater mobilizing effect than—as was the traditional Marxist conviction—patient and painstaking political education. Although the members of the Aktionsrat shared New Left ideas, they criticized the fact that student activists did not take into account the problem of women's oppression. Aktionsrat members started to rebel against their male colleagues, asking them to support women in their struggle for the liberation and equality of both sexes.[28]

The Aktionsrat developed an action strategy based on the idea that "the private was political." If actually existing relationships between men and women and parents and children reflected the dominant structures of society, these power relations could only be overcome by the transformation of "private" relationships. The members of the Aktionsrat did not restrict these activities to the level of theoretical reflection. In the spring of 1968, they opened the first "antiauthoritarian child care center" in West Berlin, which served not only as a model for similar projects elsewhere in West Berlin but also in other German cities. The kindergartens occupied hastily renovated former small storefronts (*Tante-Emma-Läden*). The project of the so-called

Kinderläden was linked to the transformation strategy of the New Left, which placed the idea of counterinstitutions as effective means to change society on center stage. Monika Seifert, the initiator of the Kinderläden-like *Frankfurter Kinderschule*, declared that "each counterorganization challenging the institutions of our present-day society will broaden the basis of the antiauthoritarian movement."[29]

Theoretically, the Kinderläden experiments referred to the *Studien über Autorität und Familie*[30] elaborated in the 1930s and 1940s by the Frankfurt Institute for Social Research and the institute's research on the "authoritarian personality."[31] From the antiauthoritarian point of view, rigidity and repression in traditional education severely compromise the free development of an individual by causing a lack of willpower and promoting voluntary subordination to authorities. Against this nefarious development the Kinderläden defended instructional principles emphasizing the child's autonomy and freedom. The antiauthoritarian position crucially referred to Theodor Adorno's expression that "an education that wants to prevent the repetition [of fascism] has to concentrate on the young child."[32] The initiators of the Kinderläden, mainly parents of small children who were usually loosely connected to the student movement, studied not only the aforementioned works of the Frankfurt School but also the related writings of Herbert Marcuse, Erich Fromm, and Wilhelm Reich.[33] At the end of the 1920s, the latter had worked on studies on the larger implications of the Russian Revolution and particularly on the role of sexuality in the transformation process. His analysis, entitled *The Sexual Revolution*, was first published in Paris in 1930 and reprinted in Germany in 1966.[34] Reich emphasized the importance of a child's free sexual development. His main argument was that social transformation presupposes sexual liberation. It was this idea, combined with Herbert Marcuse's reinterpretation of psychoanalysis, that influenced the normative orientation of the antiauthoritarian child care activists in the late 1960s.

On a more practical level, the activists were inspired by two innovative concrete educational experiences and projects: the Summerhill Schools, founded in 1921 by Alexander S. Neill (a summary of their experiences was published in German as a paperback in 1969)[35] and the Moscow Child Laboratory. A description and analysis of this early Soviet educational experiment dating back to the 1920s was reprinted in 1968 by the Kommune 2, which was centrally engaged in the Kinderläden affair.[36] Both projects were based on the idea that children were able to handle their needs without any help from adult "educators."

This concept of "self-regulation" led to two reflections. First, the initiators of the Kinderläden appealed to society as a whole to take care of its children. If the prevention of the formation of authoritarian personalities was a collective duty, society had to guarantee conditions in which free development of individuality was possible.[37] Second, the antiauthoritarian concept of education in the late 1960s attributed more importance to the educating person than was the case in both the Summerhill Schools and the Moscow Child Laboratory. As it revalorized the work of child rearing, the antiauthoritarian conception of society thus elevated the work of many women. Mothers (and fathers) could contribute to social and political transformation by refusing to transmit capitalist principles of competition and efficiency to the next generation. The women's movement of the 1970s expanded on these themes, advocating public recognition of women's work in society; thus, one may talk of a partial transfer of normative elements from one particular protest movement to its successor.

But the legacy of 1968 did not only concern the normative dimension. The women engaged in the Kinderläden projects also acquired organizational skills and mobilization know-how.[38] Many of them joined the free-abortion campaign in 1971 and soon became women's movement activists.[39] Therefore, it is not at all astonishing that many forms of action and organization of the women's movement stem from the action repertoire of the antiauthoritarian movement. At the origin of antiauthoritarian activism in the 1968 era was the "action concept" *Aufklärung durch Aktion* (Enlightenment through Action), which implicitly and explicitly rejected "enlightenment" through theoretical instruction. Such action-oriented concepts also influenced feminist mobilization strategies. The Aktionsrat also served as a model for women in some other cities in West Germany.[40]

Thus, the activities of women in 1968 contributed to the rise of a communication structure that could be reactivated as late as three years after the demobilization of the German movement of 1968. The successful mobilization of the German abortion campaign was partly due to a central element of social movements: their capacity to mobilize and to tie together existing networks by means of "personal relations, that is to say through a complex structure of immediate interaction."[41]

THE FRENCH CASE

What does the French case suggest about the relation between the ideas and practices of 1968, on the one hand, and the rise of the women's movement and the struggle for free abortion, on the other? As far as the cognitive dimension was concerned, the French activists of 1968 were as much influenced by the ideas of the New Left (Nouvelle Gauche) as their German comrades. They put the category of "alienation," introduced by the young Marx, at the center of their reflections on power relations in society. This keyword, more than the mature Marx's category, "exploitation," allowed New Left activists to relate the project of emancipation to the spheres of production *and* reproduction, at the same time facilitating their understanding of revolution not purely in political terms but equally in terms of the transformation of everyday life.

This attention to everyday transformation can be seen clearly in a manifesto entitled "De la misère en milieu étudiant" (On the Poverty of Student Life), published in 1966 by the *Internationale Situationiste*.[42] The authors claimed that the university was the creation of two authoritarian systems, the family and the state. By adjusting the university to the needs of industry and publicity, capitalism endeavored to submit the academic world to the principles of supply and demand. Many students reacted by an uncontrolled consumption of cultural goods. This could give them the illusion to choose and to act freely, but, the authors contended, in reality they were manipulated by the logic of capitalism. Other students coped with the situation by transforming their economic subjugation into a sort of bohemia, a lifestyle that, from the authors' point of view, was likewise merely an illusion of liberty. In sum, they argued, students unconsciously reproduced the traditional structures of capitalist class-society; this overdetermination would even go as far as dominating their erotic relations.

The alienation within family and couples was the subject of a manifesto of an action committee, "Nous sommes en marche" (We Are Marching Forward), which had been created after the events of the "Night of the Barricades" on 10 May 1968.[43] Here the committee members went so far as to put into question all present norms, especially the notions of "fatherhood" and "motherhood." They defended the idea that these repressive products of family ideology should be overcome, since such restrictions would favor the functionalization, hierarchization, and alienation of the relationships between parents and children instead of providing room for individual self-realization. Only a free, fulfilled, and autonomously governed sexuality that was not intended to serve the function of reproduction could, so the argument went, guarantee the individual's self-determination.

The supporters of the French movement, like the Germans, thus pursued an emancipatory strategy that addressed simultaneously the individual and society. On the one hand, they appealed to the collectivity to take responsibility for birthrates, child rearing, and education. On the other hand, they emphasized the individual's contribution to a society that would be free of oppression and alienation. They interpreted actually existing interhuman relationships in terms of domination and submission, identifying women and children as the main victims of such conditions. Here the activists of the movement of May 1968 recurred to the ideas of the New Left; they used the keyword "alienation" to analyze not only production but also reproduction processes. A revolution of everyday life was to challenge at the same time the cultural, political, and economic order of society.

Did French activists *act* according to these theoretical reflections? Some traces are to be found, as, for instance, the spontaneously organized *crèches sauvages* (unauthorized child care centers). The first autonomous kindergartens opened in May 1968 in the occupied Sorbonne. The initiators tried to realize the principles of what they wanted all educational institutions to be: assurance of proximity to the parent's workplace and flexible opening hours.[44] The Sorbonne project served as a model for the creation of similar institutions at the Universities of Vincennes and Nanterre.[45] In the first place, the kindergartens' objective was to share child care. This had become a necessity during the events of May 1968, when revolutionary activism was a time-consuming enterprise. In the second place, the idea was to prevent the reproduction of structures of domination.[46] The problem of women's subordination in society was not mentioned in this context, although the students were aware of the concept of "sexual segregation." The topic had been the trigger of the student protest in Nanterre in March 1967. The only group that was preoccupied with the theme of "women's liberation" and gender relationships in 1968 was the aforementioned group FMA. But FMA did not participate in the organization and realization of the crèches sauvages.

Another group that was not influenced by the Kinderläden experience traced its origins to 1968. "In the beginning," explained its leader, Antoinette Fouque, in 1979, "in October 1968, we were three: . . . three women, daughters of the antiauthoritarian revolt of May 68."[47] The circle soon became the group Psychanalyse et Politique. Fouque, a journalist and lecturer, was very much inspired by the early postwar debates in the psychoanalytical community about female sexuality.[48] In the 1960s she discovered Jacques Lacan's work. The Centre Expérimental de Vincennes, begun by Lacan in late 1968 in the newly opened University of Vincennes in the eastern banlieu of Paris, attracted highly politicized students, including Fouque.[49] Various political groups and circles, mainly sympathizing with the extreme left, were to be found here, and the debate on society's revolutionary transformation was omnipresent. In this context, it was easy for Fouque to convene a group of female students interested in the question of women's subordination. They met irregularly and at a variety of venues and had no contact with other feminist groups and associations, so that the period up to 1970 is barely documented. Yet we know that in the spring of 1970 an open clash broke out between the Vincennes women's group and male "revolutionaries" about the question of how to introduce women's oppression into reflections on general societal oppression.[50]

Inspired by the writings of Lacan and Derrida, Fouque's group did not share the essentialist view of egalitarian feminism like most of the MLF adherents but instead referred to structuralist and psychoanalytic argumentations. They put "difference" at the center of their reflections on women, and it was that notion of *différence* that became a keyword of French feminism, particularly when "exported" abroad.[51] Their reflections on how to overcome women's subordination were based on psychoanalytical knowledge favoring the individual development of the human being over collective action. Mass mobilization as attempted by the abortion campaign corresponded neither to their self-understanding as an intellectual vanguard nor to their project to change society by changing the structures of the psyche.

CONCLUSION

The comparison of the legacy and heritage of the antiauthoritarian child care centers in France and Germany leads to the following reflections. First, we can say that the project of a future nonrepressive society was common to the French and the German movement of 1968 writ large. But in France, the theme of education, though included in the agenda of the May 1968 movement, did not result in further theoretical reflections on liberation and still less on women's liberation. The link between emancipation from authoritarian personality structures and women's emancipation, propagated by the Aktionsrat, was a particularity of the German movement. This could be one of the reasons why the connection between the emancipatory demands of the German movement of 1968 and those of the women's movement some years later were more evident than in the French case.

Despite these national particularities, the examination of the various social movements that occurred between 1968 and the beginning of the 1970s shows how strongly the mobilization of the women's movements in both countries depended on the character and the development of the social movement of 1968. Christine Delphy's question—"Was '68 the trigger to the [women's] movement or was it coincidence?"[52]—must be answered in a differentiated but unequivocal way. In both France and Germany, the formation of the women's groups in the seventies was influenced by 1968 in a variety of ways.

Micromobilization Contexts

Thus, the micromobilizations of 1968 in West Berlin and other university towns in Germany and in Paris, especially at the University of Vincennes, favored the creation of the very first women's groups in the course of 1968 (the Aktionsrat and similar groups, the Groupe de Vincennes, and in a certain way FMA). Though the women's group of Vincennes remained isolated and did not get into contact with FMA until the spring of 1970, its existence is largely due to the politicized atmosphere of the *après-mai*.

The development in other countries seems to strengthen the argument that existing formal and informal networks promoted the foundation of women's groups. In the United States, for example, many radical feminists began in the civil rights and the student movements; some of them had been active in the community organizing projects of the early 1960s. Functioning communication structures and personal relations preceding the women's liberation movement contributed there to the successful mobilization of feminist groups in the late 1960s.[53] Personal ties based in local structures had a mobilizing effect that was not limited to the local. On the contrary, they contributed to the rapid diffusion of information and ideas. This diffusion was not only nationwide but also transnational and, in the case of the United States, even transcontinental. In 1970, for example, the first collection of feminist texts in the history of the French second wave women's movement was published in Paris. *Libération des femmes: Année zero* included more than ten articles written by American feminists. Two years later German feminists likewise published a collection of articles by American feminists.[54]

We have some information about the transmission channels of those crossborder phenomena. They were frequently a result of visits and exchanges. Before joining FMA in Paris in 1968, Christine Delphy had been a student in Chicago and Berkeley and an activist in the civil rights movement. We already mentioned Alice Schwarzer who, after initiating the German manifesto on abortion in 1971, kept in regular contact with the MLF. More evidence could be easily adduced to show the reality and importance of the international circulation of feminists (or those who would become feminists), and their ideas, in the 1960s and early 1970s. We now turn, accordingly, to the cognitive dimension.

Cognitive Orientation

The ideas of the New Left are responsible for a great deal of the similarity between movement histories in France and Germany. The women's movements linked up with the New Left critique of authoritarian structures in bureaucratic and interhuman relationships. They conceived of "revolution" not only with regard to the public and economic realm but also as a key element in the transformation of everyday life. The antiauthoritarian project, indeed, questioned the distinction between the public and the private. The post-1968 women's groups claimed that the "private" was "political."

From this perspective, it was not difficult for the women's movement to reinterpret the terms of "exploitation" by, for instance, challenging the distribution of housework between men and women,[55] and then to add an analysis of power relations in terms of "alienation" by broaching the issues of rape and domestic violence. Indeed, activists working in homes for battered women (*Frauenhäuser, maisons des femmes*) demonstrated how feminist ideas became internationally important. Erin Pizzey's book, *Scream Quietly, the Neighbours Will Hear*, which, in 1974, provided the initial stimulus for anti–domestic violence initiatives in Great Britain, appeared in 1975 in a French and in 1976 in a German translation and inspired the creation of many battered women's shelters on both sides of the Rhine.

The two women's movements also shared the ideas of a decentralized and antihierarchical organizational form emerging from the activist context of 1968. This was particularly the case in Germany where, from 1973 onward, women's centers and women's journals spread to almost every city.[56] But the French MLF likewise adhered to the antihierarchical organizational model.

Dynamics of Interaction

The New Left project to promote antiauthoritarian interactions among partners, parents and children, colleagues, and others partly remained theory even within the antiauthoritarian movement. On the level of the interaction between the first women's groups and the male "revolutionaries," it is clear that the women's explicit break with male forms of activism had to do with the fact that even inside the movement of 1968, the antiauthoritarian principles were realized at best only partially. Even the Kommune 2, whose explicit aim was to practice an antiauthoritarian way of life, failed in the attempt to realize complete equality between the sexes. In their report on the community experiment of 1967–1969, Kommune 2 activists noted that the requirements of a "revolutionary praxis" were not attuned to the different modes in which men and women experienced their respective reality.[57] There is much evidence that the behavior of left-wing men toward women did not differ decisively from societal norms. The best example of the persistent male ignorance with regard to women's oppression was their reaction to Helke Sander's speech in September 1968:[58] Male SDS representatives remained silent. What had rather changed were the expectations of left women with regard to the dominant rhetoric of equality and liberation in 1968.

Remembering 1968

This discrepancy between "revolutionary" discourse and "revolutionary" reality explains the ambivalent attitude of the women's movements toward 1968. For the French and for the German women's movements of the 1970s—and even up to the present—1968 has become a founding myth, sometimes in the form of a countermyth, since many radical feminists in both movements describe 1968 as a mostly male-dominated movement and criticize the "sexual revolution" as part of a sexual order favoring female discrimination. Other groups or persons stress the explosive effect of 1968 and its challenge to the social and sexual order. However, apart from these differing opinions, both fractions of the women's movement admit the significance of 1968, whether by directly referring to the ideas of 1968 or by criticizing their unsatisfactory realization.

To summarize, it is true that 1968 has influenced collective memory. But it is also true that 1968 was not only a turning point in terms of retrospective identification. The legacy of 1968 cannot be exclusively relegated to the level of memory work and mythmaking. The feminist echoes of 1968 are also audible and visible at the level of mobilization contexts, cognitive orientations, and interaction dynamics.

NOTES

1. Ronald Fraser, ed., *1968: A Student Generation in Revolt* (London: Chatto & Windus, 1988); Hervé Hamon and Patrick Rotman, *Génération*, 2 vols. (Paris: Seuil, 1988).

2. Arthur Marwick, *The Sixties: Cultural Revolution in Britain, France, Italy, and the United States, c. 1958–c. 1974* (Oxford: Oxford University Press, 1998).

3. See, for instance, Ingrid Gilcher-Holtey, *"Die Phantasie an die Macht": Mai 68 in Frankreich* (Frankfurt: Suhrkamp, 1995).

4. Claus Leggewie, "1968: Ein Laboratorium der nachindustriellen Gesellschaft? Zur Tradition der antiautoritären Revolte seit den sechziger Jahren," *Aus Politik und Zeitgeschichte* 38/1, no. 20 (1988): 3–25. On 1968, see Detlev Claussen, "Chiffre 68," in *Revolution und Mythos*, ed. Dieter Harth and Jan Assman (Frankfurt: Fischer, 1992), 219–28.

5. Friedhelm Neidhardt and Dieter Rucht, "The Analyses of Social Movements," in *Research on Social Movements: The State of the Art in Western Europe and the USA*, ed. Dieter Rucht (Frankfurt: Campus, 1991), 421–64.

6. On this, see, for instance, Karl-Werner Brand, "Kontinuität und Diskontinuität in den neuen sozialen Bewegungen," in *Neue soziale Bewegungen in der Bundesrepublik Deutschland*, ed. Roland Roth and Dieter Rucht (Bonn: Bundeszentrale für Politische Bildung, 1987), 40–54; Ulrich K. Preuß, "Die Erbschaft von '1968' in der deutschen Politik," in *Opposition als Triebkraft der Demokratie. Bilanzen und Perspektiven der zweiten Republik: Jürgen Seifert zum 70. Geburtstag*, ed. Michael Buckmiller and Joachim Perels (Hannover: Offizin, 1998), 149–63.

7. According to Dieter Rucht, new social movements are characterized by a skepticism toward so-called modernization processes, a decentralized organizational structure, and a transformation strategy focusing on both structural and individual/psychological changes. Sociologically, new social movements are rooted in the new middle classes. See Dieter Rucht, *Modernisierung und neue soziale Bewegungen: Deutschland, Frankreich und USA im Vergleich* (Frankfurt: Campus, 1994), 154. The theoretical literature on new social movements has been mushrooming in the last fifteen years. For an overview, see Russell J. Dalton and Manfred Kuechler, *Challenging the Political Order: New Social and Political Movements in Western Democracies* (Cambridge: Polity, 1990); Doug McAdam, John D. McCarthy, and Meyer N. Zald, eds., *Comparative Perspectives on Social Movements: Political Opportunities, Mobilizing Structures, and Cultural Framings* (Cambridge: Cambridge University Press, 1996); and Ansgar Klein, Hans-Josef Legrand, and Thomas Leif, eds., *Neue soziale Bewegungen: Impulse, Bilanzen, Perspektiven* (Opladen: Leske & Budrich, 1999).

8. Article 317 of French penal law was originally enacted in 1920. During the Vichy Regime, punishment included the death penalty. After 1944, this particular clause was

removed from the books, but abortion remained illegal up to the mid-1970s. The German equivalent to Article 317 was Paragraph 218, which stemmed from the *Bürgerliche Gesetzbuch* in 1871. During the Third Reich, punishment included, as in France, the death penalty. The Federal Republic decided to keep Paragraph 218 in a (slightly mitigated) version dating back to the Weimar Republic. For the history of Paragraph 218 in the first half of the twentieth century, see Atina Grossmann, *Reforming Sex: The German Movement for Birth Control and Abortion Reform 1920–1950* (New York: Oxford University Press, 1995). For France, see Anne Cova, *Maternité et droits des femmes en France (XIXe–XXe siècles)* (Paris: Economica, 1997).

9. Ute Frevert, "Frauen auf dem Weg zur Gleichberechtigung—Hindernisse, Umleitungen, Einbahnstraßen," in *Zäsuren nach 1945: Essays zur Periodisierung der deutschen Nachkriegsgeschichte*, ed. Martin Broszat (Munich: Beck, 1990), 113–30.

10. "Wir haben abgetrieben," *Stern*, 6 June 1971.

11. In the language of social science, a direct intermediary in the sense in which Alice Schwarzer performed this role is a "direct-relational link." For the distinction between "direct" and "nondirect relational ties" in transnational diffusion processes, see Doug McAdam and Dieter Rucht, "The Cross-National Diffusion of Movement Ideas," *Annals of the American Academy of Political and Social Science* [AAPSS] 528 (1993): 56–74.

12. See Stevie Jackson, *Christine Delphy* (London: Sage, 1996).

13. Mouvement de liberté de l'avortement, "Le gouvernement intensifie la repression contre l'avortement," leaflet from June 1971 in Bibliothèque et Documentation Internationale Contemporaine [Paris], Fonds MLF 1/2.

14. See Remy Rieffel, "Gisèle Halimi," in *Dictionnaire des intellectuels français*, ed. Jacques Julliard and Michel Winock (Paris: Seuil, 1996), 584–85.

15. Some weeks after the publication of the manifesto, Halimi and other prominent persons, among them Simone de Beauvoir, founded an association, Choisir, which attempted to defend women accused of abortion. In contrast to some other, more radical feminist groups, this organization tried to obtain the reform of abortion legislation by legal means. See Choisir, *Avortement: Une loi en procès: L'affaire de Bobigny: Sténotypie intégrale des débats du tribunal de Bobigny (8 novembre 1972)*, with a preface by Simone de Beauvoir (Paris: Gallimard, 1973).

16. "374 Frauen wollen die bürgerliche Moral stürzen. Die Staatsanwaltschaft ermittelt schon," *Abendzeitung*, 2 June 1971.

17. "Frauen gegen den Abtreibungsparagraphen," *Frankfurter Allgemeine Zeitung*, 3 June 1971.

18. "Betonte Gelassenheit," *Frankfurter Rundschau*, 5 June 1971.

19. "Frauenaktion 50," "Protokoll vom Plenum des 4.8.1971 im Club Voltaire, Frankfurt," in Frauen-Mediaturm Köln (Cologne), Collection PDFB 1.

20. Anne Tristan and Annie de Pisan, *Histoires du MLF* (Paris: Calmann-Lévy, 1977), 65.

21. The year 1970 was the year of Delphy's landmark article, "L'ennemi principal," in the very first collection of French feminist writings, *Libération des femmes: Année zéro*, number 54–55 of "Partisans," a publication series by the radical publisher François Maspero, with a second edition published, again in Paris, by Maspero in 1972.

22. The quarrel between "*Psych et Po*" and the other groups within the MLF continued up to the end of the 1970s and beyond. It culminated in the conflict about the right to use the acronym *MLF*, a controversy that ended up before the courts in 1979.

23. This Berger Commission met from July to November 1973 and organized several hearings. See the "Rapport Berger," "Rapport d'information n° 930," the final report by this commission, adopted by the French National Assembly on 28 November 1974. See also Anne-Marie Devreux and Michèle Ferrand-Piccard, "La loi sur l'avortement: Chronologie des événements et des prises de position," *Revue Française de Sociologie* 23 (1982): 503–18.

24. For the history of the Aktionsrat, see Gisa Windhüfel, "Die Außerparlamentarische Opposition und die Anfänge der Neuen Frauenbewegung (1968–1970)," master's thesis, Department of Sociology, University of Bochum, 1994.

25. For the concept of micromobilization structures, see Doug McAdam, "Micromobilization Contexts and Recruitment to Activism," in *From Structure to Action: Comparing Social Movement Research across Cultures*, ed. Bert Klandermans, Hanspeter Kriesi, and Sidney Tarrow (London: JAI, 1988), 125–54.

26. See also Ute Kätzel, *Die 68erinnen: Porträts einer rebellischen Frauengeneration* (Reinbek: Rowohlt, 2002).

27. For the characterization of the New Left/Neue Linke/Nouvelle Gauche, see Ingrid Gilcher-Holtey, *Die 68er Bewegung: Deutschland, Westeuropa, USA* (Munich: Beck, 2001).

28. See Helke Sander's speech at the SDS annual meeting on 13 September 1968 in Frankfurt, in *Autonome Frauen: Schlüsseltexte der neuen Frauenbewegung seit 1968*, ed. Ann Anders (Frankfurt: Fischer, 1988), 39–47.

29. Monika Seifert, "Zur Theorie der antiautoritären Kinderläden," *Konkret* 3 (1969): 43.

30. Max Horkheimer, Erich Fromm, and Herbert Marcuse, *Studien über Autorität und Familie* (Paris: Alcan, 1936).

31. Theodor W. Adorno, *The Authoritarian Personality: Studies in Prejudice* (New York: Harper, 1950).

32. Theodor Adorno, "Erziehung nach Auschwitz," radio presentation, Hessischer Rundfunk, 18 April 1974, in *Gesammelte Schriften* 10/2 (Frankfurt: Suhrkamp, 1977), 76.

33. Concerning the links between these social scientists, see Rolf Wiggershaus, *Die Frankfurter Schule: Geschichte, theoretische Entwicklung, politische Bedeutung* (Munich: dtv, 1997).

34. Wilhelm Reich, *Die sexuelle Revolution: Zur charakterlichen Selbststeuerung des Menschen* (Frankfurt: Fischer, 1966).

35. The original English-language edition was first published, with a foreword by Erich Fromm, as Alexander S. Neill, *Summerhill: A Radical Approach to Child Rearing* (New York: Hart, 1960). The Summerhill model became very popular in Germany; a German translation appeared as *Theorie und Praxis der antiautoritären Erziehung: Das Beispiel Summerhill* (Reinbek: Rowohlt, 1969).

36. See Kommune 2, "Kindererziehung in der Kommune," *Kursbuch* 17 (1969): 147–78. The report, entitled *Versuch der Revolutionierung des bürgerlichen Individuums*, was published in West Berlin in 1969 by the Oberbaumpresse. By the late 1960s, this Soviet experiment generated few echoes outside the West German context.

37. See Helke Sander's speech at the SDS Annual Meeting in 1968, in *Autonome Frauen*, 44.

38. For the analytical distinction between the normative dimension and organizational skills in the cognitive praxis of social movements, see Ron Eyerman and Andrew Jamison, *Social Movements: A Cognitive Approach* (Cambridge: Polity, 1991).

39. To mention but one example, Sigrun Fronius, mentioned earlier, became in 1977 a member of the editorial board of an important German feminist revue, *Courage*.

40. Similar groups existed in Frankfurt, Münster, Munich, Hamburg, and Bonn.

41. Friedhelm Neidhardt, "Einige Ideen zu einer allgemeinen Theorie sozialer Bewegungen," in *Sozialstruktur im Umbruch*, ed. Stefan Hradil (Opladen: Leske & Budrich, 1985), 197.

42. Internationale Situationiste, "De la misère en milieu étudiant, considérée sous ses aspects économique, politique, psychologique, sexuel et notamment intellectuel et de quelques moyens pour y remédier, Strasbourg, AFGES, 1966," in *Enragés et situationistes dans le mouvement d'occupation*, ed. René Viénet (Paris: Gallimard, 1986), 219–43. The English translation can be consulted most conveniently in Dark Star Collective, ed., *Beneath the Paving Stones: Situationists and the Beach, May 1968* (Edinburgh: AK Press, 2001), 9–27.

43. See Ingrid Eichelberg and Wolfgang Drost, *Mai 1968: Une crise de la civilisation française: Anthologie critique de documents politiques et littéraires* (Frankfurt: Lang, 1986), 54–58.

44. "La crèche-garderie," *Le Mouvement Social* 64 (1968): 118.

45. "Les crèches sauvages vers la révolution," in Michel A. Burnier, *La France sauvage* (Paris: Éditions Publications, 1970), 38–42.

46. Interview with Monique Dental, September 1997, Paris. In 1968, Dental was a student at the University of Vincennes and initiated, among others, the kindergarten in the Sorbonne.

47. Antoinette Fouque, "Le mouvement des femmes: Féminisme et/ou M.L.F.," in *Mouvement sociaux d'aujourd'hui: Acteurs et Analystes*, Colloque de Cerisy-la-Salle 1979, ed. Alain Touraine (Paris: Ouvrières, 1982), 225–49.

48. Janine Chasseguet-Smirgel, *La sexualité féminine* (Paris: Payot, 1964); *La psychanalyse* 7 (1964), a special issue of this journal dedicated to the topic of female sexuality.

49. Elisabeth Roudinesco, *Histoire de la psychoanalyse en France*, vol. 2: *1925–1985* (Paris: Seuil, 1986).

50. See Françoise Picq, *Libération des femmes: Les années-mouvement* (Paris: Seuil, 1993). See also the firsthand description of this dispute by Juliette Mitchell in her *Women's Estate* (London: Penguin, 1971).

51. Elaine Marks and Isabelle de Courtivron, *New French Feminism: An Anthology* (New York: Schocken, 1981). For opposing views, see Claire Duchen, *French Connections: Voices from the Women's Movements in France* (London: Routledge, 1987). See also Christine Delphy, "The Invention of French Feminism," *Yale French Studies* 97 (2000): 166–97.

52. Christine Delphy and Monique Wittig, "French Feminists' Interview," *Off Our Backs* 1 (1980): 6.

53. See Sarah Evans, *Personal Politics: The Roots of Women's Liberation in the Civil Rights Movement and the New Left* (New York: Knopf, 1979), and Sarah Evans, "Decade of Discovery: 'The Personal Is Political,'" in *Global Feminisms since 1945*, ed. Bonnie G. Smith (London: Routledge, 2000), 141–63.

54. Arbeitskollektiv der Sozialistischen Frauen Frankfurt/Main, ed., *Frauen gemeinsam sind stark! Texte und Materialien des Women's Liberation Movement in den USA* (Frankfurt: Roter Stern, 1972).

55. See, for instance, Christine Delphy, *Close to Home: A Materialist Analysis of Women's Oppression* (London: Hutchinson, 1984).

56. The largest collection of German feminist journals, located in the *Frauen-Mediaturm Köln*, registers 383 journals founded between 1970 and 1980. For the French feminist press, see Chantal Bertrand-Jennings, "La presse des mouvements de libération des femmes en France de 1971 à 1982," in *Féminité, Subversion, Ecriture*, ed. Suzanne Lamy and Irène Pagès (Toronto: Remue-Ménage, 1983), 15–49.

57. Kommune 2, *Versuch der Revolutionierung*, 151.

58. See note 28.

III

1989

9

The Global Context of 1989

Jarle Simensen

The democratic revolutions in Eastern Europe around 1989 lend themselves to dramatic, voluntarist descriptions, portraying the actions of individuals and activist groups, their organization and strategies, in bringing down authoritarian regimes. Networks between activists in the different Eastern European countries played an important role, and the effect of mutual impulses and chain reactions was of obvious significance.[1] However, this fact may also point in the direction of common *structural* conditions in the area—the soil being ripe for the seed.

Some scholars have explored such approaches to the problem. Jürgen Kocka, for example, invokes general modernization theory: A modern industrial economy, whether of a socialist or capitalist nature, will create social groups, particularly middle strata, who even under authoritarian regimes develop networks and proceed to demand space for nongovernmental organizations and political participation. Moshe Lewin provides a similar explanation of the background to Mikhail Gorbachev's reforms.[2] The formula is simple: In the long run modernization points toward democracy, although history provides numerous examples of periods of modernization under authoritarian rule.

A special variant of modernization logic, of particular relevance to developments in Eastern Europe, refers to the fact that the new information technology demands openness, flexibility, and decentralization to be fully productive. This was a logic accepted by Gorbachev when he introduced his glasnost campaign, and it stood in striking contrast to the 1950s and 1960s, when there was a widespread belief, also in the West, that centralized management of the economy was a key to accelerated development.

However, general modernization theory, when applied to Eastern Europe, fails to explain the *abrupt* nature of the events of 1989. An interesting point

of departure for any causal analysis is the fact that the collapse of communism seemed to take everybody by surprise, political leaders as well as academic observers.[3] This naturally became a cause for concern, not least in the
discipline of political science, with its ambition toward generalization and
prognosis; a debate soon started on the consequences of 1989 for theory in
the discipline.[4] But so-called structural history was also touched by the problem. Thus, Kocka concludes that other causes must be added to modernization theory in order to explain the unexpected: the Tocqueville effect (i.e.,
classes on the rise spurred on to revolution by concessions from the regime),
the role of personalities, the autonomy of the political sphere, and the effect
of external events on national developments. All of this can be seen as concessions to a more voluntarist interpretation. Kocka also makes the important
point that history is a "probability discipline"; human behavior and historical
process can never be wholly explained by causal statements. The past, in
other words, must be given back some of the openness of the present.

THE GLOBAL CONTEXT: THE
"THIRD WAVE" OF DEMOCRATIZATION

The main argument of this chapter is that the democratic risings in Eastern
Europe should be seen in a *global* context. Parallel to the events in Eastern
Europe, a process of democratic reform ran its course in Latin America,
Africa, and Asia. By the beginning of the 1980s, most Latin American countries were under some form of military rule; by 1992, all except two had
elected heads of state. As late as the beginning of 1989, thirty-eight out of
forty-five African countries were under military or one-party regimes, and in
the opinion of a prominent Africanist writing at that time, "it is unlikely that
new African democracies will be created in the coming years."[5] Within a few
short years, thirty-one African countries had become multiparty states with
elected assemblies. Similar pressures for democratic reform were increasing
in Asia, from the overthrow of the Marcos regime in the Philippines in 1986,
via the first free elections in South Korea and Taiwan in 1987, to the democratic risings in China and Thailand in 1989 and 1992.[6]

This is what Samuel Huntington calls "the third wave of democratization
in the modern era."[7] In his scheme of periodicities, the first wave started with
the revolutions in the Americas in the early nineteenth century and culminated with the establishment of the new democracies at the end of World
War I. The second wave is represented by the Allied victory in 1945 and the
subsequent decolonization process in the Third World. Both waves, however, were followed by reverse movements toward authoritarianism. The
third wave began with the fall of the dictatorships in Spain and Portugal in
1975–1976 and culminated in the years immediately after 1989. On the face

of it, the extent of this wave is impressive: The number of democratic countries—we will return to definitions—rose from 78 to 138, and the percentage of democracies out of the total number of countries from 44 percent to 72 percent.

However, the notion of a "third wave" needs to be broken up. The process of democratization differed in *rhythm* and *chronology*. In Latin America, a number of countries had experienced a pendulum-like change between forms of democracy and authoritarianism ever since independence in the nineteenth century; there, the "third wave" started already in the first half of the 1980s, influenced *inter alia* by the events in Spain and Portugal. In Asia as well, the pressure for democratic reform was, as we have seen, apparent before 1989, stimulated by specific local conditions. In Eastern Europe, the reform movements of Poland and Hungary built up their strength over several years before the crisis of 1989.

The *form* of political transition also varied. The authoritarian starting points differed: one-party systems, military regimes, personal dictatorships. In some cases, typically in Latin America, the regime was in control of the process of transformation; in other cases, authoritarian regimes collapsed or were overthrown and replaced as a result of popular action or pressure, as in the Philippines, Argentina, and Romania. Finally, there were cases in which democratization resulted from a process of negotiation between the government and opposition groups, as in the many "Round Table" arrangements of Eastern Europe.

Finally, it is necessary to distinguish among *results*, as there are many forms of democracy. A minimum criterion is multiparty elections to a national assembly. But examples abound as to how this can be combined with various forms of discrimination against political opposition, manipulations at elections, curtailment of personal freedoms, limited constitutional powers for the assembly, and continued privileges for military or oligarchic elites. The concepts of "militarized democracies" in Latin America and "authoritarian democracies" in Asia indicate the limitations of such "formal democracies." The contrast is clear to what we may call "real democracies" or "liberal democracies," based on plural societies, rule of law, a neutral military, and personal freedoms.[8] The third wave divided almost equally between the two categories of democracy up to its culmination in 1992.

INTERNATIONAL RELATIONS, MODERNIZATION THEORY, AND DIFFUSION

International relations as a subdiscipline of political science developed during the Cold War and in America (and Scandinavia) was dominated by the schools of "realism" and "neorealism." They took the sovereign nation-state as the basic unit of analysis and emphasized the struggle for power and security in an anarchic international system determined by mutual threat perceptions.

Up to a point, the realist approach can explain what happened around 1989: The new armament spiral during the 1980s proved the superior economic and technological power of the United States, and clearly made even Soviet military leaders aware that internal reform was needed to protect superpower status. The new conciliatory policy toward the West implied that Soviet forces would not be used to protect the regimes of Eastern and Central Europe, a necessary precondition for the subsequent victory of the democratic revolutions. However, realist theory, with its concentration on relations between states, had little to say about the domestic reasons for the weakening and final dissolution of the Soviet Union—namely, nationalism, liberal ideas, and social movements. The same could be said about Eastern European studies in general; they had concentrated on regimes, elites, and interstate relations under Soviet hegemony to the neglect of Eastern European societies, from where the democratic reform movements rose.[9]

In the Third World, the end of the Cold War and the fall of the Soviet Union drastically weakened economic and military support for Marxist-oriented regimes and undermined the prestige of the socialist model of development. The Americans, on their side, reduced their support of authoritarian regimes that had been their allies during the Cold War, particularly in Latin America, and in some cases began pressing for reform, as in Chile after 1985 and Zaire and Kenya in the early 1990s. All Third World regimes lost international bargaining power when the Cold War ended. However, economic and political reform in Latin America and Asia had, as noted earlier, started well before 1989. Thus, the end of the Cold War cannot be considered either a necessary precondition or a sufficient cause for the democratization in these regions, even if it accelerated the process.

Modernization theory is clearly of relevance to explain not only the Eastern European but also the global process of democratization—although Kocka, for one, is hesitant on this point. Middle-class groups of liberal inclination spearheaded the reform movements in Latin America during the 1980s, in shifting alliances with labor and popular forces. New middle classes also played an important role in the opposition against authoritarian regimes in East and Southeast Asia, from the Philippines in 1985 to Thailand in 1992. Developments in China raised the question of whether it would be possible for a communist regime to carry out economic reforms without losing political control—that is, modernization without democracy.

But modernization theory, as it relates to separate but parallel national processes, can only take us part of the way toward explaining 1989; the main problem is that the level of modernization differed too widely among the main regions to explain the global and simultaneous character of the democratic movements. Thus, the African risings, although led by oppositional elites, did not have much of a modern middle class in their support but relied mainly on students and the urban populace.

A third approach, focusing on cross-border diffusion of ideas and impulses, turns attention to a crucial element in the revolutions of 1989—as in previous periods of international unrest, such as 1789, 1848, 1918, and 1968. In comparison to these past events, television now provided a powerful new instrument for the transmission of images and ideas; this was manifest in the chain reactions in Eastern Europe. Similarly, TV images from the risings in Eastern Europe and China were transmitted to the rest of the world with immediate effect. In Cameroon, the local police was dubbed "Securitate," and students in Togo named their square of demonstration in the capital "Tiananmen."

However, it is difficult to specify the causal effect of the mass media in setting off the risings. Nobody will claim that external impulses could be a *sufficient* cause in and after 1989, in the manner that an infection can be a sufficient cause of an inflammation. But external impulses must be given weight as contributory and releasing factors, important to the timing of events.

Our conclusion must be that neither international relations, nor modernization, nor diffusion can provide a full explanation of the similar and largely simultaneous processes of democratization in the different regions of the world around 1989. Reflection on the global aspects of 1989 may lead us in the direction of the concept of "international society," "world society," and "global society." This means *inter alia* that the sharp distinction between internal and external causes of national development ought to be replaced by a notion of interaction within larger systems, with a range of actors besides the state, from multinational firms and networks of private organizations to international media and institutions.[10] The argument that follows is that the democratization processes around 1989 can only be fully understood against a background of such global systemic and normative integration.

1989 AND ECONOMIC GLOBALIZATION

Failure of economic performance within an increasingly globalized economy can be considered the most general underlying cause behind the demise of authoritarian regimes around 1989.

The expansion of the world market has been a central theme in the discipline of history, with special attention to its development under the liberal international regime before 1914 and its new period of expansion under the Bretton Woods institutions after 1945. However, from the 1970s it is possible to talk of a "quantum leap" in integration, driven by a combination of international capital, new technologies, and a liberalization of trade regimes. The concept of "globalization" gained currency from about 1990 to characterize this process.[11] The volume of exports in relation to gross national product roughly doubled from 1960 to 1990, the stock of international bank lending increased ten times from 1980 to 1990, at the same time as liberalization and new technology increased capital mobility enormously. A radical new feature was the internationalization of *production* through the multinational corporations. The International Monetary Fund (IMF) rose in importance in its role as a global lender of last resort and a global financial watchdog. All of this meant that weak economic performance was quickly punished by the global market. When this had consequences for welfare and living standards in the countries concerned, it was bound to have political consequences. Let us look more closely at the effects in the different regions.

There is reason to argue, more than hitherto has been the case, that the global economic context was important in explaining the political collapse in Eastern Europe.[12] True, the socialist camp had been largely sealed off from the capitalist world market, but it had always presented itself as an alternative to the doomed capitalist system: "Catch up with and overtake the West" was a standard slogan since Khrushchev. When the Western system proved to be superior in all regards, from information technology to basic consumer goods, this was bound to have serious consequences for the legitimacy of the regimes and for the self-confidence of the ruling elite. A guiding idea for Gorbachev was that reintegration in the global economy was the only way to obtain new technology and break out of stagnation. This demanded an entirely new ideological orientation, deemphasizing class conflict on a world scale, underlining the joint interests of humanity, and launching the concept of a "European house" or a "common European home."[13] Membership in the international agreement on tariffs and trade, GATT, became a high political priority. In this situation political reform was a necessity, to achieve not only economic productivity but also international creditworthiness. But Gorbachev had underestimated the forces he let loose: the frustrated nationalities, popular disillusionment, and the democratic movements in the satellite states in Eastern and Central Europe.

In explaining the crises in the Third World, the relevance of globalization is even more apparent. Both Latin America and the earlier colonies in Africa and Asia had seen a tendency toward authoritarian governments and state-directed, protected national economies after World War II, justified by prevailing theories in development economics at the time, and favored by elites eager to milk the economy for personal profit. The standard problems of political decay and low productivity in authoritarian states then emerged beginning in the 1970s, and state finance got out of control in one country after another in Latin America and Africa. Currency manipulations and uninhibited printing of money led to hyperinflation, destructive of the legitimacy of any regime.

The crisis in the 1980s was set off by the confrontation with the realities of the global economy in the form of the debt problem. Here the steep rise in oil prices after 1973 had a crucial, double effect. The flood of petrodollars pumped new lending capacity into the global capital system, leading to reckless lending and borrowing. At the same time, the increased oil import bill took a larger share of the foreign currency earnings of poor countries. Combined with falling prices on other raw materials and fluctuating dollar values, this brought the malfunctioning national economies in Latin America and Africa into bankruptcy, starting with the Mexican declaration of nonpayment in 1982.[14]

The ensuing rescue operations in the form of joint action by the threatened American banks, the IMF, and the U.S. government provided a vivid illustration of the new level of interdependence in the global economy. The conditionalities imposed by the IMF and the World Bank in the form of financial discipline, realistic budgets, and economic liberalization represented a degree of international intervention unheard of since the days of informal imperialism in the Middle East and China in the nineteenth century. African critics talked of "recolonization."[15]

The connection between economic and political reform was not straightforward. The IMF and the World Bank were initially satisfied to see structural adjustment implemented by authoritarian regimes, as in the case of Augusto Pinochet's Chile in the early 1980s; a strong regime might be best suited to carry out the unpopular measures needed. However, after the fall of communism and the pressure for democratization from different quarters, the IMF/World Bank as well began to include human rights and multiparty democracy among their conditional ties; the importance of democracy to good governance and economic performance became standard currency in the new discourse. The pressure on authoritarian and bankrupt regimes increased when bilateral aid donors lined up behind the international financial institutions. When large-scale credit and aid were withheld from President Arap Moi in Kenya in 1991, it did not take long before multiparty elections were conceded. Previous Marxist-oriented governments, as in Angola and Mozambique, announced multiparty elections on the eve of their departure to Washington to negotiate loans with the World Bank.

The austerity programs imposed by the IMF predictably led to increased popular discontent. This was a separate causal element in the democratic risings in the dozen or so African countries around 1989. It is not easy to unravel the various threads that went into these risings. Urban discontent with worsening material conditions, particularly the removal of food subsidies under the new policies of budgetary stringency, was politically dangerous. At the bottom there was a simmering exasperation with despotic governments. Thus, demonstrators might combine demands for democratic elections with protest against the IMF and foreign influence in general.[16] When elected regimes in their turn took over responsibility for the austerity programs, this became a strain on their legitimacy, which was part of the explanation for the later backlash against liberal reform, in both Eastern Europe and the Third World. The precise role of international financial institutions in the process of democratization—and in the later backlash against liberal reform both in Eastern Europe and many countries of the former Third World—remains to be charted.

1989, CIVIC ORGANIZATIONS, AND GLOBAL SOCIETY

It is an extraordinary phenomenon that all the approximately 190 discrete, "sovereign" units in the international system are organized according to the same nation-state model, with the same paraphernalia and the same claim to international status; in this sense, global political culture has been homogenized to a surprising degree. Meanwhile, the international state system has produced an ever-increasing number of common institutions, at both regional and global levels—military, economic, and cultural—with the United Nations family as the most comprehensive, although not the most effective. The growth of international law and institutions for its promotion is a substantial expression of global normative integration. International conventions regulate ever new sectors, and the UN Declaration of Human Rights has become a universally recognized code, even if interpretations differ. In Eastern Europe, it was of material importance that human rights were written into the Helsinki Accord of 1975; thus, the stipulations about free travel were immediately used by opposition groups in Eastern Europe. Regard for the Helsinki Accord may also have spelled the final end to the Brezhnev doctrine, which claimed the right of armed Soviet intervention in order to bolster threatened communist regimes.[17]

When we come to the political actors behind the democratic movements, the concept of a global society based on normative integration becomes immediately relevant. In Eastern Europe, the ground for 1989 had been prepared by Solidarity, Charter 77, the Hungarian reform movement, and the muted East German opposition. Churches, peace organizations, environmental groups, and informal networks formed the special profile of the "velvet revolutions." Their immediate link-up with parallel groups in the West was an important feature of developments in 1989. In the Soviet Union, the peace movement of the 1980s, with its close ties to similar movements in the West, was of particular importance. It created new space for political debate by being able to play on official Soviet peace and disarmament ideology.[18] There was a paradox here, in that the crisis in the East was stimulated not only by the contrast with the material success of the West but also by contact with Western antiestablishment groups critical of the capitalist economy, many of them with roots in 1968.

Immanuel Wallerstein later provided an interpretation of 1989 that transcended this paradox: There is an alternative model of modernity to capitalism, rooted in the Enlightenment, emphasizing human freedom rather than material growth, and the contradiction between those two versions of modernity is at the bottom of the moral and institutional crisis of our time. In this perspective, Wallerstein regards 1989 as a continuation of 1968, both "revolutions" representing a protest, based on the idea of "people's sovereignty," against the capitalist world system, Soviet "state capitalism" included. In all regions of the world, the risings around 1989 therefore represented a challenge against the classes that sustain the capitalist world economy. This incipient alliance between "progressive" forces both East and West, according to Wallerstein, lost out after the end of the Cold War to the overwhelming forces of global neoliberalism.[19]

Civic organizations played a particularly important role in preparing the ground for the democratization process in Latin America, utilizing their international connections to the full. Civil society on a European model was an integral part of the political tradition in this region, and even military regimes tended to proclaim democratic government as the norm and their own rule as time-limited emergency operations. When left-wing groups and guerrilla movements were weakened by the dwindling of Soviet support during the late 1980s and American support of authoritarian regimes was reduced, the road was eased toward compromise and a controlled transition to civilian rule. This was a reform process with its own profile, different from the revolutions in Eastern Europe and the popular risings in Africa.

There were parallels in South Africa, where civic organizations had continued to play a role under apartheid, even among the disenfranchised and suppressed nonwhite population. Churches could profit from strong international connections; the Catholic Church openly flouted aspects of apartheid. Black trade unions were recognized by the government. The regime's desire for political legitimacy in the West, and the strain of carrying the status of a political outcast, must be part of the explanation for why apartheid was gradually abandoned. When the ban on multiracial political organization was lifted in 1984, the United Democratic Front could spring up almost overnight, and its new suppression two years later proved to be the last frantic measure before the great turn of 1990.

But the South African revolution as well was part of the global wave. In 1989, the Communist Party of South Africa adopted a new program that accepted negotiations, and the general secretary of the party, Joe Slovo, in January 1990 circulated a document entitled "Has Socialism Failed?" in which he raised the possibility of multiparty democracy. This was part of the background to the release of Nelson Mandela and the beginning of constitutional reform.[20]

In Black Africa, economic weakness and dependence meant that the regimes were particularly vulnerable to external pressure once international norms of democracy and human rights were activated. The reports of

Amnesty International and the International Commission of Jurists were of great influence. The latter played a leading part in arranging conferences of lawyers and journalists to prepare the ground for a Charter of Human Rights that was finally adopted—in a castrated form—by the Organization of African Unity in 1990. And once the demands for elected government were unleashed, international networks immediately went into play. When President Kenneth Kaunda resisted demands for multiparty elections in Zambia, the international trade union movement mobilized, and when the IMF and bilateral aid organizations at the same time threw their weight behind the demand for multiparty elections, Kaunda was forced to concede.[21]

Compared to Latin America and Africa, it may seem that nongovernmental organizations with international networks played a less important part in East and Southeast Asia. In many countries, the emerging "authoritarian democracies" stressed the importance of control and collective duties, rather than individual rights and unlimited freedom. The former prime minister of Singapore, Lee Kuan Yew, was a prominent spokesperson for this view—in a would-be Confucian tradition—insisting that economic reform must come before political freedom; from his point of view, the Soviet Union was wrong in its priorities and China right.

Let us return to the question of the social basis of the democratic movements. Eric Hobsbawm, with his ambition to write global social history, finds a common precondition for the political risings around 1989 in what he calls "the growing urbanization of the globe." In his structural interpretation, the world at the end of the twentieth century was in a state of social crisis, with an increasing political gap between rulers and ruled.[22] The middle classes who mobilized in citizen movements clearly carried common features in all regions of the world, logically enough given the universal character of modern higher education and the employment of its candidates in the bureaucracies and economies of the modern homogenized nation-state. Immanuel Wallerstein finds a common cause behind 1989 in a universal squeeze on these same middle classes, whose numbers in the golden years of the world economy after 1945 had been inflated far beyond what the productive base could carry, and which after the recession of the 1970s in many countries found the ground cut from under their feet.[23]

Since the 1970s, students and intellectuals had continuously drawn attention to the lack of democratic rights under military dictatorships in Asia and Latin America. African universities were in a state of frequent turmoil, and students and intellectuals were overrepresented among political prisoners. In the risings around 1989, students were often in the vanguard, regularly so in Africa. The role of students in international revolutionary movements is an old story, related to the international character of the university, the capacity of the students for international communication and their mobile nature as a social group.[24]

Global consciousness was clearly most in evidence among elite groups, but not exclusively so. The events in 1989 revealed the enormous attraction of Western mass consumer society as a cultural model for broad strata of the population, in both Eastern Europe and the rest of the world. It meant that specific material standards, styles and products were taken as criteria for self-realization and a meaningful modern life. The importance of this demonstration effect in the political breakdowns of the socialist countries can scarcely be overestimated. Western popular youth culture, as expressed in dress, style, and rock music (including its verbal content), transmitted an aggressive message of personal freedom and opposition to established norms.

The modern mass media had a special function in this connection. The media in their material aspect represent systemic integration at the highest level. In 1989, they provided channels for diffusion of political impulses and means of coordination during political actions. Nowhere was this more important than in Eastern Europe. But tactics at Tiananmen Square were coordinated through telefax with student groups in America, and TV coverage was skillfully manipulated with an awareness of the global audience. It was no longer possible for the nation-state to control the flow of information.

Fukuyama's argument from 1989 about the "End of History" represented the most pointed statement at the time of the belief in global normative integration.[25] Inspired by Hegel's idealistic interpretation of world history, Fukuyama could regard 1989 as a final victory in the progress of the idea of freedom, although there might be delays and setbacks in its realization, including a reversal to aggressive, even fascist forms of nationalism in Russia. (This is not the place to go into the controversies Fukuyama created and the relative disfavor into which his views have fallen since they were first published.)

CONCLUSION

Let us sum up some of the arguments for seeing the democratic risings in Eastern Europe in 1989 in a global perspective. The first is that their impact in other regions of the world is a topic of obvious significance; everywhere it acted as a stimulus to similar movements, although the causal weight of such external impulses is difficult to specify. We have stressed that some of the democratic risings in Latin America and Asia started well before the events in Eastern Europe; Tiananmen also came earlier in the year of 1989. Whether the knowledge of such Third World risings played any role for the opposition in Eastern Europe remains an open and unresearched question, although it is known that events in Chile were closely watched in Poland.

A second gain relates to the general advantage of comparison, regardless of the question of influence. With regard to the social basis of the opposition, we have found a general pattern, with middle-class groups and students predominating and part of the urban populace mobilized at critical moments. We have seen historians like Hobsbawm and Wallerstein groping for an explanation of 1989 in global social history. Voluntary organizations everywhere played an important role, frequently acting in international networks. In Eastern Europe, the contact with activist groups in the West, where peace and the environment were central issues, was of particular importance. Common to all these groups and organizations, both local and international, was a consciousness of universal democratic values that could translate into practical agendas for local political reform. Some have talked of a "global civil society" in embryo.[26]

However, the most general precondition for the democratic revolutions we have found in the economic bankruptcy of authoritarian, state-directed economies, dramatically revealed in their confrontation with a globalized economy driven by an advanced stage of technology. When the International Monetary Fund and the World Bank added human rights and multiparty elections to their conditionalities, combined external and internal pressures led authoritarian regimes to succumb. This was a highly relevant perspective also in Eastern Europe, where integration in the world economy was increasingly seen as the only way out of stagnation, and where the human rights section of the Helsinki Accords acted as a beacon.

A structural argument of this kind may be criticized as a neoliberal version of modernization theory writ large. Globalization is an uneven, multifaceted, and contradictory process that may create its own counterforces; the resurgence of ethnicity and religious fundamentalism is a case in point, and its challenge to democracy is obvious. Many of the formal democracies established around 1989, especially in Africa and the former Soviet Union, have fallen back into forms of authoritarian rule. Thus, between 1992 and 1995, the number of authoritarian countries increased from thirty-eight to fifty-three, the percentage of such countries going up from 20 percent to 28 percent of the total.[27] Where formal democracy has been retained, in many places it has become a sham, with the leaders manipulating the elective system and hampering opposition by foul methods.

From a radical position, the new, formal democracies can be seen as a manifestation of "low-intensity democracy," the result of a global strategy by the United States as the hegemonic power, in alliance with local ruling classes, to preempt the revolutionary potential of the 1989 risings.[28] If basic class and hegemonic interests are threatened, the forces of economic globalization might in given situations also work in favor of authoritarian rule, both at home and abroad, in contradiction of the trend toward normative integration manifest in the democratic wave of 1989.

NOTES

1. The state of this research is summarized in Mary Kaldor and Ivan Vejvoda, *Democratization in Central and Eastern Europe* (London: Pinter, 1999).

2. Jürgen Kocka, "Überraschung und Erklärung: Was die Umbrüche von 1989/90 für die Gesellschaftsgeschichte bedeuten könnten," in *Was ist Gesellschaftsgeschichte? Positionen, Themen, Analysen*, ed. Manfred Hettling and Claudia Huerkamp (Munich: Beck, 1991); Moshe Lewin, *The Gorbachev Phenomenon: A Historical Interpretation* (Berkeley: University of California Press, 1991).

3. Sidney Tarrow, "Aiming at a Moving Target: Social Science and the Recent Rebellions in Eastern Europe," *PS: Political Science and Politics* 24, no. 1 (1991): 12–20; Timur Kuran, "Now Out of Never: The Element of Surprise in the East European Revolution of 1989," *World Politics* 44, no. 1 (October 1991): 7–49; Barry Buzan, "The Present as a Historic Turning Point," *Journal of Peace Research* 32, no. 4 (1995): 385–98; Christian Meier, "Die 'Ereignisse' und der Umbruch des Weltsystems," *Merkur* 44, no. 495 (1990): 376–86.

4. Lucian W. Pye, "Political Science and the Crisis of Authoritarianism," *American Political Science Review* 84, no. 1 (March 1990): 3–21; Fred Halliday, *Rethinking International Relations* (Basingstoke, U.K.: Macmillan, 1994); John Gaddis, "International Relations Theory and the End of the Cold War," *International Security* 17, no. 3 (1992): 5–58; Torbjørn L. Knutsen, *A History of International Relations Theory* (Manchester: Manchester University Press, 1997). Early historiographic surveys of research on the democratization in Eastern Europe in Martin Rady, "1989 and All That," *Slavonic and East European Review* 73, no. 1 (January 1995): 111–16; and Philip Longworth, "1989 and After," *Slavonic and East European Review* 71, no. 4 (October 1993): 701–71.

5. Henry Bienen, "Authoritarianism and Democracy in Africa," in *Comparative Political Dynamics: Global Research Perspectives*, ed. Dankwart A. Rustow and Kenneth Paul Erickson (New York: HarperCollins, 1991), 226.

6. A general introduction to the problem of democratization in the Third World is Larry Diamond, Juan J. Linz, and Seymour Lipset, eds., *Democracy in Developing Countries*, 4 vols. (Boulder, Colo.: Lynne Rienner, 1988); comparative perspectives on Asia appear in Gerardo L. Munck and Carol Skalnik Leff, "Modes of Transition and Democratization: South America and Eastern Europe in Comparative Perspective," *Comparative Politics* 29, no. 3 (April 1997): 343–63. On democratic reform in Africa: John A. Wiseman, ed., *Democracy and Political Change in Sub-Saharan Africa* (London: Routledge, 1995); Claude Ake, *Democracy and Development in Africa* (Washington, D.C.: Brookings Institution, 1996); Richard Joseph, "Democratization in Africa after 1989: Comparative and Theoretical Perspectives," *Comparative Politics* 29, no. 3 (April 1997): 363–83; Taye Assefa, Severine M. Rugumamu, and Abdel Ghaffar M-Ahmed, eds., *Globalization, Democracy and Development in Africa: Challenges and Prospects* (Addis Ababa: Organization for Social Science Research in Eastern and Southern Africa, 2001). See also *Africa Today* 43, no. 4 (1996), a special issue on democratic reform.

7. Samuel Huntington, *The Third Wave: Democratization in the Late Twentieth Century* (Norman: University of Oklahoma Press, 1991); Samuel Huntington, "How Countries Democratize," *Political Science Quarterly* 106, no. 4 (Winter 1991): 579–616.

8. The criteria underlying the two types of democracy go back to Joseph Schumpeter, *Capitalism, Socialism and Democracy* (London: Allen & Unwin, 1947), and Robert Dahl, *Polyarchy: Participation and Opposition* (New Haven, Conn.: Yale University Press, 1971).

9. John Gaddis, "The Cold War, the Long Peace and the Future," in *Beyond the Cold War: New Dimensions in International Relations*, ed. Geir Lundestad and Odd Arne Westad (Oslo: Scandinavian University Press, 1993).

10. Martin Shaw, *Global Society and International Relations: Sociological Concepts and Political Perspectives* (Cambridge: Polity, 1994); Roland Robertson, *Globalization: Social Theory and Global Culture* (London: Sage, 1992); William E. Connolly, "Democracy and Territoriality," *Millennium* 20, no. 3 (1991): 463–84; an early introduction of the concept of "world society" is John W. Burton, *World Society* (Cambridge: Cambridge University Press, 1972).

11. Useful guides for our purpose to the literature and debates on globalization are Jan Aart Scholte, *Globalization: A Critical Introduction* (Basingstoke, U.K.: Palgrave, 2000); Peter Dicken, *Global Shift: Transforming the World Economy* (London: Chapman, 1998); and David Held, Anthony McGrew, David Goldblatt, and Jonathan Perraton, *Global Transformations: Politics, Economics and Culture* (Oxford: Polity, 1999). The discipline of history is a latecomer to the field; introductions are Bruce Mazlish and Ralph Buultjens, eds., *Conceptualizing Global History* (Boulder, Colo.: Westview, 1993), and Anthony G. Hopkins, ed., *Globalization in World History* (London: Pimlico, 2002).

12. Jacques Lévesque, *The Enigma of 1989: The USSR and the Liberation of Eastern Europe* (Berkeley: University of California Press, 1997). See also the documents introduced by Lévesque in *The Cold War International History Project Bulletin*, no. 12/13 (2002); Ed A. Hewett with Clifford C. Gaddy, *Open for Business: Russia's Return to the Global Economy* (Washington, D.C.: Brookings Institution, 1992); György Péteri, "On the Legacy of State Socialism in Academia," in Péteri, *Academia and State Socialism: Essays on the Political History of Academic Life in Post-1945 Hungary and East Central Europe* (Highland Lakes, N.Y.: Atlantic Research and Publications, 1998), 227–55. On the World Bank in Eastern Europe, see Janine R. Wedel, *Collision and Collusion: The Strange Case of Western Aid to Eastern Europe, 1989–1998* (New York: St. Martin's, 1998).

13. Mikhail Gorbachev, *Socialism, Peace and Democracy: Writings, Speeches and Reports* (London: Zwan, 1987); Mikhail Gorbachev, *Memoirs* (London: Bantam, 1996).

14. Barry Eichengreen and Peter H. Lindert, eds., *The International Debt Crisis in Historical Perspective* (Cambridge, Mass.: MIT Press, 1989); Michael P. Claudon, ed., *World Debt Crisis: International Lending on Trial* (Cambridge, Mass.: Ballinger, 1986); Penelope Hartland-Thunberg and Charles K. Ebinger, eds., *Banks, Petrodollars, and Sovereign Debtors: Blood from a Stone?* (Lexington, Mass.: Lexington, 1986).

15. The field of structural adjustment studies was a growth industry during the 1990s. An introduction to its political aspects is Stephen Haggard and Steven B. Webb, eds., *Voting for Reform: Democracy, Political Liberalization and Economic Adjustment* (New York: Oxford University Press, 1994). For an early critical perspective, see John Cavanagh, Daphne Wysham and Marcos Arruda, eds., *Beyond Bretton*

Woods: Alternatives to the Global Economic Order (London: Pluto, with Institute for Policy Studies, 1994). For Africa, see Peter Gibbon, Yusuf Bangura, and Arve Ofstad, eds., *Authoritarianism, Democracy and Adjustment* (Uppsala: Nordiska Afrikainstitutet, 1992).

16. Lars Rudebeck, ed., *When Democracy Makes Sense: Studies in the Democratic Potential of Third World Popular Risings* (Uppsala: AKUT, 1992); Michael Bratton and Nicolas Van de Valle, "Popular Protest and Political Reform in Africa," *Comparative Politics* 24, no. 4 (1992): 419–43.

17. Daniel Thomas, *The Helsinki Effect: International Norms, Human Rights, and the Demise of Communism* (Princeton, N.J.: Princeton University Press, 2001); David Held, *Democracy and the Global Order: From the Modern State to Cosmopolitan Governance* (Cambridge: Polity, 1995); Richard Falck, "The Infancy of Global Civil Society," in *Beyond the Cold War: New Dimensions in International Relations*, ed. Geir Lundestad and Odd Arne Westad (Oslo: Scandinavian University Press, 1993); Eileen McCarthy-Arnolds, David R. Penna, and Debra Joy Cruz Sobrepeña, eds., *Africa, Human Rights and the Global System: The Political Economy of Human Rights in a Changing World* (Westport, Conn.: Greenwood, 1994); Claude E. Welsh, *Protecting Human Rights in Africa: Strategies and Roles of Non-Governmental Organizations* (Philadelphia: University of Pennsylvania Press, 1995).

18. Helmut Anheier, Glasius Marlies, and Mary Kaldor, eds., *Global Civil Society 2001* (Oxford: Oxford University Press, 2001); Matthew Evangelista, *Unarmed Forces: The Transnational Movement to End the Cold War* (Ithaca, N.Y.: Cornell University Press, 1999).

19. Immanuel Wallerstein, "The End of What Modernity," *Theory and Society*, 24, no. 4 (1995): 471–88; Immanuel Wallerstein, Giovanni Arrighi, and Terence K. Hopkins, "1989, the Continuation of 1968," *Review: Fernand Braudel Center for the Study of Economies, Historical Systems, and Civilizations* 15, no. 2 (Spring 1992): 221–42.

20. "The decline and collapse of communism in Eastern Europe and Russia put a new complexion on things. The ANC was formerly an instrument of Russian expansion in Southern Africa; when that threat fell away, the carpet was pulled from under the ANC; its base of financing, counseling and moral support had crumbled. It was as if God had taken a hand—a new turn in world history. We had to seize the opportunity." President F. W. de Klerk in 1990, quoted in Willem de Klerk, *F. W. de Klerk: The Man in His Time* (Johannesburg: Ball, 1991), 27.

21. McCarthy-Arnolds et al., eds., *Africa, Human Rights and the Global System*.

22. Eric Hobsbawm, *Age of Extremes: The Short Twentieth Century* (London: Joseph, 1994), 458.

23. Wallerstein et al., "1989, the Continuation of 1968."

24. Seymour Lipset, *Student Politics* (London: Basic Books, 1967); Donald K. Emmerson, ed., *Students and Politics in Developing Nations* (London: Pall Mall, 1968); W. J. Hanna, *University Students and African Politics* (London: Africana, 1975).

25. Francis Fukuyama, "The End of History?" *The National Interest* 16, no. 3 (Summer 1989): 3–18.

26. Falck, "Infancy of Global Civil Society," in *Beyond the Cold War*.

27. On the backlash for democracy: Larry Diamond, "Is the Third Wave Over?" *Journal of Democracy* 7, no. 3 (1996): 20–37; Julius Ihonvbere, "Where Is the Third Wave? A Critical Evaluation of Africa's Non-Transition to Democracy," *Africa Today*

43, no. 4 (1996): 343–68; Samuel Huntington, "Democracy for the Long Haul," *Journal of Democracy* 7, no. 2 (1996): 3–14.

28. Barel Gills and Joel Rocamora, "Low Intensity Democracy," *Third World Quarterly* 13, no. 3 (1992): 501–25; broader perspectives on the social basis of democratization in Robin Luckham, Anne Marie Goetz, and Mary Kaldor, *Democratic Institutions and Politics in Contexts of Inequality, Poverty, and Conflict: A Conceptual Framework*. Working Paper 104 (Brighton, U.K.: Institute of Development Studies, 2000); Janine R. Wedel, *Clans, Cliques, and Captured States: Rethinking "Transition" in Central and Eastern Europe and the Former Soviet Union* (Helsinki: n.p., 2001).

10

The Development of a Green Opposition in Czechoslovakia

The Role of International Contacts

Miroslav Vaněk

In the last third of the twentieth century, the state of the natural environment on Earth became one of the main problems of contemporary civilization. It was defined by environmental studies, which emerged as an academic discipline linking philosophy with the methods of the social and natural sciences. Individual persons, groups, social movements, political parties, and government organs of various political systems spoke out on the topic with increasing urgency. It is not easy for a contemporary historian to address these developments, because the problem has yet to be solved either at the global level or in any one country whose development the historian analyzes, despite all the great social and political changes that took place in the period under discussion in this article.

The specific features of the environmental problem in Czechoslovakia are the result of geography and political and economic developments since the end of World War II. The borders of postwar Czechoslovakia, a country with a long industrial tradition, coincided (until the Bohemian lands and Slovakia went their separate ways in 1993; this article will focus on the Czech case) with natural boundaries on more than two-thirds of their total length—that is, with mountain ranges that partially enclosed the country in a natural basin. Those natural boundaries held in the emissions of an increasing number of factory and power plant smokestacks. After the Communist takeover in late February 1948, the Iron Curtain separated Czechoslovakia in almost every sense from its neighbors to the West. The country, which became politically, economically, and militarily part of the Eastern bloc of Marxist-Leninist states controlled by the Soviet Union, was forced to change the structure of its industrial production and adapt it to the great-power needs of the Soviet Union, regardless of the damage that would be done to the natural environment (particularly by the machine and chemical industries). After a quarter of a century of Communist rule, however, it was easy to see that the megalomaniacal ambitions of the Five-Year Plans, which aimed "to catch up to and overtake" the states of the capitalist West, were unrealistic, except in one respect: the extent of damage done to the natural environment.

By the beginning of the 1970s, the state of the Czechoslovak environment had become such a serious problem, with ramifications for whole sectors of the population, that the Communist regime was forced to pay attention to the problem. This was in part due to the growing international attention to environmental concerns. In particular, two important international conferences in the 1970s drew attention to the global nature of environmental problems and conveyed to the Czechoslovak leadership emphatic warnings that neither the mountain ranges nor the Iron Curtain would prevent the toxic waste of Czechoslovak industry from penetrating neighboring countries by air and water. In 1972, on the basis of broad-based international initiatives, the UN Conference on the Human Environment met in Stockholm; in 1975, the environment was an important topic at the Conference on Security and Cooperation in Europe (CSCE), in Helsinki. Both of these conferences drew participants from the Eastern bloc countries into the debate on the natural environment and helped to force their governments to take a somewhat more accommodating, active position on environmental protection.[1]

That this topic appeared on the agenda of these prestigious and influential international meetings testifies to the differences in the approach of the Western democracies and the East bloc countries toward environmental problems. The industrialized countries of the West had felt the negative impact of environmentally destructive industrial production roughly fifteen to twenty years before the countries of the Eastern bloc and, for economical, environmental, and social reasons, began with that head start to change and adapt the structure of their industries. The more developed modern technologies preferred by the countries of the West seemed less harmful to the environment in both the exploitation of natural resources and the processing of those resources, and they produced more attractive products, which to an increasing extent were recyclable. Scientific research into the impact of industrial production on the natural environment often ran up against the more or less open resistance of producers, cartels, and commercial interests, but it was not restricted or sabotaged by the government organs and institutions of those countries. These, in turn, faced growing pressure from civil action groups, social movements, and, ultimately, political parties, which came generally to be known as "Green" parties. These political parties tended to be on the left of the political spectrum, and their members and supporters used essentially conventional methods of political competition (with varying degrees of radicalism). The topic of the natural environment became explicitly political (which may have led to its sometimes being used for political ends), but even the most radical adherents of the Green movement and parties refrained from attacking the democratic systems themselves; nor did the Western democracies threaten the existence or freedom of the Green parties merely on account of their activities, but at most fined some of their excesses. Although these countries also struggled with environmental issues, they were at least openly debated by experts, politicians, and the general public.

In the Soviet bloc states, by contrast, the search for ways to repair and prevent damage to the natural environment ran up against ideology and power politics. Czechoslovakia, whose leadership took part in the two aforementioned conferences and signed the Helsinki Final Act, had come to these conferences with rather different terms and conditions. According to precise indices, Czechoslovakia, beginning in the 1970s, came to hold first and second place in destruction of the natural environment in Europe. The north Bohemian basin was among the most polluted regions of the world. The deplorable state of the environment was, logically, reflected in the economy, the health of the population, and the social-political sphere.[2] Moreover, the regime radically limited civil liberties and human rights. Even the basic social certainties (almost no unemployment, with a nearly acceptable level of health care and social security) became increasingly dubious in light of the damage done to the natural environment, whose catastrophic impact on the health of the population (particularly children) could no longer be concealed.

Yet Czechoslovakia had a long, eventful tradition of environmental conservation movements and societies, stretching back to the nineteenth century. The tradition had been violently interrupted during the Nazi German Occupation of 1939–1945 and again after the Communist takeover of February 1948; it was not until 1958, at the instigation of the zoologist Otakar Leiský, that another attempt was made to resurrect the tradition with the first modern voluntary organization, called TIS (Yew Tree)—Association for the Protection of Nature and the Countryside. From its beginnings, this organization struggled to maintain its independence; it was, for one thing, probably the only association in the Czechoslovak Socialist Republic with a founding charter that did not mention the leading role of the Communist Party. In the 1970s, after TIS had grown to sixteen thousand members, the regime forced it to disband.[3] The strictures of the Communist state, combined with a tradition of environmental protection, led to the formation of a specifically Czech (or Czechoslovak) kind of "conservationist," who in character was quite the opposite of the Western adherent of modern environmentalist movements. Among the qualities of the Czech conservationist were humility, self-realization in small-scale local volunteer work, a traditionally romantic attitude to nature and to historical monuments, as well as a complete absence of political goals and personal ambition.

Although the Iron Curtain was not hermetic, it severely limited the perception and understanding of modern Western political and social trends.

The lack of information and almost total absence of communication with the populations of the Western democracies became one of the main factors influencing the typical Czech conservationist's attitude to Green movements and parties. Many Czech conservationists were, paradoxically, at first wary of Western Greens. Internal resistance toward the Czechoslovak Communist regime—though not expressed in words and deeds—led to mistrust of and an aversion toward all parties, trends, and movements that in the West had declared themselves leftist or rather were often simply labeled as such.[4] The radicalism (even if often closer to anarchism than to the old left) of the Green parties and movements in the West, which placed them on the left in their own countries, was a product of their zeal for environmental protest and of their age (Western Greens tended to be young), but in Czechoslovakia this aspect was largely distorted and seen as evidence of their "leftist" leanings and consequently of attitudes that Czech conservationists were unable to identify with.

The information barrier, of course, worked in two directions and led to the fact that until very recently (if not in fact to the present day), Western Greens perceived Czech environmentalists as submissive, opportunistic, and ineffective romantics, whose tree-planting, well-cleaning, and recording of individual zoological and botanical species did not correspond to the actual urgency of the state of the environment and to modern attempts at finding solutions to it. This misunderstanding can reasonably be seen as one of the chief reasons for the total absence of spontaneous contact between Czech and Western adherents of environmentalism through the early 1980s and why there were no signs of collaboration, not counting the Western media (e.g., Radio Free Europe), which, by broadcasting to the East, at least tried to weaken the information barrier on environmental questions.

Despite the warnings about the urgency of environmental issues at the conferences in Stockholm and Helsinki, the talks (particularly in Helsinki) were concerned mainly with human and civil rights, defining the inalienability of those rights for the population of the civilized world, including the countries behind the Iron Curtain. The Communist states (including Czechoslovakia in the early years of normalization), however, accepted these principles in a purely formal way and in practice did not undertake any official changes in their domestic politics. But because these regimes also had to show a certain willingness to make concessions regarding the principles declared by these conferences, they adopted at least a slightly more benevolent and active position on environmental questions.

It must also be stressed here that environmentally oriented activity in Czechoslovakia in the 1970s, in comparison with the West, contained paradoxical features. Coinciding with the Stockholm conference, the Czechoslovak government set up a Commission for the Natural Environment in 1972, though no ministry of the environment with power at the federal level was established till the end of 1989.[5] The government entrusted relevant institutes in the Czechoslovak Academy of Sciences with the preparation of a theoretical basis for the work of the commission, and it also took steps toward greater public involvement in environmental activities, though the immediate impulse for this came, once again, from an academic body. The Institute of the Natural Environment at the Academy of Sciences came up with the idea of forming a youth organization for environmental conservation. According to Director Emil Hadač, the institute was thus also able to address the problem of the "low political commitment" of its employees (only three were members of the Communist Party). To deflect this charge, the staff of the institute established a branch of the Socialist Youth Organization (SSM) in their institute and oriented its activity toward nature protection.[6] The Central Committee of the Czech SSM declared 1974 to be "Conservation and Natural Environment Development Year." The key part of the official campaign that soon followed was the Brontosaurus Project, which was carefully coordinated with other institutes of the Academy of Sciences, the Czech Government Council for the Natural Environment, and other ministries in charge of various sectors of the natural environment. The campaign was also given much publicity in the mass media, particularly in magazines and programs with young readers and audiences.[7] The success of what had originally been conceived as a one-off event gave rise, with the consent of state organs, to the countrywide Brontosaurus Movement, which rejuvenated what was by then the merely formal and senseless activity of the SSM.[8]

In 1975, when Czechoslovakia became a signatory to the Helsinki Final Act on Security and Cooperation in Europe, its organs (in accord with Article 5 of the act, which also related to environmental questions) started planning another controlled initiative, aimed, on the one hand, at the protection of the natural environment and, on the other, at defusing the potential for spontaneous activities in Czechoslovak society. Three years later, in 1978 the Czechoslovak government issued a decree entrusting the Ministry of the Arts and Culture with the establishment of an ecologically oriented organization. The next year, the organization appeared as the Czech Union of Conservationists (ČSOP). Once again, the Czechoslovak Academy of Sciences played an important role.[9]

The proclaimed task of the Czech Union of Conservationists was also a cover for the tacit role that it was meant to play—namely, to replace TIS, which had proved irksome to the Communist regime and so was suppressed in 1979. This was done in such a way that the ČSOP would appear to TIS members to be its legal, natural successor. The Union of Conservationists essentially copied the hierarchic structure of the Czechoslovak Communist Party. A system of district, city, and central committees; auditing and control commissions; functionaries; and conferences enabled the regime to control all the activity of the organization and also make the ČSOP conform to the official principle of "democratic centralism," which, particularly in the sphere of finance, re-stricted any independent action by its local organizations. The number of lo-cal organizations and individual members of ČSOP and the Brontosaurus Movement, however, grew from the moment of their establishment to the end of the 1980s; by 1989, ČSOP had twenty-eight thousand individual mem-bers registered and nine hundred local organizations.[10]

Although the Brontosaurus Movement used the term *movement* in its name, and this term was thus automatically encoded in the public con-sciousness, it remains a question whether an environmentally oriented movement actually existed in Czechoslovakia in the late 1970s and early 1980s, or merely various organizations. Both initiatives had been established at the order of government and Communist Party organs (more or less moti-vated by the two international conferences), and they developed under their supervision and with their consent or at least forbearance. This was a process that was essentially the opposite of the typical emergence and de-velopment of Green movements and parties in Western democracies. In the West, the emergence of such initiatives was inspired and brought about by the spontaneous activity of the public, "from below," which in turn instigated scholarly research on environmental topics, organized public activities, and pursued concrete action by government bodies. In Czechoslovakia, by con-trast, the fundamental impetus came "from above"; only after academic in-stitutions had become interested was the general public involved. Charac-teristic features of a social movement (spontaneous emergence, dissemination by natural channels of communication, independent activity, and the opportunity to act as a pressure group) were therefore missing in Czechoslovakia.

The absence of such features cannot, however, be attributed to the lack of a sense of environmental conservation in Czechoslovak society in the late 1970s, but only to the likelihood of surveillance and, possibly, persecution by the regime of any independent activity. In 1985, for example, the envi-ronmental activist Pavel Křivka was imprisoned for eighteen months for, among other things, having written a letter to his friend in West Germany, in which he described the critical state of the environment in Czechoslovakia. Environmental activists and conservationists in Czechoslovakia in the late 1970s and early 1980s also had to resolve the moral dilemma of whether ac-tivity within official organizations was an expression of loyalty to the exist-ing regime and consequently a form of collaboration (or at least submission and opportunism), or whether it was an activity that was essentially positive, despite its taking place in regime-controlled organizations. The dilemma was intensified by rational doubts about whether it was at all possible to develop positive, meaningful, and effective environmental protection when members of these organizations faced regime censorship of information concerning the true state of the natural environment.

However serious and pressing this dilemma, grassroots conservationists generally did not pose this question so explicitly. As Brontosaurus activist Eliška Nováková put it:

> We were concerned with the "little" questions of the environment—if there is such a thing, and if the conservation of the natural environment can be compartmentalized like that. We didn't want to get mixed up in the big questions that were politically not up for discussion anyway. We were concerned instead with small-scale work to awaken people to the problems. We assumed that unless environmental awareness entered everyday life, there was no point in doing anything. Apart from that, the Socialist Youth Organization leaders would not have allowed us to take on the "big" environmental questions. We saw the point in what we were doing in the fact that young people were finding out about our activity and their parents were finding out from them. The young generation was environmentally more aware. That was how we wanted to make a breeding ground for future conservationists. We tried mainly to educate.[11]

The scholarly literature, interviews with environmental activists, and my own research have confirmed that unlike Green initiatives in the West, there was no attempt in Czechoslovakia in the late 1970s and early 1980s—and actually could not have been—to influence decision making in politics or the bureaucracy. If the Czech conservationists at that time had any of the characteristics of an opposition, then it was an opposition that tended to be implicit and internal. What they were trying to do with their "small-scale work" was, on closer examination, essentially in opposition to the government orientation toward extensive economic growth or, later, at least to the maintenance of the status quo of consumption at any price—that is, at the price of the devastation of the natural environment.[12]

Given this focus, it is not surprising that throughout this period the only contact with Western ecological and environmentalist currents took place at the official level, either in connection with the two big international conferences or among academics; if the general public heard about their meetings, it remained unaffected. The sole exception to this lack of public interest in environmental protection was, indirectly, the emergence of the Charter 77 movement. The Charter 77 signatories concentrated on upholding human and civil rights and exposing cases of their abuse by the regime; they based their campaign on the signatures of the Czechoslovak politicians on the Helsinki Final Act. Although they did not begin to pay more attention to the "rights of nature" until the 1980s (in response to both the continuing devastation of the environment and the opportunities yielded by Mikhail Gorbachev's glasnost), the Chartists, immediately after their emergence, gained access to Western mass media, such as Radio Free Europe, BBC, and Voice of America. The broadcasts of these stations, which a growing number of Czechs and Slovaks listened to (secretly, at the risk of regime persecution), soon included reports and discussions on the most pressing environmental questions in Czechoslovakia, and thus the public was at least informed about them.

Things began to change in 1983. In that year, the two military opposing blocs, NATO and the Warsaw Pact, began to base a new generation of atomic weapons in the countries of Western and Eastern Europe. In the West, politically diverse peace movements expanded and radicalized, protesting against both the expansion of the nuclear weapons of their own countries and the threat these weapons posed to the natural environment of the whole planet. Czechoslovakia had, admittedly, no spontaneously formed, independent peace movement, nor was the parallel between the threat posed by nuclear weapons and the potential environmental consequences of this threat expressed directly. Yet some young Czechs did voice protests, as early as the autumn of 1983, against the basing of Soviet midrange missiles on Czechoslovak territory (young East Germans expressed similar protests). Charter 77 reacted to the report of the basing of missiles with a document addressed to the Czechoslovak government. It demanded that Czechoslovaks should be able to meet informally with representatives of Western peace groups. The Czechoslovak secret police had kept under surveillance a number of petitions against the basing of nuclear weapons in Czechoslovakia. Yet in February 1984, Czechoslovak president Gustáv Husák and members of the Czechoslovak government were presented with a petition, signed by 939 citizens, against the basing of nuclear weapons in Czechoslovakia. Several thousand more citizens signed it later that year.[13] Although these protests did not openly express the link between the threat posed by nuclear weapons and the threat of the gradual devastation of the natural environment (by military and nonmilitary use of nuclear power), it was perhaps expressed on their behalf by the British historian Timothy Garton Ash, who had visited Czechoslovakia in early 1984: "Unlike the philosophical, literary and historical interests of Charter 77, the questions of peace and environmental pollution meet with an immediate general response. You do not need to be an intellectual to feel threatened by missiles and acid rain."[14]

The growing tension between the two military blocs was also reflected in an intensified friction in the internal politics of the Communist regime. Czechoslovaks heard about the "ideological deviation" of the West constantly. Even Czechoslovak fans of punk music were persecuted, labeled disseminators of Western pacifism and nonsocialist environmental thinking.[15] An aggressive campaign by the party-run mass media (particularly the papers *Tribuna* and *Rudé Právo*) attacked modern music and, above all, the way of life of some young people who did not identify with the imposed conspicuous consumption or the conformity of their parents' generation.

In the first third of the 1980s, the young generation began to gain prominence among environmentalists, as well as among peace activists, fans of rock music, and persons interested in religious and philosophical questions. Members of this generation either had not experienced the trauma of August 1968 at all or had at most experienced it only as children; they were therefore not marked by fear and caution, with no experience of the existential worries of their parents. Moreover, although this generation was brought up under a Communist regime, it never identified with its ideology. For the most part, it tended not to see the members of Western environmentalist parties and movements as left-wing, and it wanted to share their interests as well as the free access to information that Westerners now enjoyed thanks to developing technology.

Nor could the regime, despite all the repression, manage to maintain the information blockade on domestic environmental information. Evidence of this is the dissemination of the first analysis of the state of the environment in Czechoslovakia, the results of which eventually made their way to both the public at home and, by "underground" channels, abroad. This analysis was prepared in the autumn of 1983 by the Environmental Section of the Biology Society of the Czechoslovak Academy of Sciences at the direct impetus of the government and its premier, Lubomír Štrougal. This "government assignment" freed up information about the true state of the Czechoslovak natural environment, which had hitherto been kept secret even from experts. The report drew disquieting conclusions from the data and made a number of critical observations on the socioeconomic and, in particular, health impact that the present state of affairs would have. Although the whole report (published in a very limited number of copies) was meant only for the eyes of government functionaries, it was leaked and published in December 1983 in Charter 77's *samizdat* periodical *Informace o Chartě* (*Infoch*).[16]

The publishing of this classified report in the small "dissident ghetto" of Charter 77 signatories did not hit the regime as hard as did its publishing by the media abroad. As early as January 1984, part of it appeared in the Paris daily *Le Monde* and was quoted in broadcasts of the Voice of America and Radio Free Europe. In February 1984, about one-third of the report was published in the *Tageszeitung*, Berlin, and the whole report was published in the émigré journal *Listy* (of the Czechoslovak socialist opposition in exile). Finally, on 7 June 1984, a substantial part of it was published in the Hamburg weekly *Die Zeit*, under the title "Top Secret—Ecological Bankruptcy in the East Bloc."[17]

This publicity was a blow to the regime in a sensitive area. No investigation or search for culprits could hide the facts that Czechoslovakia was, ecologically speaking, among the most devastated countries in Europe and that its regime was unable either to protect the environment or to keep its own information secret. According to an adviser to Lubomír Štrougal, the premier reacted to the information leak with the words: "The fact that the news was printed by the Charter in *Infoch* was not particularly worrying, considering the number of copies in which the bulletin was printed and therefore its negligible influence on the public. [. . .] Its being broadcast by the Voice of America and Radio Free Europe, however, was too much."[18] Moreover, the report was published at a time when Vasil Bil'ak, the chief Communist ideologue, was preaching the view that ecologists were the "enemies of socialism."

The publishing of the report had an international impact as well. Foreign delegations visiting Czechoslovakia afterward (particularly those from West Germany) rarely failed to ask their hosts about the natural environment in Czechoslovakia. The widespread publicity of the report was thus important not only for the actual information it provided but also because it demonstrated the permeability of the barrier between Czechoslovakia and the West, thus leading to some Western pressure on Czechoslovakia to solve its serious environmental problems.[19] In this way Czech awareness of the deplorable state of the natural environment in Czechoslovakia gradually increased. Still, the government changed neither its fundamental approach to environmental questions nor its attitude to the extent the public should be informed about serious environmental crises. That was fully manifested after 26 April 1986, the day of the accident at the atomic energy plant in Chernobyl.

With the meltdown at Chernobyl, the last shred of the Czechoslovak public's already reduced confidence in the Communist government institutions and bodies also melted down. In comparison with the countries of Western Europe, Czechoslovakia took far weaker, far less effective measures to protect the public from potential health damage as a result of the nuclear accident. The main government response was not to warn the public and inform them but "to calm them down." For example, the secret police confiscated leaflets that appeared in at least four Czechoslovak regions in late May, which contained, among other things, an appeal from the citizens of Austria asking Czechoslovak citizens to think twice about building a nuclear plant near the Austrian border. In connection with this incident, the Czechoslovak secret police detained five Austrian students in Prague. Whereas the Czechoslovak mass media urged the public—after an increase in radioactivity in Czechoslovakia was officially admitted (five days after the accident)—only to observe the rules of general personal hygiene, the Austrian leaflets warned that radioactive contamination remained dangerous and provided specific instructions about what steps to take, including how to prepare food (especially for babies, children, and pregnant and nursing women).[20] Nor was confidence in the government restored by propaganda tricks—for example, when Czechoslovak Television ran footage of the Ukraine claiming that life and work in the collective farms near Chernobyl was taking place as usual and that vegetables could be eaten directly from the fields, even without washing them. The most important sources of reliable information were, as before, Radio Free Europe and BBC, whose audience rose, in the weeks after the Chernobyl catastrophe, to nearly half of all Czechoslovaks who listened to radio.[21] These forbidden sources would not have as many listeners again, except during the first week after the demonstrations of November 1989.

The evidence thus suggests not only that Western neighbors were well informed about the environmental situation in the Soviet bloc but also that no leaflets or other information of any considerable quantity were disseminated by Czechoslovaks themselves. By contrast, clear criticism, though not particularly hard-hitting, of the existing atomic energy program of the countries of the Council for Mutual Economic Cooperation (COMECON) and demands for the revision of that program were heard in the neighboring countries— Poland, Hungary, East Germany, and even the Soviet Union itself—after Chernobyl.[22] In Kraków, two thousand persons came together to protest the lack of information available to the public concerning the nuclear accident; only the Czechoslovak public kept timidly quiet. The loss of faith in the Communist government organs, however, led after all to a gradual loss of fear, which in subsequent years manifested itself in the accelerating emergence of new citizens' initiatives and movements and the radicalization of existing official organizations.

From the environmentalist point of view, an important though not direct result of the Chernobyl accident was that the population finally realized that atomic energy could be a source of danger, whether as missiles or power plants. This awareness helped environmentally oriented groups to find a common language and platform with members of peace initiatives and movements—a convergence similar to the one west of the Czechoslovak border.

In the last three years before the changes of November and December 1989, practically all Czech citizens' initiatives, from Charter 77 to the nascent activities among the young generation (the Independent Peace Association, the John Lennon Peace Club, the Bohemian Children), were oriented also to environmental matters and focused attention on the current state of the natural environment. Among the young members of the Brontosaurus Movement and, to a certain extent, ČSOP, there was also an increasing number of people who realized that repairing the damage already done to the natural environment required that the causes and culprits be identified. Meanwhile, with the gradual thaw that came about as part of Gorbachev's perestroika and glasnost, the greater part of the public no longer could perceive work in the area of environmental protection, even that of the independent citizens' initiatives, as being something particularly dangerous.

At least some youth moved in 1987–1989 from a conservationist platform to the kind of activity the regime called "illegal" and "oppositional." In the book *Sto studentských revolucí* (One Hundred Student Revolutions), several university students who later actively joined the 1989 revolution recalled the linking of conservation of the natural environment to questions that went beyond "mere" conservation. An example is the interview with Jindřich Petrlík, the founder of the environmentalist organization Children of the Earth:

> As very young environmentalists in the 1980s we were not all isolated. We had information about Greenpeace; we established our first contacts. Some of us were proponents of anarchism; some of us listened to Punk and New Wave, alternative music and the underground. Young people from Brontosaurus repaired historical Churches and roadside crosses, and, for example, some of the most active fighters in the battle to save Stromovka Park, in Prague, were, in addition to the Bohemian Children, members of one of the Prague branches of Brontosaurus.[23]

The convergence of positions and interests among environmentally oriented activists and members of other independent groups was, to be sure, important for subsequent developments. An environmental protest did take place in 1987, but only thanks to an external impetus—namely, at the initiative of several young Austrians from a branch of Greenpeace. On the first anniversary of the Chernobyl accident, they hung a banner over the National Museum on Wenceslas Square, Prague, warning in large letters in Czech of the possibility of other catastrophes at other nuclear plants (e.g., Temelín, then under construction near the Austrian border). The police arrested the Austrians, drove them to the border, and expelled them from the country. Whereas environmental movements elsewhere in Europe—the Polish Freedom and Peace movement being no exception—made their disgust with the antienvironmentalist arrogance of industrial systems spontaneously, noisily, and resolutely clear, the silent Czechs had to import their one and only outcry from the "lands of hard currency," as the saying went.[24]

This pattern of "imported" protest continued through mid-1989, yet domestic politics would also begin to play a role. In late May 1989, Premier Ladislav Adamec convened in Prague a meeting of government representatives from neighboring countries to discuss environmental problems in the region.[25] During that meeting, activists of the citizens' initiative "Prague Mothers" walked up and down the streets of downtown Prague with babies in strollers and small children at their sides, and they presented to the assembled statesmen a petition concerning the dreadful quality of the air the youngest generation was being forced to breathe. In the presence of this audience, the police could not use the Plexiglas shields, batons, and water cannons that had proved so effective in dispersing past demonstrations.

The following week, an international meeting of young people on environmental and peace issues convened in Vimperk, southern Bohemia. This four-day "Bohemian Forest Ecological and Peace Meeting 1989" was attended by about 1,500 young people from environmental and peace groups from twenty-seven countries. ČSOP, the Socialist Youth Organization, and the Czechoslovak Peace Committee organized the event. The public discussions and meetings were attended by official as well as independent environmental organizations from Czechoslovakia and abroad, including Czechoslovak émigrés who had found not only asylum abroad but also a chance to express their views on the environment. Among the participants of the Vimperk meeting was Milan Horáček, a founder of the West German Green Party and a member of the Bundestag.[26] The Czechoslovak secret police had detailed information about Horáček's work as editor in chief of the German version of *Listy* and about his contacts with Czechoslovak émigré leaders. But because the West German Green Party made its participation in the Vimperk meeting conditional upon allowing Horáček to attend, the regime had no choice but to issue him the required tourist visa. Horáček then appeared, on 2 June, in a discussion on environmental issues in Czechoslovakia and abroad. He pointed out Gorbachev's positive attitude toward the possibility of several political parties existing in a Communist state and recommended to the Czechoslovak environmental movement that it start a political party similar to the Greens in Western Europe.[27]

Whereas a few years before 1989 the arrival of a Czechoslovak émigré— especially an émigré delivering a public speech and agitating for the formation of a non-Communist political party—would have been impossible, indeed almost inconceivable, the situation had changed much in the interval. Calls for dialogue with the regime enabled the convening of a series of forums on the environment, which were held in Brno, as well as a relatively large petition in support of the environment in the Chomutov region and another petition against the construction of a dam in the Křivoklát area, and the emergence of the independent Ecology Society and its *samizdat* magazine *Ekologický Bulletin*. Before anyone could take steps toward the founding of a Green Party in Czechoslovakia, the whole internal political situation changed so radically that there would be no time for setting out ecological positions for the nearest future.

Until the 1980s, for all practical purposes, the development of environmental awareness in Czechoslovakia was without external influences, because, with the exception of a short spell in the 1960s, the country was isolated by the Iron Curtain. In the 1970s and particularly in the 1980s the official organs of the Western countries had a certain influence, but that could neither change the nature of the Czechoslovak economy nor change the attitude toward the natural environment, which had (within the logic of Communist ideology) been degraded to the level of collective property for which nobody bore any personal responsibility. The environmental movements of Western Europe and the United States, and the Greens in the 1980s, could make their influence felt in Czechoslovakia only with difficulty, because their activity and positions were concealed both by the artificially formed information barrier and by the label of "left-wing thinking," which in Czechoslovakia tended to lead to long-term misunderstandings rather than to efforts to work together. In the late 1980s, however, the heterogeneous official and independent environmentalist streams in Czechoslovakia joined together in the citizens' initiatives to focus attention on the seriousness of environmental issues; from them they adopted methods of coming out in public, which, in the last few years before November 1989, may be called political.

The Communist regime never explicitly stated that it did not recognize the attempts to protect the natural environment or rejected those attempts. It merely shunted conservation aside as a luxury for which the country must first earn the money to pay—most effectively by developing extensive machine and chemical production using energy produced from burning low-grade brown coal. Not even the changes in the political regime and social system in November and December 1989, however, were able to do away entirely with the short-sighted attitude, running across the whole Czechoslovak political spectrum, that the population of the country must first earn the money to pay for environmental measures. Not even the changes in ownership and social relations during the last twelve years have overcome the deeply rooted prejudice that nature, the country and the whole planet are the global property of humankind, to be disposed of without responsibility toward future generations and the planet on which *Homo sapiens* is but one of many biological species. But the great changes of November and December 1989 have at least provided essential social conditions and prerequisites forcing those with anthropocentric attitudes to put their arguments in competition with more ecological attitudes.

NOTES

1. Miroslav Vaněk, "Zelené mládí: Ekologické aktivity mladé generace v osmdesátých letech," in *Ostrůvky svobody: Kulturní a občanské aktivity mladé generace v 80. letech v Československu*, ed. Miroslav Vaněk (Prague: Votobia, 2002), 238–40; Barbara Hicks and JoAnn Carmin, "Finding the 'Social' in Movements: International Triggering Events, Transnational Networks and Environmentalism in Post-Communist Central Europe," paper presented at the Fourth International Conference of the International Society for Third-Sector Research, Dublin, Ireland, July 2000, 6–7.

2. Miroslav Vaněk, *Nedalo se tady dýchat: Ekologie v českých zemích v letech 1968–1989* (Prague: Maxdorf, 1996), 12–18.

3. Vaněk, *Nedalo se tady dýchat*, 12–18.

4. See Václav Havel, "An Anatomy of a Reticence," in *Václav Havel or Living in Truth*, ed. Jan Vladislav (London: Faber & Faber, 1986), 164–95.

5. Hicks and Carmin, "Finding the 'Social,'" 6.

6. Vaněk, "Zelené mládí," 242.

7. Jan Velek, "Akce Brontosaurus," *Mladý Svět* 16, no. 3 (April 1974): 8–9.

8. Vaněk, "Zelené mládí," 243.

9. Vaněk, *Nedalo se tady dýchat*, 40–41.

10. There are no separate numbers for Brontosaurus membership. During its entire existence, it was a part of the Socialist Youth Union and did not have its own list of members.

11. Vaněk, *Nedalo se tady dýchat*, 40–41.

12. Hana Librová, "Kreuzwege und Paradoxa der tschechischen Umweltbewegung," in *Sborník prací Filozofické fakulty Brněnské university*, G 34 (Brno: Filozofická fakulta Masarykova univerzita Brno, 1991).

13. Petr Blažek, "Dejte šanci míru," in *Ostrůvky svobody*, ed. Vaněk, 90–95.

14. Timothy Garton Ash, *The Uses of Adversity: Essays on the Fate of Central Europe* (New York: Vintage, 1990), 69–70.

15. Miroslav Vaněk, "Kytky v popelnici," in *Ostrůvky svobody*, ed. Vaněk, 188, 191, 203–4.

16. Vaněk, *Nedalo se tady dýchat*, 69.

17. Wolf Oschlies, *Böhmens Fluren und Heine sterben: Zur Umweltkatastrophe in der Tschechoslowakei* (Cologne: Böhlau, 1985), 8.

18. Vaněk, *Nedalo se tady dýchat*, 69–70.

19. Vaněk, *Nedalo se tady dýchat*, 70–71.

20. Cited in Vaněk, *Nedalo se tady dýchat, 82*.

21. Vaněk, *Nedalo se tady dýchat*, 83.

22. Vaněk, *Nedalo se tady dýchat*, 84.

23. Milan Otáhal and Miroslav Vaněk, *Sto studentských revolucí: Studenti v období pádu komunismu v Československu—životopisná vyprávění* (Prague: Nakladatelství Lidové noviny, 1999), 94–116, 638–39.

24. Petr Blumfeld, "Můj kraj, stejně jako tvůj kraj, jde do . . . ," *Ekologický Bulletin* 9 (March 1989): 12–13.

25. Vaněk, "Zelené mládí," 268.

26. Vaněk, *Nedalo se tady dýchat*, 124–25.

27. Vaněk, "Zelené mládí," 267–68.

11

A Transcontinental Movement of Citizens?

Strategic Debates in the 1980s Western Peace Movement

Patrick Burke

The opening plenary of the third European Nuclear Disarmament (END) Convention in Perugia in July 1984 was under way. The city's mayor had greeted the thousand-strong audience in the Teatro Turreno. Without warning, a group of peace activists, with red cloths tied around their mouths and holding placards, climbed onto the stage. The placards carried the names and symbols of those independent peace groups and human rights groups— from Central Eastern Europe and the Soviet Union (CEE/SU), as well as from Turkey and the Israeli Occupied Territories—whose invited representatives had been refused permission by their governments to travel to the convention. The protesters stood in silence for only a few minutes, then left the stage.[1] Their public demonstration, however, ensured that one issue dominated the convention: the virtual absence of "independents"[2] and the simultaneous presence of delegates of some official peace committees from Eastern Europe.

The question of who from CEE/SU, and under what conditions, should be invited to the END Conventions had been controversial since the planning of the second convention in West Berlin in 1983.[3] The organizers of the Perugia protest were Western peace activists who had become increasingly dissatisfied with the policies of the Liaison Committee toward official and independent actors in CEE/SU. (The Liaison Committee, the permanent organizing committee of the conventions, met every two to three months to plan the next convention.) In essence, they thought that the Liaison Committee was emphasizing ties with the peace committees at the expense of relations with, in the words of an open letter cowritten in early 1984 by one of the protesters, Dieter Esche, "our real partners in Eastern Europe, independent peace groups and movements."[4]

At the end of the convention, the protesters and others set up a new grouping, the European Network for East–West Dialogue, or "Network," the purpose of which was precisely to concentrate on relations with independent groups in the East. At its founding, the Network consisted mainly of small Western peace groups; even though later some larger West European peace organizations became involved, many of the important mainstream peace groups never did.

The protest at Perugia, and the setting up of the Network, are an important part of a larger story: the attempts by some Western peace groups in the 1980s to create an alliance with independent groups and movements in CEE/SU. Some have called the dialogue that ensued between these groups East and West a "détente from below," in analogy to the concomitant relationships between Western peace groups and state bodies in the East, such as the official peace committees.

After sketching the contours of the Western peace movement of the 1980s, this chapter outlines the conceptual frame within which this "Ostpolitik" was conducted; it then tells the story by focusing on the work of one key character in it: the British peace group END.[5] A central theme of the chapter is the tensions within sections of the Western peace movement to which this Ostpolitik gave rise: tensions both between groups who pursued "détente from below" and those who were skeptical of its value, and tensions within groups committed to that détente. British END was one such group. These strains, this chapter argues, illustrate the difficulties inherent in the attempt to create a transsystemic alliance in the Cold War, an attempt that raised the question of how to combine Western peace movement demands for détente and disarmament with demands for human rights and democracy in the Soviet bloc.

A TRANSNATIONAL MOVEMENT

Between 1979 and the mid- to late 1980s, almost every West European country witnessed tens, occasionally hundreds of thousands, even millions of people campaigning against nuclear weapons. The catalyst for the rise of the West European peace movements was NATO's "dual-track" decision of 12 December 1979. This entailed the deployment of 464 Tomahawk cruise and 108 Pershing II U.S. medium-range nuclear missiles in five West European countries—the United Kingdom, the Netherlands, Belgium, West Germany, and Italy; simultaneously, the United States would negotiate with the Soviet Union for the nondeployment of these missiles in return for the removal of Soviet theater nuclear weapons, the SS-20s. The dominant issue of the peace campaigns was halting the proposed deployment of cruise and Pershing II missiles.

The movements were national—the publicly visible high points of the peace campaign were the huge national demonstrations in many West European capitals in the autumn of 1981 and 1983—and much of the peace campaigning took place locally. However, together, these movements also constituted a transnational social movement; that is, in Sidney Tarrow's definition, they were "connected networks of challengers" both "rooted in domestic social networks" and "organized across national boundaries," and engaged in "sustained contentious interaction with opponents—national or nonnational."[6]

The movements were connected in two ways. First, they shared a "collective action frame";[7] that is, they agreed that a particular set of issues was a problem, offered a solution to that problem, and specified an agent of the solution. The problem was, in broad terms, the nuclear arms race and the Cold War but, first and foremost, Western nuclear weapons, and, specifically, cruise and Pershing II missiles. The solution was nuclear disarmament but, immediately, nondeployment of the new NATO missiles. An agent of that solution would be, of course, peace movements.

Second, the movements were linked both informally and organizationally, and at various levels.[8] For example, activists from northern Europe took part in the peace camp at Comiso in Sicily; women from West Germany, Holland and Sweden were among the thirty thousand who encircled Greenham Common air base on 12 December 1982; there were international rallies (e.g., in Brussels at Easter 1981) and marches (the Scandinavian women's march from Copenhagen to Paris in the summer of 1981); and activists spoke at meetings abroad (e.g., in Britain, on the 1983 "Five Nations" and the 1984 "Beyond the Blocs" speaking tours) and at mass rallies (in Bonn in 1981 or London in 1983).[9]

There were also more institutionalized, longer-term networks of, and links between, movements—for example, the International Peace Coordination and Communication Centre (IPCC), under whose auspices representatives of nonaligned peace groups in Western Europe and the United States met regularly to plan tactics and strategies; and, from the end of 1981, the END Conventions and the Liaison Committee—sometimes called the END Convention process—which brought together nonaligned movements, political parties, trade unions, churches, and other institutions.[10] The political framework for the convention process was provided by the END Appeal, the signing of which was a condition of participating in the process.

However, as has been indicated, the Western peace movement also contained another a kind of transnational element. From the early 1980s, some groups engaged in dialogue, and tried to work with, actors in CEE/SU; they were motivated to do so by the desire to create some kind of "transcontinental movement."[11] They conducted this work both inside and outside the convention process; the political framework for this work was provided mainly by the 1980 END Appeal.

Drafted largely by the British historian E. P. Thompson, and signed by thousands of activists in Western Europe, as well as by a handful of individuals in CEE/SU,[12] the appeal framed the Cold War, and the alternative to it, in both military and civic-cum-political terms. Its authors wanted the appeal to provide a nonaligned, pan-European framework for national peace campaigns. The threat, the appeal states, is posed not just by nuclear weapons but by the whole confrontation, political and military, between East and West: the Cold War. The appeal establishes a causal link between the Cold War and restrictions on civil rights—"in the East as well as the West." And both sides *share* responsibility for the Cold War and its consequences: "Guilt lies squarely upon both parties."

The response to the threat is, first, to demand the creation of a European nuclear weapons–free zone: "We must act together to free the entire territory of Europe, from Poland to Portugal, from nuclear weapons, air and submarine bases, and from all institutions engaged in research into or manufacture of nuclear weapons. We ask the two superpowers to withdraw all nuclear weapons from European territory."

The appeal, however, also addresses the Cold War directly: "Our objectives must be to free Europe from confrontation, to enforce detente between the United States and the Soviet Union, and, ultimately, to dissolve both great power alliances." The means to the ends advocated in the appeal are not primarily the actions or policies of states; they lie, rather, above all "in our own hands": "People "of every faith and persuasion" need to create a "European-wide campaign," a "trans-continental movement in which every kind of exchange takes place." Some exchanges, then, will be between representatives of states, while other, "less formal"—and, the appeal strongly implies, more significant—will be among institutions, groups, and individuals outside state structures.[13] The appeal thus did something that many peace campaigns in the West avoided: It called explicitly for an end to the post–World War II status quo in Europe, and it asked not for statesmen to negotiate but for "ordinary people" to campaign for this end.

DISPUTES AND TENSIONS

Supporters of the appeal emphasized different aspects of the project it sketched out, above all with regard to East–West relations. Some stressed the creation of a European nuclear weapons–free zone. In its East–West work, this strategy tended to promote contacts with official bodies in the East—and was thus labeled by some "détente from above"—and was skeptical about the value of "détente from below." This approach was pursued, broadly speaking, by political parties and trade unions and organizations linked to them, though it was also largely favored by peace organizations such as the

British Campaign for Nuclear Disarmament (discussed later) or the Bertrand Russell Peace Foundation. This understanding of the Western peace movement's strategy in general, and of the END campaign in particular, was similar to the approach of the West German Social Democratic Party (SPD): namely, that détente and nuclear disarmament could and should be kept separate from the question of human rights and democracy in CEE/SU. As such, and by favoring contacts with "officials" rather than cooperation with independents, this approach did not raise the question of the legitimacy of the regimes in CEE/SU.

Others, while supporting the idea of a nuclear weapons–free zone in Europe, increasingly emphasized that part of the project that called for an end to the Cold War and for Europe to go "beyond the blocs."[14] This approach prioritized the dialogue with independent groups in the East (though for the most part not to the exclusion of contacts with official bodies). This approach was followed by peace groups including British END; in France, CODENE; in West Germany, the Greens and, in West Berlin, the East–West Dialogue Group; in the Netherlands, IKV; and in the United States, the Campaign for Peace and Democracy, East and West.[15] Many of these groups either cofounded or subsequently became involved in the European Network for East–West Dialogue. This strategy, because it treated as essential components of its campaign independent groups in CEE/SU that were regarded as illegitimate by their own regimes, did implicitly question the legitimacy of those regimes.

In the convention process—within which much of this East–West work was most visibly conducted—the two strategies gave rise to continuing tension and occasional sharp disputes between their respective proponents. (This was an example of how, in Mary Kaldor's words, the goal of building a "transcontinental movement of citizens" was not "widely accepted"—indeed, was "bitterly contested"—in the Western peace movement.[16]) These differences surfaced above all in the regular debates on the Liaison Committee about who from CEE/SU should be invited to the next convention and under what conditions. For example, should only signatories of the appeal be invited as full participants, with nonsignatories attending as observers only? Should only independent activists be invited? Official peace committees and independents? Should the presence of officials be conditional on that of "unofficials"? Was this sensible, given that unofficial activists would almost certainly not be able to attend? (If this happened, there would be no CEE/SU presence at all the conventions, which some felt would undermine the END commitment to dialogue with the East.) These debates sometimes boiled over into the convention itself; one such occasion was the 1984 END Convention in Perugia. These two approaches to East–West relations were pursued side by side within the framework of the convention process until the end of the decade. By the time of the preparations for the END Convention in Coventry in 1987, one British END activist could note that there was a "fundamental divergence of peace movement perspectives" between these "two very differently motivated tendencies" on the Liaison Committee.[17]

BRITISH END

The East–West contacts conducted in the spirit of the END Appeal also, however, created tensions *within* groups committed to the END project. British END was one such group. In order to understand why this was so, we must first examine the nature of British END and its East–West work.

Established in 1980 to promote the END Appeal—Edward Thompson was its best-known founder—British END was an intellectual pressure group disseminating ideas and information, above all in its publications.[18] It concentrated on three areas. It promoted the END idea in Britain—in the peace movement, in political parties and trade unions, and in the churches. It stimulated links between the British peace movement and peace movements elsewhere in Western Europe and helped to foster cooperation amongst nonaligned West European and U.S. peace groups. And it developed its own, and helped other peace groups develop their, East–West ties. British END was very small: When it was a nonmembership organization (until 1985), its registered supporters numbered around two thousand;[19] after 1985, it acquired no more than about six hundred members.

While its East–West work was by no means all that END did, this activity did become an increasingly important element in the group's campaigning as the decade progressed. The distinctive approach of British END to East–West campaigning was sketched out in the END Appeal and was elaborated above all by Thompson. In publications and internal documents, as well as in speeches, he developed arguments for what he called in his 1982 pamphlet *Beyond the Cold War* a "détente of peoples rather than states," a "politics of peace, informed by a new internationalist code of honour, conducted by citizens."[20] The Cold War, he argued, had made the "cause of 'peace' and the cause of 'freedom'" fall apart. The rise of the Western peace movement and the first responses to it from CEE showed, he claimed, that "these two causes are returning to one cause—peace and freedom—and as this happens, so, by a hundred different channels, the transcontinental discourse of political culture can be resumed."[21]

Within a political framework constructed largely by the writings and speeches of Edward Thompson, British END's East–West work developed along two tracks: on the one hand, developing a relationship with independent groups and individuals in CEE/SU; on the other, establishing links with official bodies. The independent forces included, in Czechoslovakia, Charter 77, the human rights group founded in 1977, the Jazz Section,[22] and the Independent Peace Association, set up in 1988; in Hungary, individuals in the Democratic Opposition, an intellectual grouping that emerged in the late 1970s, the Peace Group for Dialogue, established in 1982, and, from the mid-1980s, students who went on to form the FIDESZ, a political party that played an important role in the transition to democracy; in Poland, leading figures in Solidarity, KOS (the Committee for Social Defense), created in 1982 after the imposition of martial law, and Freedom and Peace, an independent human rights and peace group founded in 1985; in the German Democratic Republic (GDR), the autonomous peace movement often called—after its most distinctive symbol—Swords into Ploughshares, Women for Peace (both of these emerged in 1982), and the Peace and Human Rights Initiative, set up in 1986; and, in the Soviet Union, the Moscow Trust Group, created in 1982.

DIALOGUE

At the heart of British END's (and other Western peace groups') relationship with independent groups in CEE/SU was precisely its participation in a *dialogue* with them—that is, in an exchange of ideas in letters, statements, articles, and face-to-face discussions.

In END's case, the written dialogue included Thompson's correspondence with Charter 77 signatory Jaroslav Šabata (a key figure in Charter 77's participation in the dialogue); official END statements or letters written in response to statements or letters by, for example, KOS or Charter 77; and, of course, the END Appeal, along with some of Thompson's early writings, which were translated into some of the Eastern European languages.[23] Most of the face-to-face contacts took place in CEE/SU, as, for most of the decade, with the exception of a small number of Hungarians and Poles, most activists from Soviet bloc countries could not visit the West. Many END activists traveled to the CEE/SU: Lynne Jones and Mark Salter, for example, traveled regularly and frequently to Poland between 1981 and 1989, meeting a wide range of activists; there was a flurry of visits to the Peace Group for Dialogue in Hungary between September 1982 and July 1983 (when the group was dissolved)—not just by prominent British END figures such as Edward Thompson and Mary Kaldor but by less well-known activists such as Stephen Tunnicliffe of the END Churches Lateral Committee. British END supporters also traveled to the Soviet Union, Czechoslovakia, and, in Yugoslavia, Slovenia.

In the course of these exchanges, ideas were diffused in both directions. Interlocutors on each side of the East–West dialogue have pointed to the influence of these exchanges on their ideas.[24] For END, arguably the single most important idea that came from the East was the notion that peace was "indivisible." Perhaps the most coherent *written* expression of this idea came in a series of statements, letters, and articles written between 1981 and 1985 by Charter 77 signatories, writing collectively and individually, including Václav Havel, Jaroslav Šabata, and Jiří Hájek.[25] The "indivisibility of peace" refers to the notion that there can be no peace *between* states if there is no peace (i.e., justice and respect for human rights) *within* states—and, by implication, that to campaign for the former but not the latter is both politically shortsighted and morally indefensible. Linking peace between states and internal democracy was not foreign to the END frame. The END Appeal had not only stated that the Cold War entailed the erosion of civil rights in East and West—thus implying that ending the Cold War would remove a profound threat to civil rights. It had also declared that supporters of the appeal would defend the right of all citizens to take part in the East–West exchange. That is, END supporters would, as part of their work, uphold the rights of association and expression (at least of those engaged in this work). However, the notion of the indivisibility of peace went further: It placed the building of peace between states and respect for human rights and freedom on the same footing. It made the achievement of the former conditional on the latter: "To guarantee peace it is necessary to eliminate violence and injustice within states and guarantee respect by the state authorities in all countries of human and civil rights."[26]

The "indivisibility of peace" was also brought home to END campaigners by the way that END's (and other Western groups') interlocutors in CEE/SU were treated by their authorities—for example, the imprisonment for their participation in the dialogue with the Western peace movement not just of human rights campaigners, but even of peace campaigners who had openly opposed the deployment of *Western* missiles.[27]

In short, the original END linking of peace and civil rights, coupled with END activists' openness to the stronger notion of the indivisibility of peace and their experience of having people in CEE/SU they were in dialogue with—and often knew—being arrested and imprisoned—all this combined to persuade at least some British END activists that democracy in CEE/SU must be part of the END strategy. Indeed, Kaldor has argued that, by the end of the 1980s, there was a "growing consensus" among those who took part in the East–West dialogue—and, therefore, among END activists—that "democracy in Eastern Europe was the best strategy for ending the Cold War," but democracy "could be best achieved within the framework of a détente process and a winding down of the arms race." She contrasts this with the stance of some in the East and West who considered peace or human rights to be achievable only sequentially. Thus, in the Western peace movement there were those "who argued that human rights would follow disarmament and that the worst evil was nuclear weapons;" in the East, meanwhile, there were those "who argued that the Soviet Union only [understood] force and the West therefore needed to be strong; . . . disarmament would only be possible after the fall of communism."[28]

Some Eastern activists have indicated that the Western peace movements, or individual activists, influenced their work in various ways. Gerd Poppe, for example, a leading peace and human rights campaigner in the GDR, has written that the END Appeal, as well as Thompson's essay "Notes on Exterminism, the Last Stage of Civilization," helped shape the thinking of some GDR activists. These analyses and others, he writes, indicated to their GDR readers that a "'new international' of emancipatory and antimilitarist movements was needed."[29]

However, in the East, too, the strategy of dialogue and cooperation between Western peace groups and independent groups in the East was (to quote again Kaldor on Western peace activists) sometimes "bitterly contested," rather than "widely accepted."[30] This was evident in the differing statements made about the Western peace movement by activists in CEE/SU. The dissident milieu in Czechoslovakia could produce not only Jaroslav Šabata's statement that "the western European independent peace movement has intrinsically the same aims as ourselves" but also Václav Racek's sharp criticism of the same movement.[31] Racek (a pseudonym) not only argued that there was no possibility of a Western-style peace movement emerging in CEE/SU and therefore of any pan-European campaign of the kind envisaged in the END Appeal. He also claimed that the peace movement did not understand the specific threat to peace posed by the "totalitarian system." His "alternative strategy for the repair of Europe" included the demand that the "peace movement should support the military forces of Western democracies as *instruments* of human rights confronting totalitarian systems."[32]

RELATIONS WITH "OFFICIALS"

At the same time, British END maintained relations with officialdom in the East, which meant, for most of the 1980s, official peace committees, organizations whose function was to help mobilize domestic opinion behind their own regimes' foreign and defense policies, and to conduct relations with foreign peace movements.

The relationship between British END and the peace committees was quite different from its relations with independent actors in the Soviet bloc.[33] While British END activists treated the latter as potential partners in a transcontinental movement against the Cold War, they regarded the former as necessary, even fruitful, contacts, but not as possible allies. Thompson, who played a key role in shaping British END's policies toward

CEE/SU, arguably reflected a consensus within British END on this issue when he wrote that

> we recognise that Eastern Councils perform useful functions of communication and diplomacy. . . . We welcome occasions to meet them. But we cannot acknowledge them as equal partners in a transcontinental peace movement. . . . [To do so] could only be upon the premise . . . that no responsibility of any kind for Europe's crisis lies with the Soviet Union or the Warsaw bloc.[34]

Peace committees and other official bodies in the East, for their part, were—particularly in the first half of the decade—suspicious of, and sometimes hostile toward, British END and other parts of the nonaligned peace movement. In June 1983, for example, just before the "Prague Assembly for Peace and Life, against Nuclear War," a conference organized by the pro-Moscow World Peace Council, the Czechoslovak Communist Party circulated a document to activists and functionaries describing END ("active mainly in Great Britain") as an "organisation with explicit anti-communist and anti-Soviet function."[35] In addition, some END activists were denied entry to countries in the Soviet bloc, and one was arrested and interrogated for four days by the GDR authorities in December 1983. At the same time, as we have seen, the authorities in CEE/SU were harassing some of the independent activists in their own countries engaged in dialogue with Western peace groups. As a result, much of British END's relationship with officialdom in the Soviet bloc consisted of protests against the treatment of East European activists and of END visitors. Indeed, British END ran support campaigns for harassed CEE/SU activists throughout the 1980s.

The fundamental cause of this mutual suspicion was the basic difference in outlook between British END and the regimes of the Soviet bloc. British END blamed both sides for the Cold War, championed independent activists in CEE/SU, and raised the question of human rights abuses in the Soviet bloc. It thus posed an implicit challenge to the legitimacy of the Warsaw Pact regimes. These regimes, in turn, blamed the nuclear arms race and the Cold War on the West, treated independent groups as opponents, and regarded the raising of human rights issues as interference in their internal affairs.

Despite these tensions, British END maintained a relationship with the peace committees and other official bodies in the East. Partly this derived naturally from the aim of promoting "every kind of exchange" as part of a "trans-continental movement";[36] partly, for some END activists, this was— alongside talking with independent activists—one way to "build bridges" to, and "break down enemy images" of, the East. It was also seen as a way of increasing the space in which independent CEE/SU activists could operate. And, finally, British END activists thought they could use these channels to try to influence the thinking of the Soviet bloc regimes.[37]

THE CAMPAIGN FOR NUCLEAR DISARMAMENT

British END also tried to involve other groups and organizations in the West in the dialogue. It did this partly by publicizing the dialogue. With its own publications, briefing sheets for activists, internal reports by END activists about their trips to the CEE/SU, articles by END activists in the left and mainstream press, and the occasional book (e.g., Thompson's *Zero Option* and *The Heavy Dancers*), British END was a key source of information in English on independent peace activities in the East and on the East–West dialogue.

British END was also trying actively to disseminate its ideas within other organizations. In Britain, one such organization—which British END wanted to influence perhaps more than any other—was the Campaign for Nuclear Disarmament (CND). Founded in 1958, and by 1983 with about one hundred thousand national members, CND was the dominant organization in the British peace movement. CND had a national agenda: Its campaigning remit was unilateral nuclear disarmament by Britain and, in the immediate term, preventing the deployment of cruise missiles and of Britain's own Trident missile system. This "historic focus on British unilateralism," James Hinton has argued, "may well have inhibited CND in its attempt to develop . . . an active Europeanism."[38] Nevertheless, CND did have international policies, formulated above all by its International Committee. These policies focused on the END Convention process, the International Peace Coordination and Communication Centre, as well as broadly promoting "a process of dialogue" with the peace committees of the Soviet bloc.[39]

There was a much broader spectrum of views about CEE/SU in CND than in British END. While some activists were explicitly pro-Soviet, and others, by contrast, identified with the END approach, a much wider range of opinion was simply more concerned about U.S., rather than Soviet, nuclear weapons and foreign policy. Hinton argues that "while the great majority of CND activists agreed that Russia bore some share of responsibility for keeping the Cold War going . . . few . . . shared Thompson's sense of an ongoing engagement against Soviet, as well as American, power in Europe."[40] Nevertheless, Thompson was just one of a number of END activists who served on CND's International Committee, promoting a nonaligned East–West politics and the idea of détente from below. Arguably, this involvement not only, in Jane Mayes's words, "inspired CND to be more internationalist." It was also an important counterweight to those International Committee members who were strongly pro-Soviet or simply skeptical of East–West dialogue from below. Yet CND never became strongly involved in the East–West citizens' dialogue. British END could not persuade it of the value of this work for CND's core program. CND did use the restrictive concept of "peace rights" to speak out in defense of some peace activists in CEE/SU (and Turkey) who were being harassed by their regimes; but it was careful to avoid addressing the question of human right abuses, let alone the lack of democracy, in CEE/SU.

British END's East–West work, then, tried to combine three different elements. British END was one of a number of peace groups in the West to take part in a transcontinental dialogue with independent forces in CEE/SU. These forces challenged some of the assumptions of the END frame; nevertheless, this dialogue arguably produced a consensus about the interdependence of democracy in CEE/SU and détente and disarmament. British END also maintained relations with official peace committees, organizations whose frame clashed fundamentally with its own and that, for much of the 1980s, were hostile to British END and its sister groups in the West. And British END was trying to involve in the East–West dialogue from below other Western peace groups. One of these, CND, was reluctant to become involved in the pan-European citizens' dialogue. The tensions created by trying to combine these three elements in one strategy occasionally surfaced, as described next.

EAST–WEST POLITICS IN BRITISH END

The protest at Perugia and the founding of the Network, as we have seen, were the work of Western peace activists who wanted to prioritize the dialogue with independent groups in the East. These events reflected strains within the Western peace movement over its relationship with CEE/SU, specifically between two currents in the END Convention process.

The protest at Perugia and the founding of the Network also gave rise, in late 1984 and early 1985, to an increasingly fractious row within British END. Some wanted the organization to join this new entity; others opposed this move. The dispute, which surfaced at regular meetings of British END's Coordinating Committee, in memos and letters, and at specially convened meetings, reached a crisis in February 1985, just after the Network's first public event, a seminar on the fortieth anniversary of the Yalta conference. British END had formally decided not to sponsor the seminar. One reason for refusing was that, in its view, the rejection of the division of Europe symbolized by Yalta had become associated with Western "cold-war propaganda" advocating the rollback of Soviet hegemony only; another was that the seminar was taking place outside the "mainstream of the peace movement."[41] Mary Kaldor and three of the four staff members, however, plus a handful of other END activists, attended the seminar; indeed, Kaldor spoke at it. Shortly after their return, Edward Thompson, furious at what he saw as an undermining of an agreed position, announced his provisional withdrawal from British END.[42]

In the arguments about the Network within British END, activists advocated two different approaches to the East–West dialogue from below. Some argued, among other things, that in the two existing transnational peace movement forums of the Western peace movement—the IPCC and the Convention process—East–West politics were marginalized. They favored British END's joining a new body that would concentrate on the dialogue with independents. These activists tended to downplay or not to address the possible deleterious effect on END's relations with CND and other mainstream peace organizations should END join the Network. Such effects might include these groups distancing themselves from British END, thus reducing the possibility of its influencing them. They would do this because British END was becoming involved in an organization, the Network, that would be too much concerned with an issue irrelevant to, or even harmful to the interests of, the Western peace movement: human rights and democracy in CEE/SU.

Others, most notably Thompson, the most influential opponent of the Network within British END, argued that British END must remain committed to the strategy that was at the heart of END's strategy for ending the Cold War: "plural" dialogue.[43] His central objection was that the Network strategy would undermine this strategy.[44] He argued this case forcefully in a series of internal letters and memos in early 1985 and, in somewhat coded form, in *Double Exposure*: "To be effective, the dialogue between East and West must engage widening constituencies of citizens." In the East, it must not, on the one hand, "be co-opted by official diplomatic organs"; while, on the other, "it must not be short-circuited into a few advanced intellectual groups," such as Charter 77 and KOS—on which, Thompson feared, the Network would concentrate.[45] These groups, though admirable and important, were in a sense "Westerners"; that is, they wrote and acted partly with an eye to Western responses. The moments of breakthrough had come, he claimed, when Eastern Europeans had "thrown up their own forms": the Peace Group for Dialogue, the Moscow Trust Group or Swords into Ploughshares.[46] And in the West, the dialogue "must involve majority peace movements" such as CND.[47] The large Western nonaligned movements, Thompson argued, had not been brought into the Network.[48] In addition, the Network's strategy of concentrating on independent CEE/SU groups undermined another aspect of the "plural dialogue": the need to engage Eastern "officials."[49]

Eventually, the crisis in END caused by the row over the Network subsided. As the Network arguments threatened END's cohesion—Thompson's threat to withdraw was only the most dramatic expression of this threat—the Coordinating Committee dropped the issue. Thompson did not leave British END, and END did not join the Network.

From 1985, the Network became a channel for significant parts of the East–West citizens' dialogue. The most comprehensive statement written (and signed) by activists in East and West was an initiative of the Network: the "Helsinki Memorandum," or *Giving Real Life to the Helsinki Accords*. Of three seminars, unique in their location, size, and breadth of participation, that brought together West European (and U.S.) and independent Eastern activists, the idea for the first—in Warsaw in May 1987—grew out of discussions between Jacek Czaputowicz of the host organization Freedom and Peace, and Dieter Esche of the Network;[50] the second—in Budapest in November of that year—was cosponsored by the Network.[51]

Meanwhile, in the second half of the 1980s, British END continued its CEE/SU work. END activists were frequent visitors to Poland and, with other Western groups, worked closely with Freedom and Peace; in Czechoslovakia, they maintained relations with Charter 77 and established them with the Jazz Section and the Independent Peace Association; they ran or participated in national and international defense campaigns in defense of peace and human rights activists in Czechoslovakia; they continued to support the Moscow Trust Group and to visit the GDR; and they opened relations with Slovenian peace activists. At the same time, the *END Journal* continued to publicize the dialogue and to promote the idea of détente from below. British END supporters even participated as observers at planning meetings of the Network. And though British END campaigners played only a minor role in the drafting of the Helsinki Memorandum, they were active participants in the seminars. In other words, once British END had decided not to join the Network, it continued its East–West work alongside, and sometimes participating in, the Network. At the same time, détente from below, though always contested, continued to be conducted within the convention process.

CONCLUSION

Why, then, is the Network episode significant? It is of interest to the student of the Western peace movement of the 1980s because it was in the arguments about the Network that the tensions within the East–West component of the END project were sharply (and, in the case of the Perugia demonstration, dramatically and publicly) revealed. These tensions were rooted in the difficulties inherent in a strategy of creating a movement, in the Cold War, that would span borders not only between countries but also between social systems. This strategy raised the question of how to combine the Western peace movement's demands for détente and disarmament with the need for human rights and democracy in CEE/SU, whether this need was voiced explicitly or was merely implicit in the treatment of independent groups by their regimes. While détente required stable East–West relations, the demand for democracy and human rights in CEE/SU implied a transformation of state–society relations. Insofar as this challenged the legitimacy of the regimes in the Soviet bloc, it potentially augured destabilization instead.

The tensions manifested themselves on two levels. First, within the END Convention process, groups committed to the pan-European citizens' dialogue and those skeptical of its value disagreed continually about the convention's relations with the East. Here, two kinds of pan-European strategy possible within the framework of the END project coexisted: "détente from above" and "détente from below." The Network was created when enough proponents of détente from below felt that the convention process could not function properly as a forum for this dialogue.

The tensions were also evident within one group, British END, as it tried to reconcile its commitment to the dialogue with its commitment to its relationship with CND while also talking to official bodies in the East. On the one hand, British END's close engagement with independent groups in CEE/SU meant that the lack of human rights in, and the need for the democratization of, that region became an increasingly important issue for the organization. On the other hand, British END was a committed part of the British and West European peace movement. British END's main partner in the United Kingdom, CND, which it wanted to influence, had little interest in linking its peace campaign with the issues of civil rights and democracy in CEE/SU, or in promoting a strategy of cooperation with independent groups in the East. The same was true of some peace organizations outside the United Kingdom and political parties in Britain and abroad.

This dilemma, in principle, faced all Western peace groups involved in the East–West dialogue. The Network represented one solution to the dilemma: The peace groups in it had decided that they would simply concentrate on developing close relations with independent groups in CEE/SU, largely ignore official peace committees, and, crucially, not concern themselves with trying to bring into the dialogue reluctant Western peace groups. END, by contrast, offered another solution, with the tensions this created surfacing most sharply in the arguments about the Network: to try, until the end of the decade, to bridge the gap between the Western peace movement and independent peace and human rights groups in Central Eastern Europe and the Soviet Union, while keeping open the channels to the "officials."

NOTES

The author would like to thank Padraic Kenney, Gerd-Rainer Horn, and Barry Buzan for their help with this chapter.

1. There are accounts of the protest in the Convention's daily newsletter, *Convention News*, in END Archive, private collection (Brighton, U.K.).

2. Western peace activists variously called the nonstate groups in CEE/SU with which they were in contact "independents," "unofficials," "dissidents," "our friends," and "our partners." The term *independents*, which I use in this chapter, highlights the

most significant characteristic of these groups: that they were independent of their respective regimes. *Officials*, in turn, refers to the state-sponsored peace committees of CEE/SU.

3. END Conventions were held between 1982 and 1992, each year but one in a different country, and attended by between 600 and 2,500 supporters of the END Appeal.

4. Dieter Esche, Jürgen Graalfs, and Walther Grunwald, "Some Remarks about the Controversy Concerning the East–West Dialogue," *Listy: Documents of Independent Peace Movements East-West* 2 (n.d.): 3–7. The authors were members of the Liaison Committee.

5. The convention and the Liaison Committee, on the one hand, and the British group END, on the other, were separate entities. Both had as their political framework the END Appeal. END was just one of many groups and organizations represented on the Liaison Committee and at each convention. It is important to note that there was no pan-European organization called END. Though END was not referred to at the time as British END, I will do so for purposes of clarity.

6. Sidney Tarrow, *Power in Movement: Social Movements and Contentious Politics* (Cambridge: Cambridge University Press, 1998), 184.

7. Tarrow, *Power in Movement*, 109–11.

8. See Tarrow, *Power in Movement*, 184–85.

9. For details of some of these events, see "Peace Camp Inspiration," *END Journal* 6 (October–November 1983): 6 (on Comiso); April Carter, *Peace Movements: International Protest and World Politics since 1945* (London: Longman, 1992) (on Greenham Common); Tony Simpson, "Brussels—Easter 1981," and Rip Bulkeley, "'Is There Anyone Here from Bonn/Leiden?'" *END Bulletin* 5 (Summer 1981): 20–21; "It's a Long Way to Paris," *END Bulletin* 6 (Autumn 1981): 8–10 (on the Scandinavian march); "Five Nations Supplement," *END Journal* 6 (October–November 1983); "Beyond the Blocs Speaking Tour," *END Journal* 12 (October–November 1984): 32.

10. The term *nonaligned* was used in the 1980s to denote those Western peace groups—the great majority—that opposed the nuclear weapons of both sides; in other words, that were not pro-Soviet. It is important to note that the term also covers groups that supported the END Appeal but were skeptical about the dialogue with independent groups in the East.

11. "Appeal for European Nuclear Disarmament," in *Protest and Survive*, ed. E. P. Thompson and Dan Smith (Harmondsworth, U.K.: Penguin, 1980), 225.

12. For example, in Czechoslovakia, the Jazz Section. Part of the official Musicians' Union, the Jazz Section provided a forum for a wide range of cultural activity in Czechoslovakia until the authorities suppressed it and imprisoned its officers in 1986. The Jazz Section joined END in 1983. See its letter to END in *END Journal* 4 (June–July 1984): 28.

13. All quotations from "Appeal for European Nuclear Disarmament," in *Protest and Survive*, 223–26.

14. See, for example, Edward Thompson, "Beyond the Blocs," *END Journal* 12 (October–November 1984): 12–15; Mary Kaldor, "Beyond the Blocs: Defending Europe the Political Way," *World Policy Journal* 1, no. 1 (Spring 1984): 1–21.

15. CODENE: Comité pour le Désarmement Nucléaire en Europe; IKV: Interkerkelijk Vredesberaad (Inter-Church Peace Council).

16. Mary Kaldor, "Bringing Peace and Human Rights Together," lecture series, "The Ideas of 1989" (London: London School of Economics, Centre for the Study of Global Governance, 2000), 7.

17. Pat Chilton, report on END Convention Liaison Committee meeting, 3–5 April 1987, in END Archive. Chilton was a member of British END.

18. These included *END Bulletin* (1980–1983), *END Journal* (1982–1989), as well as pamphlets and books.

19. "Supporters" were subscribers to *END Bulletin* and *END Journal*.

20. E. P. Thompson, *Beyond the Cold War* (London: Merlin, 1982), 29 and 31.

21. Thompson, *Beyond the Cold War*, 26.

22. See note 12.

23. For example, *Beyond the Cold War*, which was published in *samizdat* in Budapest (see Ferenc Köszegi and E. P. Thompson, *The New Hungarian Peace Movement* [London: END/Merlin, n.d.], 5); and "Notes on Exterminism, the Last Stage of Civilization" in *Exterminism and Cold War*, ed. Edward Thompson et al. (London: Verso, 1982), 1–33, which was read in independent circles in the GDR (see Gerd Poppe, "Zur Entwicklung des grenzüberschreitenden Dialogs" in *Die Bürgerbewegungen in der DDR und in den ostdeutschen Bundesländern* [Opladen: Westdeutscher, 1993], 205–6).

24. For Western examples, see Mary Kaldor, "Bringing Peace and Human Rights Together," passim; and "A Movement for Peace and Democracy," in *Demokratische Reformen und europäische Sicherheit* (Bonn: Friedrich-Ebert-Stiftung, 1989), 101. For an Eastern example, see Poppe, "Zur Entwicklung des grenzüberschreitenden Dialogs."

25. The phrase "the indivisibility of peace" is first used in Charter 77's document of 15 November 1981, "Statement on West European Peace Movements," in *Voices from Prague: Documents on Czechoslovakia and the Peace Movement* (London: END/Palach, 1983), 22–23.

26. Charter 77, "Open Letter to Peace Movements," *Voices from Prague*, 24.

27. An example of the former was the Charter 77 signatory Ladislav Lis, arrested and imprisoned in 1983 and 1984; of the latter, Bärbel Bohley and Ulrike Poppe of Women for Peace in the GDR, who were arrested in 1983.

28. Kaldor, "Bringing Peace and Human Rights Together," 7.

29. Poppe, "Zur Entwicklung des grenzüberschreitenden Dialogs," 205–6.

30. Kaldor, "Bringing Peace and Human Rights Together," 7.

31. Jaroslav Šabata, "Letter to E. P. Thompson," in *Voices from Prague*, 53.

32. Václav Racek, "Letter from Prague," in *Voices from Prague*, 16.

33. For most of the 1980s, British END's bilateral contacts (with "officials") were limited to peace committees in three countries: the Soviet Union, the GDR, and Hungary.

34. E. P. Thompson, "What Kind of Partnership?" in *The Heavy Dancers* (London: Merlin, 1985), 164–65. A few British END activists expressed great skepticism about the pursuit of these contacts. See, for example, John Keane, "Civil Society and the Peace Movement in Britain," *Thesis Eleven* 8 (January 1984): 5–22. Keane was a member of British END's Czechoslovak Task Group.

35. "Who's Paying the Piper?" *END Journal* 9 (April–May 1984): 9.

36. "Appeal for European Nuclear Disarmament," 225.

37. For claims about the success of these last two aims, see Kaldor, "Bringing Peace and Human Rights Together," 8–9; Tair Tairov, "From New Thinking to a Civic

Peace," in *Europe from Below: An East–West Dialogue*, ed. Mary Kaldor (London/New York: Verso, 1991); and Alexei Pankin, "Soviet New Thinking," lecture series, "The Ideas of 1989" (London: London School of Economics, Centre for the Study of Global Governance, 2000).

38. James Hinton, *Protests and Visions: Peace Politics in 20th Century Britain* (London: Hutchinson Radius, 1989), 188. Hinton, a professional historian, was an early END activist and a leading figure in CND.

39. Jane Mayes, "Introducing CND's International Work," undated paper, in END Archive. Mayes was the "linkperson" (i.e., chairperson) of the International Committee.

40. Hinton, *Protests and Visions*, 186–87.

41. Letter from Peter Crampton (chair of END) "[t]o all members of the provisional secretariat of the European Network for East–West Dialogue," 14 January 1985, in END Archive.

42. Letter to British END Coordinating Committee, 9 February 1985, in END Archive.

43. E. P. Thompson, *Double Exposure* (London: Merlin, 1985), 150.

44. Other objections included the fear that CEE/SU authorities would see the Network as a directive center for dissident activities and that this would bring down the authorities on the Easterners' heads even harder than normal.

45. Thompson, *Double Exposure*, 150.

46. Letter to Paul Anderson (deputy editor of *END Journal*), 10 March 1985, in END Archive.

47. Thompson, *Double Exposure*, 150.

48. "END and the East" (internal discussion document for British END), 21 March 1985, in END Archive.

49. Thompson, *Double Exposure*, 151.

50. Padraic Kenney, *A Carnival of Revolution: Central Europe 1989* (Princeton, N.J.: Princeton University Press, 2002), 115.

51. "Hungarian Meeting a Success," *END Journal* 31 (December 1987–January 1988): 8. The third seminar, disrupted by the authorities, took place in Prague in June 1988.

12

Opposition Networks and Transnational Diffusion in the Revolutions of 1989

Padraic Kenney

How do social movements learn about one another and decide to adopt similar strategies, tactics, or styles? Transnational diffusion is still a relatively new field of social movement research. As Doug McAdam and Dieter Rucht have noted, most relevant scholarship "tend[s] to think of social movements as discrete entities that arise independently of one another; hence the search for unique causes."[1] Yet especially in moments of broad international change, unique causes must be illusory. Marco Giugni suggests three possible explanations for similarities across movements in different countries: globalization; structural affinity; and diffusion of information, people, and ideas.[2] The first two have been easiest to study; diffusion, again, has been neglected. Social movement scholars have largely focused on diffusion among Western democracies, between which travel is a simple matter and within which access to ideas is relatively unfettered. Across nondemocratic societies, diffusion is even less likely to be studied; one exception is the work of Vincent Boudreau, who in a study of democratic movements in Southeast Asia questions such influence, doubting that the Philippine struggle for democracy may have had an impact on the much later Indonesian movement.[3]

To understand how or why international networks of social movements work, the revolutions of 1989 are an essential case. It is one thing to show that activists with similar goals and/or strategies are operating in different countries at the same time. It is quite another to determine precisely what was conveyed and to whom. The year 1989 should stand next to the years 1968 and 1945 (and earlier examples, such as 1918 and 1848) as dates emblematic of the power of revolutionary ideas to jump barriers of language and politics to affect an entire continent. Upsurges of popular protest against communist rule appeared to cascade miraculously across the region, from Poland to Hungary, East Germany, Czechoslovakia, and on to the Soviet Union. Though many commentators at the time used the language of the miraculous to describe the events, historians should know better. Essays in this volume have established without a doubt that such transnational influences do occur, with some regularity. But how does this happen?

In this chapter, I will use the example of the Central European revolutions of 1989 to consider the praxis of diffusion and to offer a typology of diffusion processes. This is no easy task in Central Europe, where the political change appears to take place nearly simultaneously. In what follows, I will propose that active transnational diffusion (as opposed to that brought about by structural factors, such as world war or natural disasters) can be categorized into six modes of contact: *command, text, legend, pilgrimage, courier,* and *convocation.* After briefly discussing the first two of these, I will focus on the last four, with particular attention to the influence of two Polish movements of the years 1985–1989: the Freedom and Peace movement and Polish-Czechoslovak Solidarity. As we will see, Poland rightly belongs at the center of any transnational analysis of the fall of communism.

COMMAND

Scholars who have thought about the dynamics of this "miracle year" usually choose one of two explanations for this simultaneity. The most popular focuses on the accession to Kremlin leadership of Mikhail Gorbachev, who emboldened liberalizing and democratic impulses throughout the Soviet empire. Indeed, if we want to understand why Communist leaders gave up the ghost so rapidly, even in the bloc's darker corners, Gorbachev is quite important. This I call diffusion by *command*; in Gorbachev's case, this often meant the absence of command. Within a short time after becoming Communist Party general secretary in early 1985, he initiated sweeping reforms (and what is more important for Central Europe, talked boldly about those reforms) in the economy, and then in politics and international relations. From Gorbachev, economic reformers and democratic thinkers got the signal to push their ideas, while hard-liners found they could no longer rely on Soviet tanks, or Soviet subsidies, to prop up their policies. Eastern European Communist leaders, still accustomed to following Kremlin signals slavishly, offered echoes of Gorbachev's slogans: restructuring the economy (perestroika), openness in the media (glasnost), and democratization. Gorbachev used visits to Central Europe, and also to the West, to alert those leaders to the need to rescue socialism with new approaches.[4]

TEXT

A second focus—popularized especially by Timothy Garton Ash[5]—is on the dissident intellectuals, like those associated with Czechoslovakia's Charter 77. Responding in part to the Helsinki Accords of 1976, these men and women explored their common rights and common Central European identity. In their *samizdat* journals (e.g., *Beszélő* in Hungary, *Krytyka* in Poland, and *Střední Europa* in Czechoslovakia) and in the Western press (e.g., *East European Reporter, Labour Focus on Eastern Europe, Gegenstimmen,* and *La Nouvelle Alternative*), they could communicate indirectly with their peers through text. An essay like Václav Havel's "Power of the Powerless" (1978) could gain great influence throughout the region, changing the way dissidents saw their regimes and the potential of opposition.[6]

This is an important story, worthy of further study. But I want to focus on forms of transnational contact that, as I suggested at the outset, have received the least attention: those between social movements. In so doing, I will be interested in diffusion not so much of ideas but of strategies, tactics, style, and materials. My intention here is not to test models of diffusion[7] or to provide a comprehensive survey of cross-national networks in Central Europe. Instead, I hope to provide a framework for a more systematic exploration of diffusion processes.

Both of the movements used as examples here were small (Freedom and Peace with perhaps two hundred to five hundred active participants; Polish-Czechoslovak Solidarity with a few dozen). Freedom and Peace (Wolność i Pokój, or WiP), for a brief time among the best-known movements in Central Europe, staged a number of actions in protest of the military oath, the imprisonment of conscientious objectors, and environmental degradation (especially related to Poland's nuclear energy program). Polish-Czechoslovak Solidarity (PČS), as the name suggests, built ties between neighbors whose relations had traditionally been marked by suspicion.[8] Both drew from a generation younger than that of the intellectuals mentioned earlier; most active participants had been in high school or even elementary school when Solidarity had flourished in 1980–1981; none could remember the ideological struggles of 1968. In contrast to Solidarity, which survived in the underground and still boasted hundreds of thousands of dues-paying members, international recognition, and leaders with decades of experience, these new movements had far fewer resources of any kind. Their influence would depend on new channels and resources that they themselves would create—though the resources and name recognition of their elder sibling were also essential assets. The two movements offer prime examples of the modes of contact I wish to explore in the rest of this chapter.

LEGEND

I use the term *legend* to denote activism that responds to stories one has heard about the exploits of other movements. Most often, these stories are spread by underground or foreign media. In contrast to *text*, however, the intellectual content of the message is less important than the style of opposition and specific tactics. International media, especially Radio Free Europe, play a critical role. But to think of the media themselves as actors would be misleading. The social movements themselves—and this was especially true of Freedom and Peace—provided news of their activities by telephone and later would devise other means of spreading their fame, as we shall see. The audience for this information also played an active role, choosing the information it found most useful and twisting what they heard to their own ends.

Zsolt Keszthelyi, a student of English and French literature in Budapest, had been fascinated by Solidarity from his high school days in southern Hungary, where he followed it avidly on Radio Free Europe. In Budapest, he tried unsuccessfully to specialize in Polish studies. In 1984, an older friend gave Keszthelyi the address of two young Poles, Małgorzata Tarasiewicz and Adam Jagusiak, who had initiated contact with Hungarian students by placing advertisements on a university bulletin board while visiting Budapest. Tarasiewicz and Jagusiak would soon be participants in Freedom and Peace, and they found much in common with Keszthelyi when he visited them in Sopot (near Gdańsk). They talked about anarchism, militarism, and the tarnished traditions of Polish-Hungarian friendship.[9] Keszthelyi was interested both in peace issues and in nationalism. He helped to start a samizdat journal, *Vox Humana*, that focused on the taboo subject of Hungarian national consciousness. This combination of interests is very much like that of many in WiP; it was therefore not surprising that Keszthelyi would, in 1987, follow their lead and refuse to serve in the army. Keszthelyi knew just what to do. "I got the recipe," he says. "Write your ideas, write openly what you think, and send it to the military together with your [military registration] book. And this is what I did."[10]

Keszthelyi's letter of 18 February 1987 explained his reasons in WiP language.

> I don't have trust in the "popular-democratic" army, which is subordinate to a government that was not chosen by a popular vote based upon competing political programs. I think that by this refusal, as in my fight for a free press, I can contribute to the creation of a society free from fear, in which the administration of public affairs will be based upon responsibility and individual conscience, and not upon uncritical faith, or on fear.[11]

Arrest and conviction were virtually certain; in April, Keszthelyi received a three-year sentence. At his appeal hearing, Keszthelyi connected his fate directly to the Polish cause: Hearing about the bravery of Father Jerzy Popiełuszko (murdered by security police in 1984) had made him feel like a Pole, he declared; now, he was being sentenced by representatives of the same system that had murdered the Polish priest as well as the leader of 1956, Imre Nagy.[12]

Oleh Olisevych, in Lviv, in western Ukraine, was another who grew up in the shadow of the Polish legend. Lviv had been a part of Poland before 1939, and many in the city speak or at least understand Polish; Polish-language broadcasts were a popular (though somewhat risky) source of information. Olisevych—who refused to use Russian, the lingua franca even in the hippie community—taught himself Polish this way. Soon, he had established contact with his Polish peers. In September 1987, he led a group of fellow hippies in Lviv in Soviet Ukraine's first demonstration of the Gorbachev era. Their action was reported in a Moscow samizdat bulletin, a copy of which made it to Warsaw. WiP's Jacek Czaputowicz was inspired to send a letter (in English, which they stuck to despite Olisevych's knowledge of Polish) to the address published in the bulletin. Over the next two years, Czaputowicz and Olisevych exchanged news of their respective groups (Olisevych called his Doviria, or "Trust") and clippings about youth culture in the Soviet Union and Poland. Olisevych hoped they might be able to coordinate demonstrations, take part in each other's actions, and support each other's demands. Close cooperation—or even a meeting—would be impossible until 1989—when Olisevych joined Freedom and Peace pacifists for a joint demonstration on the anniversary of the Nazi-Soviet pact of August 1939.[13]

But there is no doubt that WiP inspired the Ukrainians. About one spring 1988 demonstration, Olisevych wrote to Czaputowicz that "there were theatrical situations, just like you had not long ago in Wrocław."[14] Olisevych, as it happens, had gotten his movements confused. The demonstration he referred to had not been one organized by Freedom and Peace but by Orange Alternative, a guerrilla theater collective. Nevertheless, Olisevych clearly felt inspired by what he heard about in Poland, and he sought to import a "theatrical" style of lighthearted confrontation he associated with Poland into a very different national situation.[15]

PILGRIMAGE

The stories of Keszthelyi and Olisevych remind us that those who subscribe to the "legend" and follow the exploits of movements abroad may sooner or later visit them. For such activists, these visits are not unlike pilgrimages to a revered (if not sacred) site. The journey is both an expression of devotion or fellow feeling and a search for knowledge. It may even, as with a religious pilgrimage, take place on a special day: an anniversary (as in Olisevych's case) or the date of an expected demonstration.

Hungarian dissidents always paid special attention to Poland, ever since the two countries had posed twin challenges to the Soviet Bloc in October 1956. In the 1960s and 1970s, young Hungarians traveled to the jazz clubs of Warsaw to hear what they could not at home. In the Solidarity era, the pilgrimages acquired an explicitly political focus. Two young Budapest teachers—István Stumpf, who was completing a thesis on the establishment of communism in Poland, and Tamás Fellegi, a recent law graduate—first traveled to Poland to connect with another pilgrimage, that of Pope John Paul II in 1983. They encountered there a society that—despite the considerably greater repression in evidence less than two years after the crackdown on Solidarity and the imposition of martial law—seemed markedly freer than in Hungary. Fellegi and Stumpf attended a papal mass in Warsaw and were deeply impressed by the sight of hundreds of thousands of worshippers, some carrying Solidarity signs or singing forbidden songs. It was not just the level of freedom or the audacity of the people they met—it was the capacity for self-organization that struck them and stayed with them as they drove back to Budapest.[16]

When Stumpf and Fellegi received permission to open a residential college for young law students, the Polish lessons remained on their minds, and they proceeded to share their vision of independent self-organization. Like Zsolt Keszthelyi before them, they, too, followed Jagusiak's and Tarasiewicz's flyer, and in 1985 took some twenty students on a field trip to Gdańsk. They wanted students to experience that freedom for themselves and hoped they would learn from their Polish peers new ways of opposition. During their brief visit, the Hungarian and Polish students went to lay flowers at the monument to shipyard workers massacred during a 1970 strike— and were detained at the monument by the police for four hours. The experience emboldened the Hungarians; upon their return home, they worked to unite student activists across Hungary and founded a new periodical in the style of Polish samizdat. By the time the students returned for a last visit, in 1987, Tarasiewicz and Jagusiak were active in WiP, and their apartment turned out to be a meeting place for young activists from all over Poland. Their visit coincided with another papal pilgrimage; the Hungarian students found the apartment full of people painting Freedom and Peace banners for an upcoming papal mass for youth.

Thinking back on the Polish expeditions, Fellegi doubts that his students gained one "big lesson" from the Poles; they knew, after all, that there was no patent for success. The Polish struggle could not be reduced to samizdat essays, the pope's sermons, or Freedom and Peace banners. Poland, to the Hungarians, was about strategies for survival and techniques of successful activism in a repressive state. The Polish approach was to ignore the state, as much as possible; to act according to one's own plan, whatever the police might do. A half-dozen guests to spirit around Gdańsk was nothing to the implacable Poles. As Fellegi put it, the lesson was to be "proactive and streetwise."[17] These qualities might seem unremarkable, but they had not characterized Hungarian opposition for decades.

Gábor Fodor, one of Fellegi's students, was inspired by the trip: "We want to follow some of their ways," he thought.[18] These students were adept learners indeed. The following spring, they were among the founders of the student group FIDESZ (Association of Young Democrats); one of them, Viktor Orbán, would in 1998 become prime minister of Hungary. FIDESZ, like WiP, espoused at the beginning both a concrete politics (such as environmental causes) and a fusion of national radicalism with a radically antiauthoritarian, decentralized stance. It would play a crucial role at several key moments in the dismantling of communism in Hungary. Though FIDESZ would eventually move toward institutionalized politics (becoming a party in 1990), the early contact with Freedom and Peace seems to have been formative.

Hungarians and Poles traditionally believe they share a common history of resistance to individualist tyranny. In other Central European countries, Poland's image was generally not so positive. To East Germans in particular, Poland seemed a land of lazy hotheads.[19] Both physically (given harsher travel restrictions in the GDR) and psychologically, a pilgrimage to Poland was difficult to undertake. Yet though most East Germans were skeptical of Polish activism, there were a few who were curious.

Wolfgang Templin was one; he had learned Polish when he traveled to Krakow to study philosophy in 1976 and had discovered the nascent Polish opposition instead.[20] In 1986, Templin was one of the founders of the Initiative for Peace and Human Rights (IFM). In contrast to the more introverted, intellectual dissent that had dominated East Germany to that point, the IFM was to be extroverted and issue focused. Still, the Polish model was far away and unfamiliar. By the 1980s, Templin (like many other prominent dissidents) was barred from traveling to Poland.

One *Grenzfall* correspondent, "Björn," was able to go east, and he described his experience in "Impressions of a Trip to Poland, or, a Lesson in Civil Courage." "Björn" was Bernd Oehler, a theology student from Leipzig and a participant in the Leipzig Working Group for Justice, the only thriving IFM circle beyond Berlin. He had Polish roots: His mother, though German, had grown up in Warsaw, and Oehler had twice been there as a child. It was Templin who asked him to try to go to Poland again, on behalf of the IFM; to great surprise, he got permission to travel. In just a few short weeks, he visited all the major centers of Polish opposition. As had Templin a decade earlier, Oehler returned convinced that GDR opposition should look to Poland; the Poles were, he recalled years later, "more emancipated than we were."[21]

In his essay, Oehler avoided direct comparisons with East Germany, but the implied contrasts were easy to read. What struck Oehler most in Poland was the intensity of national expression. The ubiquitous Polish flags and national symbols, and the public role of the Catholic Church, contrasted sharply with the near-total lack of a noncommunist collective identity in East Germany; Oehler recognized these as valuable resources for the opposition. Oehler also remarked on the diversity of the Polish opposition, implicitly contrasting it to the less colorfully variegated opposition in East Germany (and especially Berlin). He observed "radicals, *Realpolitiker*, and nationalists," and came to the cautious conclusion that pluralism could be a strength of opposition. He spent much of his time, indeed, not with Solidarity but with Freedom and Peace, whose public and international stance, cemented by personal peace treaties, seemed a model for IFM. While Oehler also noted problems in Polish opposition—he bemoaned the male-dominated culture of opposition, where women were relegated to supporting roles—his conclusion was unequivocal: "One can learn from this civil courage."[22]

These pilgrimages, then, provided more than just recipes (to use Keszthelyi's term). They were a means to experience the freedom to practice one's beliefs in freedom and to witness others acting upon those beliefs. And they emboldened some pilgrims to transfer lessons gathered abroad to home, in order that others, too, might learn from that experience.

COURIER

For those who could not travel, the praxis of freedom could be made real in another way, which we might call revolutionary export. Couriers from a society more advanced in opposition methods and technology could bring news, technical assistance, and even matériel, while themselves demonstrating a more adventurous style. The example of Polish-Czechoslovak Solidarity, founded by Wrocław student Mirosław Jasiński in 1983, suggests that, at least between two similar and adjacent cultures, revolutionary export could become a full-time opposition venture.

All Jasiński had at the outset were a few contacts in Prague, notably Chartist Petr Uhl and his wife, Anna Šabatová. But they, and other Prague dissidents, were eager partners, for they knew that the Poles had a lot to offer. The Polish underground, with hundreds of periodicals and several large publishers (some with offset presses), was light-years ahead of the Czechs, where the half-dozen or so clandestine periodicals were still using typewriters and carbons. Czech readers were starved for the information about history, international politics, philosophy, literature, and the art and science of opposition that the Polish underground published. Poles also had much easier access to the West; General Wojciech Jaruzelski's halfhearted economic reforms rested in part on the hard currency brought back by thousands of Poles who traveled to Germany, Sweden, and elsewhere every year to work illegally. Some of them, at the behest of PČS, smuggled back trunkloads of banned literature from the Czech émigré communities (as well as Polish literature, of course); Poland thus became an essential channel of communication between the post-1968 political emigration and Prague, where *tamizdat* (émigré publications) found plenty of willing recipients.

Most of this baggage reached Czechoslovakia across the Karkonosze Mountains, which reach five thousand feet along the border southwest of Wrocław. Polish-Czechoslovak Solidarity couriers would stuff backpacks with fifty to eighty pounds of literature and set off through the forests. In remoter areas, it was easy enough to slip across after the border patrol had passed. As long as there was no snow on the ground (winter crossings were rare, lest couriers' tracks expose their trails), there might be two trips monthly. At a prearranged spot on the border, the goods would be handed to a Czech contact; sometimes, the Polish courier would descend to the nearest Czech village and mail packages at the post office. There were larger packages, too: photocopiers, offset printers, and even—in summer 1989—a laptop computer. These were purchased in Vienna with money from Czech émigré organizations. They were marked as being in transit to Poland and then simply "fell off the train" somewhere in Czechoslovakia.[23]

There was no thaw, no perestroika, on the tightly controlled Polish-Czechoslovak border—despite the signs that directed one to the "Trail of Polish-Czechoslovak Friendship"—until December 1989. The opportunities to annoy the Czech authorities, though, were too great to pass up. In 1985, Warsaw underground printers, working as if on contract for the Czechs, composed and published an entire edition of a Brno literary journal and then smuggled it back into Czechoslovakia. The Czech police were stunned to find that despite all their efforts, Czech samizdat now apparently had offset printers of its own.

Polish-Czechoslovak Solidarity helped to destroy the isolation of the Czech opposition. Almost twenty years after the Prague Spring, letters from émigrés or the sounds of Radio Free Europe were almost all that reached the Czechs—and these were, after all, symbols of the border that cut the Czechs off from the world. Polish students scrambling up mountains, evading border patrols, and delivering packages invigorated the world around Charter 77 and were an inspiration for a young post-Charter opposition that emerged beginning in 1987.

In January 1987, the Czechoslovak security police arrested Brno peace activist Petr Pospíchal, PČS's main contact outside Prague. Pospíchal, a poet and Polish translator, had long been one of the most active samizdat publishers in the country; a search of his apartment turned up flyers celebrating Charter 77's tenth anniversary and much more. His Charter 77 colleagues formed a Pospíchal Defense Committee and started a petition campaign. But no sign of solidarity was more powerful than a letter Pospíchal received in prison, franked with a counterfeit Czechoslovak stamp bearing Charter 77 and PČS logos. Polish underground printers had been turning out high-quality postage stamps for years, to be sold to collectors to raise funds; this batch had been spirited over the border on New Year's Day (in a rare winter crossing) in time for the anniversary, and fooled the unsuspecting Czech authorities.[24] Not too long after, Pospíchal was freed.

Poles had a resource even more valuable than the literature they carried: activists with years of experience in organizing anticommunist resistance and protest. If giant backpacks could reach the border, then why not smuggle people as well? After months of planning in 1987, Jasiński and Ivan Lamper (a journalist for Prague's underground countercultural periodical *Revolver Revue*) brought to the Trail of Polish-Czechoslovak Friendship some of their countries' best-known opposition figures.

This was, of course, a publicity coup above all: famous dissidents meeting with impunity, in a place legally off limits. They posed proudly next to a sign reading "State Border, Crossing Forbidden." It would be easy to imagine later that these were serious planning sessions for the revolution. In truth, these theater performances for an international public (repeated in 1988 and 1989) worked on two stages. For the cameras, the prominent dissidents got to know each other and issued joint declarations about human rights. Though relatively innocuous, these were powerful expressions of the newly transnational reach of opposition. Backstage, meanwhile, Jasiński and Lamper might discuss what Czech samizdat most needed or who else should come to the next meeting. Then another shipment from Vienna or Wrocław would be arranged, and the circle of mountain climbers would expand.

Polish-Czechoslovak Solidarity had made the border into a performance space for freedom; it became the place to which one traveled to show that one was free. The September following the first summit meeting, Freedom and Peace scaled the Karkonosze Mountains to meet young Czech environmentalists (who were prevented from coming); the following summer, guerrilla theater collective Orange Alternative staged a happening there. In early spring 1989, Czechoslovakia's nascent peace and environmental movement, the Independent Peace Association, met Freedom and Peace on the border. Building on contacts established by couriers, PČS thus deconstructed the very idea of the border, taking the fear out of the barbed wire and guard towers long before they were physically removed.

CONVOCATION

The forms of contact discussed so far are essentially unidirectional: ideas, people, and materials emanate from one country to another, or people travel to a source of inspiration ("text" is a partial exception, as a samizdat or Western periodical might contain writings from several countries side by side). As transnational contacts matured, it became possible to brave multiple borders and bring activists together into one place to exchange ideas, strategies, and styles. The term *convocation* may unnecessarily imply the presence of a central authority; it does remind us, though, that the place of meeting was not irrelevant: As in a pilgrimage, activists would gather in a place of greater oppositional experience. A convocation might be a seminar, a conference, a symposium, or a festival. To meet in this way was a performance of freedom and opposition as well as a means of exchanging concrete information.

Freedom and Peace staged several such convocations. The first of these was a seminar on peace and human rights, in a Warsaw church in 1987. Some 150 to 200 guests, including prominent Solidarity activists such as Bronisław Geremek and leading Western peace activists such as Lynne Jones from Britain and Joanne Landy from New York, participated in the three-day event. There was one Czech (others were stopped at the border), a few Hungarians and Slovenes, and two students from East Germany. They all crowded into the basement of the Church of God's Mercy for three days of discussion, followed by a pilgrimage to the grave of Otto Schimek (a young Austrian soldier executed for refusing to participate in the murder of Polish civilians in 1944) some two hundred miles away in southeast Poland.[25]

The main lines of communication at the seminar were between WiP and the Western activists, to whom the Poles wanted to demonstrate that independent peace conferences and conventions (such as those held every year by European Nuclear Disarmament) were also possible under the noses of the communist authorities. "This time we won," WiP's Jacek Szymanderski exulted at the seminar's opening. "We can say that we did it!"[26] But the seminar also had meaning for Poland's Soviet bloc neighbors. Hungarian polonophiles followed suit that fall, organizing a similar event in Budapest, at the college where Tamás Fellegi taught and where FIDESZ would soon be born; Viktor Orbán gave a welcoming speech.[27] A convocation of this sort was a way of demonstrating that Central European movements played an active role in creating and maintaining transnational networks.

Freedom and Peace held another such gathering in August 1988, an "International Human Rights Conference" in a Kraków church. This conference, too, drew participants from all over the region. Even more than the 1987 seminar, this was a demonstration of impunity. Saša Vondra of Charter 77, the only Czech dissident to make it to Kraków, was astonished at the openness of the conference, in spite of the presence of an observer from the Ministry of Internal Affairs.[28] Central Europe, meanwhile, was much more in evidence than it had been before. While plenary sessions continued in the church's main hall, WiP activists and their peers from Hungary, East Germany, and elsewhere conferred and shared experiences of peace activism in a back room, away from the notice of the police and reporters. And all the participants got an unexpected glimpse of Polish opposition when Silesian coal miners, who had begun a strike about a week before the conference, showed up at the church to make their case for better pay and the return of a legal Solidarity trade union. The conjunction of conference and strikes not only contributed to the authorities' decision to agree to talks with the Polish opposition but also foretold change across the region, change that would accelerate within months.

One more convocation would play a crucial role in the fall of communism in Central Europe. The election of 4 June 1989 and the creation of a noncommunist government in September had made Poland a free and democratic country, and they gave many Poles a conscious feeling of being the elder siblings to their neighbors still struggling for freedom. In this spirit, Mirosław Jasiński of PCS planned a four-day festival of Czech culture in Wrocław, to take place on 2–5 November. To this newly free city—the home not only of PCS but of Orange Alternative and a thriving WiP circle as well—he invited scores of distinguished exiled Czech singers, poets, novelists, and essayists.

He also invited his friends from Czechoslovakia. But crossing that barrier was considerably more difficult than coming from the West to a now-free Poland. Hundreds in cars and on trains were stopped at the border by guards who confiscated their passports and sent them home. The only prominent dissident to make it was Petruška Šustrová, a former spokesperson of Charter 77. When she arrived in Wrocław, she felt she had entered another world: Everywhere she heard the unexpected sound of the Czech language, yet the conversation was utterly different, free. Šustrová got used to Poles' casual greetings in stores or on the street: "Oh, you're from Czechoslovakia! Don't worry, ma'am, communism will fall there too!"[29] In a passionate letter published just days before the Czechoslovak revolution began, she recalled her shame that the Czechs had done so little to fight for freedom in "the last immovable island of totalitarianism in Central Europe." But instead of reproach from the Poles, she heard encouragement: "Here, too, it looked for a long time as if the regime would not give in and the people had completely lost interest. Don't you dare give in to that!"[30]

Besides Šustrová, a thousand or so other Czechs made it to the festival. The vast majority of these were young; most students would not be on any police lists of suspect dissidents. They also had the energy to find more distant crossing points or the trails blazed by PCS couriers. In Wrocław, they lived in student dormitories, sharing space with veterans of WiP and other student movements. They thronged to readings, concerts, and showings of long-banned Czech films. Like Tamás Fellegi's young law students visiting Gdańsk, they had wandered into a zone of freedom, where they could think and do as they pleased.

Returning home, they brought some of this irreverent freedom with them. In Pilsen, a week after the festival, Marcel Hájek and Luboš Smatana stood up at a Union of Socialist Youth meeting and began to tell what they had seen and heard. In the audience, Jaroslav Straka was amazed to see two ordinary students ignoring threats from secret police officers in the room, carrying on as if what they had done was normal.[31]

This tone of normality and confidence, new to Czechoslovakia, was what the trips to Wrocław had given Czechs: a sense that elsewhere there were people who knew how to be free. Why, then, could it not happen here? "Those thousands of people, mostly young," wrote Šustrová, "will bring home more than just impressions from a concert and from a beautiful gathering. I think that the optimism of our Polish friends has infected them. And then, when you see with your own eyes that something can be accomplished, it stimulates you. . . . The hope we have brought home is a great foundation for the future."[32] Just days later, on 17 November, the Czechs experienced the beginning of their Velvet Revolution. There are many sources of that dramatic event, of course: news of the Berlin Wall's fall, plus the determination of a new generation of students to stage an independent demonstration. But the style and atmosphere of the Festival of Czech Culture should not be underestimated, especially when considering revolutionary events (like those in Prague) whose most prominent actors were students.

Looking at the actions initiated even by relatively modest social movements, one can come much closer to answering the question—too often neglected—of precisely what happens in such a cross-national network, in what I have called the praxis of diffusion. If we recall Keszthelyi's thanks for Freedom and Peace's "recipe" or Šustrová's call to arms from Wrocław, we can see what is passed on: not grand ideas of civil society, but concrete methods of resisting and living as if one were already free. We can see more clearly, also, who received those messages: a generation much younger than those who had created Solidarity or Charter 77; a generation that—even if it was elbowed aside at the round tables where communist power was negotiated away—is now coming to maturity in Central Europe. And that Central Europe has been built, in part, by the diffusion of ideas and tactics across once impenetrable borders almost two decades ago.

CONCLUSION

How might one apply this classification of transnational modes of contact to the analysis of revolutionary moments? It may be that modes of contact can tell us something about the revolutions themselves. For example, some modes are personal in nature, while others are indirect contacts, through print and radio. We can hypothesize that revolutionary moments linked by the former will have greater similarity (in movement style or in demands articulated) than those linked primarily by the latter. Though there is no room to explore this point here, the difference between revolutionary change in the Soviet Union (including Ukraine) and Central and Eastern Europe may be in part explained by this.

Some modes of contact function at the top of society, between elites; most others connect individuals in nonelite social movements. Additionally, elite modes are more likely to imply passive reception of information (party comrades hearing a speech made in Moscow or dissidents reading each other's texts); contact between social movements will probably involve the active acquisition of knowledge. A revolutionary moment such as that in 1989 certainly shared common ideas (human and civil rights; liberal democracy), but these are hardly blueprints for revolution sent from a command center somewhere. This was in some ways a truly decentralized revolution. In some cases (Poland, Ukraine, and East Germany), even the capital city took a backseat to opposition elsewhere in the country.

The study of transnational contacts also invites us to look more closely at the paths of influence. Some contact was linear, between two countries; in other modes (text, convocation), information is shared simultaneously among activists of many countries. Indeed, one of the main values of transnational study (as can be seen in many of the events encountered in this book) is that it helps us to understand *simultaneity*—the perplexing occurrence of surprisingly similar events at nearly the same time in separate countries. Study of the paths of transnational contact, though, requires us to ask about origins. Where, if anywhere, is the originating site of 1989?

Some movements elsewhere in the Soviet bloc also generated transnational contacts, but none to the extent of those in Poland. One is reminded of the centers of other revolutionary moments. Paris, in the years leading up to the revolutions of 1848, similarly became a destination for the radical, the liberal, and the nationalist intellectual from all across Europe. One traveled there as if on a pilgrimage, to a city of freedom and enlightenment. "Paris," wrote Polish poet Adam Mickiewicz in a lecture delivered to a Paris audience in 1840, "is the focus, the spring, the instrument. . . . By the intermediary of this great city, the peoples of Europe get to know one another and sometimes to know themselves." For Mickiewicz, the attraction was "the force of the internal movement, the mass of spiritual warmth, and the light which produces it."[33] Though Mickiewicz would not return to Poland, other intellectuals did return to Bucharest, Vienna, Rome, and Budapest, as the revolution begun in Paris found imitators across Central Europe. It would not be quite accurate to call Paris an incubator of those revolutions; one could say that a sojourn there inspired a framework of radical change essential to the furious spread of revolution that year.

A comparison between the Springtime of Nations and the "Autumn of Nations" in 1989 is not at all new.[34] But in closing with this comparison, I mean to suggest that the revolutions of 1989 moved by a similar dynamic. If they did, there is no doubt that Poland, as a whole, played the role of Paris. More than simply an inspiration or the first domino, Poland in the 1980s was both a destination and a source: for the radical, the democrat, and even the nationalist, from within the Soviet bloc and from Western Europe. They came to Poland, or learned about Poland, searching for different things; like their predecessors in Paris, they brought home revolution.

Each mode of contact that I have discussed here—legend, pilgrimage, courier, convocation—functions on two levels. At one level are the concrete effects. Would-be activists learn just what strategies or tactics have proven to attract attention or achieve particular results, as they receive information about their peers in other countries or as they visit the sites where opposition has been staged and meet its participants. They can also receive technical assistance or technology itself from more experienced social movements. In rare instances, both the relatively experienced social movements and the relative novices take the initiative to gather together, and cities like Wrocław or Kraków take on, however briefly, the role played by Paris (1848) or Petrograd (1917).

Simultaneously, each of these actions—crossing a border, holding a conference, even reading a foreign text or listening to Radio Free Europe—was a symbolic act, too. Activists in nondemocratic regimes engaged in a performance of freedom. For while regimes such as those in the Soviet bloc might tolerate (or prosecute with less diligence) some dissent, state borders were inviolable. Tightly controlled checkpoints, barbed wire, scarce passports, and distrust of foreign influence are characteristic of these regimes. These aspects are harder to challenge than, say, limits on freedom of speech. In a profound way, then, transnational activism destabilizes regimes and opens up horizons for the participants of opposition in each country. As social movements invent ways to make transnational contact real, they change the very geography of the world they inhabit.

NOTES

Earlier versions of this chapter were presented to the Program on East European Cultures and Societies at the Norwegian University of Science and Technology, Trondheim, and to the Center for Slavic, Eurasian, and East European Studies at the University of North Carolina, Chapel Hill.

1. Doug McAdam and Dieter Rucht, "The Cross-National Diffusion of Movement Ideas," *Annals of the American Academy of Political and Social Science* 528 (1993): 65. See also Donatella della Porta, Hanspeter Kriesi, and Dieter Rucht, eds., *Social Movements in a Globalizing World* (New York: St. Martin's, 1999).

2. Marco G. Giugni, "The Other Side of the Coin: Explaining Crossnational Similarities between Social Movements," *Mobilization: An International Journal* 3, no. 1 (1998): 89–105.

3. Vincent Boudreau, "Diffusing Democracy? People Power in Indonesia and the Philippines," *Bulletin of Concerned Asian Scholars* 31, no. 4 (1999): 3–18.

4. See Jacques Lévesque, *The Enigma of 1989: The USSR and the Liberation of Europe* (Berkeley: University of California Press, 1997).

5. Timothy Garton Ash, *The Uses of Adversity: Essays on Central Europe* (New York: Vintage, 1990); see also Vladimir Tismaneanu, *Reinventing Politics: Eastern Europe from Stalin to Havel* (New York: Free Press, 1992); and Barbara J. Falk, *The Dilemmas of Dissidence in East-Central Europe: Citizen Intellectuals and Philosopher Kings* (Budapest: Central European University Press, 2002).

6. Steven Lukes, "Introduction," in *The Power of the Powerless: Citizens against the State in Central-Eastern Europe*, ed. John Keane (Armonk, N.Y.: Sharpe, 1985), 12.

7. As in Giugni, "The Other Side of the Coin," for example.

8. I discuss Freedom and Peace at length in "Framing, Political Opportunities, and Civic Mobilization in the East European Revolutions: A Case Study of Poland's Freedom and Peace Movement," *Mobilization: An International Journal* 6, no. 2 (2001): 193–210; and both movements in *A Carnival of Revolution: Central Europe 1989* (Princeton, N.J.: Princeton University Press, 2002).

9. Adam Jagusiak and Małgorzata Tarasiewicz, e-mail communications to the author, 8 November and 24 November 1999.

10. Interview with Zsolt Keszthelyi, Baja, Hungary, 6 June 1998.

11. *Biuletyn WiP* (Kraków) 6 (14 March 1987).

12. See Zsolt Keszthelyi, "Kilka słów Polakom," *Serwis Informacyjny Ruchu WiP* 41 (28 June 1987).

13. Olisevych, interview, Lviv, 19 June 1988.

14. Olisewicz, Oleg (Oleh Olisevych), "Listy ze Lwowa," *Czas przyszły*, nos. 3–4 (1988–1989): 11.

15. See Kenney, *Carnival of Revolution*, chap. 5.

16. Fellegi, interview, Budapest, 8 June 2000.

17. Fellegi, interview.

18. Fodor, interview, Budapest, 16 June 1998.

19. See Dirk Philipsen, *We Were the People: Voices from East Germany's Revolutionary Autumn of 1989* (Durham, N.C.: Duke University Press, 1993), 112, 130.

20. Templin, interview, Berlin, 23 June 1999.

21. Oehler interview, Wermsdorf, 26 June 1999.

22. Björn, "Reiseimpressionen aus Polen oder Eine Lektion Zivilcourage," *Grenzfall* no. 3 (1986), reprinted in Initiative Frieden & Menschenrechte, *Grenzfall: Vollständiger Nachdruck aller in der DDR erscheinenen Ausgaben (1986/87). Erstes unabhängiges Periodikum* (Berlin: Self-published, 1989), 14–15.

23. Interview, Jasiński, 25 November 1996.

24. All the signs pointed to Pospíchal getting a long prison sentence. But a letter-writing campaign by, among others, Freedom and Peace and the East German IFM, as well as an April demonstration in Wrocław by Freedom and Peace and Polish-Czechoslovak Solidarity, contributed to Pospíchal's release in May. See "The Case of Petr Pospíchal," *East European Reporter* 2, no. 3 (1987): 19–20.

25. See Polly Duncan, "A New Generation of Opposition," *Sojourners* 16, no. 9 (October 1987): 14–19; Brian Morton and Joanne Landy, "East European Activists Test Glasnost," *Bulletin of the Atomic Scientists* (May 1988): 18–26; and *Seminarium pokojowe w Warszawie 7–9.V.87. Dokumenty* (Warsaw: Wolność i Pokój, 1987).

26. Duncan, "A New Generation of Opposition," 15.

27. Viktor Orbán, "Recapturing Life," *Across Frontiers* 4, nos. 2–3 (Spring–Summer 1988): 34–35.

28. Saša Vondra, "Akreditační číslo 1019," *Infoch* 11, no. 16 (1988): 17.

29. Šustrová, interview, Prague, 16 November 1999.

30. Petruška Šustrová, "Polské dojmy," *Sport* 4 (November 1989): 26.

31. Interview, Straka, Prague, 16 November 1999.

32. Šustrová, "Polské dojmy."

33. Quoted in Lloyd S. Kramer, *Threshhold of a New World: Intellectuals and the Exile Experience in Paris, 1830–1848* (Ithaca, N.Y.: Cornell University Press, 1988), 176.

34. See, for example, Timothy Garton Ash, *The Magic Lantern: The Revolution of '89 Witnessed in Warsaw, Budapest, Berlin and Prague* (New York: Random House, 1990), 142–49.

Bibliographic Essay

The following is not intended to be an exhaustive review either of works in transnational history (of Europe or anywhere else) or of the history of the three moments of change examined in this book. We have endeavored to list those works that we find particularly valuable as a starting point for the transnational history of these moments. Some are transnational in character; most are not. All should be useful in the creation of the kind of history we have in mind. Wherever feasible, we refer to works in English; we refer to foreign-language studies where no comparable English-language texts exist.

1945

West of the future Iron Curtain, Belgium, France, Italy, and Greece witnessed the most turbulent interactions between national and social liberation in the course of World War II resistance movements, a conflictual relationship that centrally shaped the first moment of change under investigation in this book. Yet, curiously enough, there exist no satisfactory transnational and/or comparative assessments of the phenomena of resistance and liberation to date in any language, though mention should be made of Ulrich Herbert and Axel Schildt, eds., *Kriegsende in Europa: Vom Beginn des deutschen Machtzerfalls bis zur Stabilisierung der Nachkriegsordnung 1944–1948* (Essen: Klartext, 1998); Tony Judt, ed., *Resistance and Revolution in Mediterranean Europe* (London: Routledge, 1989); Gill Bennett, ed., *The End of the War in Europe* (London: Her Majesty's Stationery Office, 1996); and the classic Gabriel Kolko, *The Politics of War: The World and United States Foreign Policy 1943–1945* (New York: Pantheon, 1990), a text first published in 1968. The very recent publication of Anna Balzarro, *Le Vercors et la zone libre de l'Alto Tortonese: Récits, mémoire, histoire* (Paris: L'Harmattan, 2002), may hopefully inspire other comparative and transnational works on this topic.

The single-most convincing study of the political but also the sociopsychological dynamic of the French resistance remains H. R. Kedward, *In Search of the Maquis: Rural Resistance in Southern France 1942–1944* (Oxford: Clarendon, 1993). For the Greek case, the equivalent keynote study is Mark Mazower, *Inside Hitler's Greece: The Experience of Occupation 1941–1944* (New Haven, Conn.: Yale University Press, 1993). Charles F. Delzell, *Mussolini's Enemies: The Italian Anti-Fascist Resistance* (Princeton, N.J.: Princeton University Press, 1961), remains the most informative English-language study for the Italian dimension; for a recent competent introduction, however, see Gustavo Corni, "Italy," in *Resistance in Western Europe*, ed. Bob Moore (Oxford: Berg, 2000), 157–82. The superior introductions to the Italian resistance remain Guido Quazza, *Resistenza e storia d'Italia: Problemi e ipotesi di ricerca* (Milan: Feltrinelli, 1976), and Claudio Pavone, *Una guerra civile: Saggio storico sulla moralità nella Resistenza* (Turin: Bollati Boringhieri, 1991). José Gotovitch, *Du rouge au tricolore: Les Communistes belges: Un aspect de l'histoire de la Résistance en Belgique* (Brussels: Labor, 1992), remains the best social history of any European Communist Party in World War II and may also serve as a comprehensive point of entry into the issues surrounding antifascist Belgian resistance movements.

The "gender of resistance" can be most fruitfully investigated in two relatively recent English-language studies utilizing very different though complementary methodological approaches: Jane Slaughter, *Women and the Italian Resistance: 1943–1945* (Denver, Colo.: Arden, 1997), and Janet Hart, *New Voices in the Nation: Women and the Greek Resistance* (Ithaca, N.Y.: Cornell University Press, 1996). Despite the availability of book-length English-language texts on women in the French resistance, an ideal starting point for the exploration of that issue remains Paula Schwartz, "Partisans and Gender Politics in Vichy France," *French Historical Studies* 16, no. 1 (1989), 126–51.

Traditional accounts of World War II resistance movements all too frequently marginalize if not overlook labor movement activism in the underground. This explicitly working-class dimension of the antifascist resistance crucially determined the sociopolitical volatility characterizing the moment of liberation in (at the very least) Romance-language Europe. Tom Behan, *The Long-Awaited Moment: The Working Class and the Italian Communist Party in Milan, 1943–1948* (New York: Lang, 1997), and Darryl Holter, *The Battle for Coal: Miners and the Politics of Nationalization in France, 1940–1950* (De Kalb: Northern Illinois University Press, 1992), are two stimulating English-language texts with the added advantage of a simultaneous close-up look at how this labor activism under Nazi occupation helped to shape the politics of the immediate postliberation era.

For a fascinating, in-depth account of pre- and postliberation militant labor actions in (the mostly francophone portions of) the Belgian state, see Rik Hemmerijckx, *Van Verzet tot Koude Oorlog 1940–1949: Machtstrijd om het ABVV* (Brussels: Vrije Universiteit Brussel Press, 2003). Adam Steinhouse, *Workers' Participation in Post-Liberation France* (Lanham, Md.: Lexington, 2001), is one of the very few English-language monographs exclusively focusing on postwar labor unrest. But special mention must be made of the French context of Robert Mencherini, *Parti Communiste, stalinisme et luttes sociales en France: Les grèves "insurrectionnelles" de 1947–1948* (Paris: Syllepse, 1998). Class struggles in immediate postwar Italy are relatively well covered in the Italian-language literature. A thorough introduction to this complex issue remains Paride Rugafiori, Salvatore Vento, and Fabio Levi, eds., *Il triangolo industriale tra ricostruzione e lotta di classe, 1945–1948* (Milan: Feltrinelli, 1974).

In what became known as the "free world," the Greek people suffered the most from the consequences of the various dynamics unleashed by the interplay of resistance, occupation, liberation, and the origins of the Cold War. The fragility of postliberation democracy under British (and later American) hegemony can best be gauged from the following works, in addition to Mazower's key work mentioned earlier: Heinz Richter, *British Intervention in Greece: From Varkiza to Civil War* (London: Merlin, 1985); John Iatrides, *Revolt in Athens* (Princeton, N.J.: Princeton University Press, 1972); John Iatrides, ed., *Greece in the 1940s: A Nation in Crisis* (Hanover, N.H.: University Press of New England, 1981); Edmund Myers, *Greek Entanglement* (Gloucester: Sutton, 1985), originally published—after much obstruction by the British state—in 1955; and Dominique Eudes, *The Kapetanios: Partisans and Civil War in Greece, 1943–1949* (New York: Monthly Review Press, 1970). Riki van Boeschoten, *From Armatolik to People's Rule: Investigation into the Collective Memory of Rural Greece, 1750–1949* (Amsterdam: Hakkert, 1991), adds a stimulating long-range anthropological dimension. Stratis Tsirkas, *Drifting Cities* (New York: Knopf, 1974), remains the superior treatment of this Greek moment of opportunity and crisis from a literary perspective.

For many activists in the resistance, liberation was conceived of as a harbinger of fundamental change going far beyond the return to the prewar status quo ante. By far the most stimulating sociopsychological study of the moment of liberation remains Alain Brossat, *Libération, fête folle, 6 juin 44–8 mai 45: Mythes et rites ou le grand théâtre des passions populaires* (Paris: Autrement, 1994). Still unsurpassed in its coverage of the sociopolitical dynamic and potential of the moment of liberation in France is Grégoire Madjarian, *Conflits, pouvoirs et société à la libération* (Paris: Union Générale d'Éditions, 1980). An important snapshot of a working-class interpretation of liberation in France is provided in Robert Mencherini, *La libération et les entreprises sous gestion ouvrière: Marseille, 1944–1948* (Paris: L'Harmattan, 1994).

David W. Ellwood, *Italy 1943–1945* (Leicester: Leicester University Press, 1985), is a rare English-language study paying serious attention to the transnational phenomenon of "liberation committees." A treasure trove of English-language primary source material on the interaction among resistance forces, liberation committees, and Anglo-American military administrations in immediate post–World War II Italy can be found in Roger Absalom, ed., *Gli alleati e la ricostruzione in Toscana (1944–1945): Documenti Anglo-Americani*, 2 vols. (Florence: Olschki, 1988 and 2001). Among the wealth of first-rate Italian-language studies of immediate postliberation Italy, the slim volume by Enzo Piscitelli, *Da Parri a De Gasperi: Storia del dopoguerra 1945/1948* (Milan: Feltrinelli, 1975), can safely be placed at the very top of the list. The recently re-published translation of a superb literary snapshot of this rapid succession of hope and deception by Carlo Levi, *The Watch* (South Royalton, Vt.: Steerforth, 1999), is a particularly powerful reminder of the promises and disappointments of the very first postwar months in the Italian state.

The medium- to long-term legacy of the period of occupation and resistance is finally beginning to get more serious scholarly attention. The collected essays in István Deák, Jan T. Gross, and Tony Judt, eds., *The Politics of Retribution in Europe: World War II and Its Aftermath* (Princeton, N.J.: Princeton University Press, 2000), are highly recommended as an epitaph for the many hopes and expectations associated with the moment of liberation in Western and Eastern Europe alike. Interesting contributions to this topic may also be found in Jan-Werner Müller, ed., *Memory and Power in Post-War Europe: Studies in the Presence of the Past* (Cambridge: Cambridge University Press, 2002). Pieter Lagrou, *The Legacy of Nazi Occupation: Patriotic Memory and National Recovery in Western Europe, 1945–1965* (Cambridge: Cambridge University Press, 1999), admirably covers the relevant experiences in Belgium, France, and the Netherlands. The classic national case study in this regard is, of course, Henry Rousso, *The Vichy Syndrome: History and Memory in France since 1944* (Cambridge, Mass.: Harvard University Press, 1992). But notice must now also be taken of the excellent portrayal of the reality and postwar myths surrounding the most famous of French *maquis*, Gilles Vergnon, *Le Vercors: Histoire et mémoire d'un maquis* (Paris: Atelier, 2002).

Only in the last decade, since the postcommunist opening of the archives, have histories of the coming to power of communism in Eastern and Central Europe really been possible. In an earlier era, when the field was almost entirely the province of political science, multicountry studies were common, and the transnational force—Stalin's intentions to "Sovietize" as much of Europe as possible—was self-evident. Today the story is more complex, but few works deal with more than one country. A rare and valuable exception is John Connelly, *Captive University: The Sovietization of East German, Czech, and Polish Higher Education, 1945–1956* (Chapel Hill: North Carolina University Press, 2000). No individual country has been as closely stud-

ied as the German Democratic Republic. From the staggering load of literature, one of the most useful for exploring the East German version of the
"communist moment" is Norman Naimark, *The Russians in Germany: A History of the Soviet Zone of Occupation, 1945–1949* (Cambridge, Mass.: Harvard University Press, 1995). On Poland, Padraic Kenney's *Rebuilding Poland: Workers and Communists 1945–1950* (Ithaca, N.Y.: Cornell University Press, 1997), is a social history of the communist revolution. Martin Myant's *Socialism and Democracy in Czechoslovakia, 1945–1948* (Cambridge: Cambridge University Press, 1981), is as yet unrivaled. Yugoslavia has also received some attention; see Carol Lilly, *Power and Persuasion: Ideology and Rhetoric in Communist Yugoslavia, 1944–1953* (Boulder, Colo.: Westview, 2001); and Melissa Bokovoy, *Peasants and Communists: Politics and Ideology in the Yugoslav Countryside, 1941–1953* (Pittsburgh, Pa.: University of Pittsburgh Press, 1998). The transformation of the early history of Communist Eastern Europe is still under way; a new generation of scholarship on these and other countries should soon appear in print.

1968

All contributors to this volume have interpreted the moment of "1968" as a moment of change that began earlier and lasted far longer than the twelve months of that fateful year. This bibliographic essay conforms to this approach. We begin by listing some recommended monographs that cover more than a single national case.

Arthur Marwick, *The Sixties: Cultural Revolution in Britain, France, Italy and the United States, c. 1958–c. 1974* (Oxford: Oxford University Press, 1998), emphasizes the cultural dimension of the "long sixties," and his tome will remain a treasure trove of information for many years to come. Chris Harman, *The Fire Last Time: 1968 and After* (London: Bookmarks, 1998), by contrast, highlights the political dimension of this period. An excellent early work is Gianni Statera, *Death of a Utopia: The Development and Decline of Student Movements in Europe* (New York: Oxford University Press, 1975). David Caute, *The Year of the Barricades: A Journey through 1968* (New York: Harper & Row, 1988), despite its limitations as a journalistic overview, covers much otherwise-neglected ground and should not be overlooked. George Katsiaficas, *The Imagination of the New Left: A Global Analysis of 1968* (Boston: South End, 1987), was one of the first historians to draw attention to the centrality of New Left thinking in the genesis of 1968. Somewhat dated but still brimming with insights is Tariq Ali, *1968 and After: Inside the Revolution* (London: Blond & Briggs, 1978); more recently, together with Susan Watkins, Ali coauthored the best English-language, illustrated coffee-table book on this transnational phenomenon: *1968: Marching in the Streets* (New York: Free Press, 1998).

Three Italian-language texts should be added to this list: the still-excellent transnational survey by Massimo Teodori, *Storia delle nuove sinistre in Europa, 1956–1976* (Bologna: Mulino, 1976); Peppino Ortoleva, *I movimenti del '68 in Europa e in America* (Roma: Riuniti, 1998); and Alberto Flores and Alberto De Bernardi, *Il Sessantotto* (Bologna: Mulino, 1998). In addition, four very recent works coming out of the University of Bielefeld target important topics in at least two crucial national contexts: Marica Tolomelli, *"Repressiv getrennt" oder "organisch verbündet": Studenten und Arbeiter 1968 in der Bundesrepublik Deutschland und in Italien* (Opladen: Leske + Budrich, 2001); Kristina Schulz, *Der lange Atem der Provokation: Die Frauenbewegung in der Bundesrepublik und in Frankreich 1968–1976* (Frankfurt: Campus, 2002); Michael Schmidtke, *Der Aufbruch der jungen Intelligenz: Die 68er-Jahre in der Bundesrepublik und den USA* (Frankfurt: Campus, 2003); and the long essay by Ingrid Gilcher-Holtey, *Die 68er-Bewegung: Deutschland, Westeuropa, USA* (Munich: Beck, 2001). Two additional German-language works also warrant favorable mention: Michael Kimmel, *Die Studentenbewegung der 60er Jahre: BRD, Frankreich, USA: Ein Vergleich* (Vienna: Wiener Universitätsverlag, 1998), and Ingo Juchler, *Die Studentenbewegungen in den Vereinigten Staaten und der Bundesrepublik Deutschland der sechziger Jahre: Eine Untersuchung hinsichtlich ihrer Beeinflussung durch Befreiungsbewegungen und -theorien aus der Dritten Welt* (Berlin: Duncker & Humblot, 1996).

Four edited volumes cannot go without mention, as they cover a broad array of topics from a wide variety of national contexts; they may also serve as excellent reference works for more detailed bibliographical searches in the respective national literatures: Aldo Agosti, Luisa Passerini, and Nicola Tranfaglia, eds., *La cultura e i luoghi del '68* (Milan: Angeli, 1991); Ingrid Gilcher-Holtey, ed., *1968: Vom Ereignis zum Gegenstand der Geschichtswissenschaft* (Göttingen: Vandenhoeck & Ruprecht, 1998); Carole Fink, Philipp Gassert, and Detlef Junker, eds., *1968: The World Transformed* (Cambridge: Cambridge University Press, 1998); and Geneviève Dreyfus-Armand, Robert Frank, Marie-Françoise Lévy, and Michelle Zancarini-Fournel, eds., *Les années 68: Le temps de la contestation* (Brussels: Complexe, 2000). A standard reference work remains the collection of interviews with student activists in a wide variety of countries: Ronald Fraser, ed., *1968: A Student Generation in Revolt* (New York: Pantheon, 1988).

No study of 1968 can be complete without detailed attention to the nonconformist cultural trends of the preceding years or the closely related phenomenon of "youth rebellion" that generally preceded the outbreak of open revolt. The central role of U.S. cultural and political ferment cannot be overlooked in this regard. Useful introductions to the American context are Morris Dickstein, *Gates of Eden: American Culture in the Sixties* (Cambridge, Mass.: Harvard University Press, 1997); Steven Watson, *The Birth of the Beat Generation: Visionaries, Rebels, and Hipsters, 1944–1960* (New York: Pantheon,

1995); and Dennis McNally, *Desolate Angel: Jack Kerouac, the Beat Generation, and America* (New York: Random House, 1979). The almost equally important British scene is evocatively portrayed in Sheila Rowbotham, *Promise of a Dream: Remembering the Sixties* (London: Penguin, 2001); and Jon Wiener, *Come Together: John Lennon in His Time* (London: Faber & Faber, 1995). The highly influential dimension of cultural nonconformism in the 1960s of the seemingly nonpolitical kind can be accessed in an exemplary fashion via the biographies of two musicians: Alan Clayson, *Jacques Brel: The Biography* (Chessington, U.K.: Castle Communication, 1996); and Sylvie Simmons, *Serge Gainsbourg: A Fistful of Gitanes* (London: Helter Skelter, 2001). An excellent point of departure for the Italian dimension of the pre-1968 period can now be found in Carmelo Adagio, Rocco Cerrato, and Simona Urso, eds., *Il lungo decennio: L'Italia prima del 68* (Verona: Cierre, 1999).

While the spotlight of the historical profession is all too often placed on the larger countries, frequently events and processes in the smaller states of the continent can be particularly insightful with regard to the mechanisms and developments under review. Thus, the Dutch experience of the *provos* and *kabouters* can be regarded as pathbreaking on a European scale due to their successful combination of cultural critique and political revolt; on these phenomena, see, above all, Virginie Mamadouh, *De stad in eigen hand: Provo's, kabouters en krakers als stedelijke sociale beweging* (Amsterdam: Sua, 1992); Yves Frémion, *Provo, la tornade blanche: Amsterdam 1965–1967* (Brussels: Cahiers JEB, 1982); and Roel van Duijn, *Provo: De geschiedenis van de provotarische beweging 1965–1967* (Amsterdam: Meulenhoff, 1985). A rare gem in this respect is the two-volume study of intellectual and political nonconformism in the Swiss capital city of Berne, Fredi Lerch, *Begerts letzte Lektion: Ein subkultureller Aufbruch* (Zurich: Rotpunkt, 1996); and Fredi Lerch, *Müllers Weg ins Paradies: Nonkonformismus im Bern der sechziger Jahre* (Zurich: Rotpunkt, 2001).

Additional volumes of special interest for an in-depth understanding of student activism in this rebellious decade include the classic Alexander Cockburn and Robin Blackburn, eds., *Student Power: Problems, Diagnosis, Action* (Harmondsworth, U.K.: Penguin, 1969); Julian Nagel, ed., *Student Power* (London: Merlin, 1969); and the collection of situationist texts, Dark Star Collective, ed., *Beneath the Paving Stones: Situationists and the Beach, May 1968* (Edinburgh: AK Press, 2001). The standard reference work for the working-class dimension of 1968 remains Colin Crouch and Alessandro Pizzorno, eds., *The Resurgence of Class Conflict in Western Europe since 1968*, 2 vols. (London: Macmillan, 1978), though special mention should be made of Dan Georgakas and Marvin Surkin, *Detroit: I Do Mind Dying: A Study in Urban Revolution* (New York: St. Martin's, 1975; recently reissued, Cambridge, Mass.: South End, 1998), a remarkable account of the interplay of black revolt in the automobile factories of Motor City, USA. The frequently neglected case of worker revolt in late-Francoist Spain may be best accessed via David Ruiz, ed., *Historia de Comisiones Obreras (1958–1988)* (Madrid: Siglo XXI, 1994).

Of the wealth of English-language texts on the French May 1968 appearing in the immediate aftermath, one may note Patrick Seale and Maureen McConville, *French Revolution 1968* (London: Penguin, 1968); Daniel Singer, *Prelude to Revolution: France in May 1968* (London: Cape, 1970; recently reissued, Cambridge, Mass.: South End, 2002); the remarkable collection of documents by Alain Schnapp and Pierre Vidal-Naquet, eds., *The French Student Uprising, November 1967–June 1968: An Analytical Record* (Boston: Beacon, 1971); Angelo Quattrocchi and Tom Nairn, *The Beginning of the End: France, May 1968: What Happened, Why It Happened* (London: Panther, 1968; recently reissued, London: Verso, 1998); and the novel by Jill Neville, *The Love Germ* (London: Weidenfeld & Nicolson, 1969; recently reissued, London: Verso, 1998).

Still one of the very best works in any language on the Italian mobilization cycle opened up in 1968 is Robert Lumley, *States of Emergency: Cultures of Revolt in Italy from 1968 to 1978* (London: Verso, 1990), but see also, among other English titles, Sidney Tarrow, *Democracy and Disorder: Protest and Politics in Italy, 1965–1975* (Oxford: Clarendon, 1989). The outstanding novel of the Italian "Hot Autumn" remains untranslated into English: Nanni Balestrini, *Vogliamo tutto: Romanzo* (Milan: Feltrinelli, 1971).

The complex issue of European New Left/far left politics before, during, and after 1968 once again cannot be adequately understood in all its complexity without a knowledge of the U.S. New Left, where three studies may provide some necessary first insights: Maurice Isserman, *If I Had a Hammer: The Death of the Old Left and the Birth of the New* (New York: Basic Books, 1987); Paul Jacobs and Saul Landau, eds., *The New Radicals: A Report with Documents* (New York: Random House, 1966); and Wini Breines, *Community and Organization in the New Left: 1962–1968* (New Brunswick, N.J.: Rutgers University Press, 1989). For the history of the British New Left, see Michael Kenny, *The First New Left: British Intellectuals after Stalin* (London: Lawrence & Wishart, 1995); and Lin Chun, *The British New Left* (Edinburgh: Edinburgh University Press, 1993).

The continental European far left oftentimes referred to itself as "new left," but, like the British "new left," it differed significantly from the American prototype in policy orientation and its penchant for Marxist theorizing, though not necessarily always in its cultural concerns and practices. The case of the Italian far left may stand for the experiences of many other national contexts; on the Italian cauldron of far left politics, over and above the work by Lumley referred to earlier, see Steve Wright, *Storming Heaven: Class Composition and Struggle in Italian Autonomist Marxism* (London: Pluto, 2002); the political biography of Europe's leading postwar artist of the left by Tom Behan, *Dario Fo: Revolutionary Theatre* (London: Pluto, 2000); the evocative collection of letters to the editor of Italy's leading far left daily newspaper, Margaret Kunzle, ed., *Dear Comrades: Readers' Letters to* Lotta Continua (London: Pluto, 1980); and, last but not least, the translated novel by Nanni Balestrini, *The Unseen* (London: Verso, 1989).

A crucial but, in the English-language context, generally overlooked aspect of 1968 is the contribution of radical Catholic activists. For France, Grégory Barrau, *Le Mai 68 des catholiques* (Paris: Ouvrières, 1998), and Denis Pelletier, *La crise catholique: Religion, société, politique en France (1965–1978)* (Paris: Payot, 2002), have opened up fruitful avenues of inquest. For Italy, note above all Mario Cuminetti, *Il dissenso cattolico in Italia, 1965–1980* (Milano: Rizzoli, 1983); Roberto Beretta, *Il lungo autunno: Controstoria del Sessantotto cattolico* (Milano: Rizzoli, 1998); and Agostino Giovagnoli, ed., *1968: Fra utopia e Vangelo* (Rome: Ave, 2000). But note also, for the U.S. context, the thoughtful study of the influence of European personalism, James H. Farrell, *The Spirit of the Sixties: The Making of Postwar Radicalism* (New York: Routledge, 1997).

Finally, special mention should be made of two books that are difficult to classify but that should be mandatory reading for any student of 1968. Michel de Certeau, *The Capture of Speech and Other Political Writings* (Minneapolis: University of Minnesota Press, 1997), is a fascinating exploration of the sociolinguistics of the 1968 revolt with manifold implications for similar processes at other times and in different historical contexts. Alessandro Portelli, *The Battle of Valle Giulia: Oral History and the Art of Dialogue* (Madison: University of Wisconsin Press, 1997), simultaneously covers the resistance experience and 1968, and it serves as a fascinating introduction to the role of memory and oral history in the popular and academic understanding of social movements. Last but not least, Kristin Ross, *May '68 and Its Afterlives* (Chicago: University of Chicago Press, 2002), is now the most serious attempt to describe and analyze the various permutations that the memory of 1968 has undergone at the hands of academic observers and the court interpreters of the powers-that-be—if only for the case of France.

Readers interested in the Prague Spring would best begin with Kieran Williams, *The Prague Spring and Its Aftermath: Czechoslovak Politics, 1968–1970* (Cambridge: Cambridge University Press, 1997). There is no good introduction in English to events in 1968 in Poland (or on student protest in that era in Yugoslavia and Hungary). Jerzy Eisler, *Marzec 1968: Geneza, przebieg, konsekwencje* (Warsaw: Państwowe Wydawnictwo Naukowe, 1991), is the standard work.

1989

The literature on 1989, while quite extensive, contains few works of a genuinely transnational character. Those interested in the central role played by change in the Soviet Union should begin with Jacques Lévesque, *The*

Enigma of 1989: The USSR and the Liberation of Eastern Europe (Berkeley: University of California Press, 1997). Among the many works on Gorbachev himself, a transnational perspective of sorts is Robert English's intellectual history of Soviet reformers, *Russia and the Idea of the West: Gorbachev, Intellectuals, and the End of the Cold War* (New York: Columbia University Press, 2000). The larger context of the Cold War and its end is treated by John Lewis Gaddis, *We Now Know: Rethinking Cold War History* (Oxford: Clarendon, 1997); while this work has been criticized for its triumphalism, it remains the broadest introduction. A very different perspective on the Cold War's end examines the role of the Pugwash movement: Matthew Evangelista, *Unarmed Forces: The Transnational Movement to End the Cold War* (Ithaca, N.Y.: Cornell University Press, 1999).

On the revolutions of 1989, Padraic Kenney's *A Carnival of Revolution: Central Europe 1989* (Princeton, N.J.: Princeton University Press, 2002), takes an explicitly transnational approach. Another work that considers cross-national similarities among social movements is John K. Glenn III, *Framing Democracy: Civil Society and Civic Movements in Eastern Europe* (Stanford, Calif.: Stanford University Press, 2001). Other works of note are J. F. Brown, *Surge to Freedom: The End of Communist Rule in Eastern Europe* (Durham, N.C.: Duke University Press, 1991); Michael Randle, *People Power: The Building of a New European Home* (Stroud, U.K.: Hawthorne, 1991); Timothy Garton Ash, *The Magic Lantern: The Revolution of 89 Witnessed in Warsaw, Budapest, Berlin and Prague* (New York: Random House, 1990); Vladimir Tismaneanu, *Reinventing Politics: Eastern Europe from Stalin to Havel* (New York: Free Press, 1993); and Gale Stokes, *The Walls Came Tumbling Down: The Collapse of Communism in Eastern Europe* (New York: Oxford University Press, 1993). While each of these generally treats the revolution as a sequence of separate national events, they all evoke the revolutionary moment and trace many of the common experiences and the common roots of virtually simultaneous change.

Finally, in the still very fresh historiography of 1989, mention should be made of works that look beyond to the consequences of that event. Two worthy of note are Tina Rosenberg's examination of retribution and justice in Poland, Czechoslovakia, and Germany, *The Haunted Land: Facing Europe's Ghosts after Communism* (New York: Random House, 1995); and Vladimir Tismaneanu's study of intellectuals after communism, *Fantasies of Salvation: Democracy, Nationalism, and Myth in Post-Communist Europe* (Princeton, N.J.: Princeton University Press, 1998). Both works offer a first look at how a transnational history of the post-1989 era might be written.

Index

About the Contributors

Aldo Agosti teaches contemporary history at the University of Turin. He is the author of several books concerning the history of the socialist and communist movements in Italy and internationally. Among his most recent works are *Togliatti* (UTET, 1996), *Bandiere rosse: Un profilo storico dei comunismi europei* (Riuniti, 1999), and *Storia del PCI* (Laterza, 2000). He has also edited an *Enciclopedia della sinistra europea* (Riuniti, 2000).

Anna Balzarro is *docteur en histoire* (École des Hautes Études en Sciences Sociales, Paris, 2001). She has presented her research in conferences at various locations from Rome to San Antonio, Texas. She has published a number of essays on aspects of resistance movements. Her most recent work is *Le Vercors et la zone libre de l'Alto Tortonese: Récits, mémoire, histoire* (L'Harmattan, 2002).

Paulina Bren recently received her Ph.D. in European history from New York University. She is currently a fellow at the Center for Humanistic Inquiry at Emory University where she is working on her book, *Closely Watched Screens: Ideology and Everyday Life in Communist Czechoslovakia*, which explores the ways in which mass culture was used to redefine socialist citizenship in Czechoslovakia during the 1970s and 1980s.

Patrick Burke is a Ph.D. candidate at the Centre for the Study of Democracy, London, and visiting lecturer in politics at the University of Westminster. The topic of his dissertation is European nuclear disarmament and the Cold War in the 1980s. He was an activist in the British peace movement in the 1980s.

Juan José Gómez Gutiérrez has a doctorate in art history and works as an independent publisher and scholar. His research interests include the history and theory of the relationship between art and politics during the twentieth century and the history of the European postwar left.

Gerd-Rainer Horn is a lecturer in twentieth-century history at the University of Warwick. His research interests include the Catalan Revolution and the moment of liberation in Western Europe (1943–1948). Publications include *European Socialists Respond to Fascism: Ideology, Activism and Contingency in the 1930s* (Oxford University Press, 1996) and *Left Catholicism: Catholics and Society in Western Europe at the Point of Liberation, 1943–1955* (Leuven University Press, 2001), coedited with Emmanuel Gerard.

Padraic Kenney is a professor of history at the University of Colorado, Boulder, where he specializes in Poland and Central Europe since 1945. He has published two books: *Rebuilding Poland: Workers and Communists 1945–1950* (Cornell University Press, 1997) and *A Carnival of Revolution: Central Europe 1989* (Princeton University Press, 2002). He is currently researching the experience of the political prisoner in twentieth-century Poland.

Arthur Marwick was appointed the first history professor at the newly founded Open University in 1969. He specializes in total war and social change, class in the twentieth century, and the influence of personal appearance since the Renaissance, and published *The Sixties: Cultural Revolution in Britain, France, Italy and the United States, c. 1958–c. 1974* in 1997. The totally revised work *The New Nature of History: Knowledge, Evidence, Language* was published in 2001.

Patrick Pasture is a research professor in history at the Katholieke Universiteit Leuven. He has been a visiting scholar at the Internationaal Instituut voor Sociale Geschiedenis in Amsterdam, the University of Paris 1, and the University of Pennsylvania. His main fields of interest are the social history of trade unionism, the welfare state, and Christendom. Publications include the coedited volumes *Between Cross and Class: Transnational History of Christian Labour 1840–2000* (Peter Lang, forthcoming 2003), *Working Class Internationalism and the Appeal of National Identity* (Berg, 1998), and the single-author monograph *Histoire du syndicalisme chrétien international* (L'Harmattan, 1999).

Kristina Schulz received her Ph.D. in history for a study of the women's movements in France and Germany, which has now been published as *Der lange Atem der Provokation: Die Frauenbewegung in der Bundesrepublik und in Frankreich 1968–1976* (Campus, 2002). Currently working in the

Department of Sociology at the University of Geneva, she is carrying out research on the material and symbolic effects of the transformation of German society since 1990.

Jarle Simensen is a professor of history at the Norwegian University of Science and Technology, Trondheim, and an adjunct professor in history at the University of Oslo. His main fields of research are African and international history in the age of imperialism. Recent books include *Norwegian Missions in African History* (Oxford University Press, 1986) and *L'Occident conquiert le monde* (Mémoires du Monde, 1994).

Miroslav Vaněk is the director of the Oral History Center in the Institute for Contemporary History of the Czech Academy of Sciences. He is the author or coauthor of three books (in Czech): *One Could Not Breathe Here: The Ecology of the Czech Lands, 1968–1989* (1996), *One Hundred Student Revolutions: Students in the Period of the Fall of Communism: Biographical Interviews* (1999), and *Islands of Freedom: Culture and Civic Activities of the Young Generation in the 1980s in Czechoslovakia* (2002).